Praise for *One Life to Give*

"With vivid details, bold strokes, and fresh insights, Fanestil has done something rare: he has offered us a new interpretation of why people fought in the American Revolution. He shows that many in the Founders' generation had absorbed an English Protestant tradition of martyrdom that dated back generations. His is a story that reveals the complexities of those times when specific religious traditions and the heated politics of a moment come together—a story about the past with resonance for our own times."
—Peter C. Mancall, Andrew W. Mellon Professor of the Humanities, University of Southern California, and author of *The Trials of Thomas Morton: An Anglican Lawyer, His Puritan Foes, and the Battle for a New England*

"This book paints a vivid and timely picture of the role that the idea of martyrdom played in our nation's Revolutionary origins. Repurposed as a wartime ideal, patriots took up arms to resist a 'tyrant' whom they were convinced represented 'a mortal threat to their liberty.' In doing so, they instilled a still potent—and potentially destabilizing—image at the root of American identity that echoes down through our nation's history, including events of recent years."
—Ann Taves, research professor and Distinguished Professor (Emerita) of Religious Studies, University of California at Santa Barbara

"Fanestil has given us a fascinating look at the Christian roots of the American Revolution. The revolutionaries, in their willingness to self-sacrifice even unto death, were formed by the Scripture, sermons, and books of their churches and preachers. This book is an engaging study of the ways we are formed by the language and practices of our faith . . . and the promise and peril that lies therein."
—Will Willimon, professor of the practice of Christian ministry, Duke Divinity School, and author of *Who Lynched Willie Earle: Preaching to Confront Racism*

"*One Life to Give* breaks new ground by connecting the American Revolution to a centuries-old spiritual inheritance: a Protestant language of martyrdom. With clear prose and engaging stories, Fanestil makes a persuasive case that religion shaped the course and outcome of the Revolution."
—Erik R. Seeman, chair, history department, University of Buffalo, and author of *Speaking with the Dead in Early America*

"As we approach the 250th anniversary of the Declaration of Independence, a rising tide of new books continues to argue about the causes and character of the American Revolution. Fanestil's *One Life to Give* focuses on personal motivation: What made men willing to die for the cause? He finds his answer in the long tradition of English Protestant martyrdom. The Revolutionary generation had been catechized by a range of texts, from reprints of John Foxe's *Book of Martyrs* (1563), the hymns of Isaac Watts, and Indian captivity narratives to revival sermons, Joseph Addison's *Cato*, and *Poor Richard's Almanac*. Patriots repeatedly referenced willing self-sacrifice for a sacred cause: they hailed the fallen at the Boston Massacre (Paul Revere), argued that patriotism could demand the ultimate sacrifice (John Hancock), demanded liberty or death (Patrick Henry), listed heroes sacrificed at the altar of liberty (Thomas Paine), and invited the virtuous to pledge their lives to the cause (Thomas Jefferson). The convicted spy Nathan Hale allegedly regretted on the scaffold that he had but one life to give for his country. To dismiss this as mere rhetoric, Fanestil persuasively argues, is to miss something vital about the fusion of politics and religion in the American Revolution."

—Christopher Grasso, Pullen Professor, department of history, William & Mary, and author of *Skepticism and American Faith: From the Revolution to the Civil War*

"Fanestil's book is an elegantly written monograph that opens an engaging new perspective on familiar historic figures and events. *One Life to Give* gives the reader a way to revisit the lives of Patrick Henry and Nathan Hale (and many others) but to see them through a new frame, a new lens, that of martyrdom. Fanestil is able to balance a regard for American heroism with a realism about American hubris. Perhaps most relevant and helpful is that this work recalls for us the long history of intertwined pulpit and politics, intertwined sermons and elections."

—Rev. Dr. Robert Allan Hill, dean of Marsh Chapel and professor of New Testament and pastoral theology, Boston University

ONE LIFE TO GIVE

To Judith,
w/ love & affection.

ONE LIFE TO GIVE

MARTYRDOM AND THE MAKING OF THE AMERICAN REVOLUTION

JOHN FANESTIL

FORTRESS PRESS
MINNEAPOLIS

ONE LIFE TO GIVE
Martyrdom and the Making of the American Revolution

All Scripture quotations are from the King James Version.

Cover image: TonyBaggett / IStock
Cover design: Lindsey Owens

Print ISBN: 978-1-5064-7414-4
eBook ISBN: 978-1-5064-7415-1
Printed in Canada

To Darrell and D.Ann, for a lifetime

Contents

Illustrations

Acknowledgments

Thank you to Peter Mancall and the USC-Huntington Early Modern Studies Institute (EMSI) for making possible my unorthodox journey to a PhD at the University of Southern California (USC). Thank you to the history faculty at USC, especially Lisa Bitel, Bill Deverell, Phil Ethington, Richard Wightman Fox, Karen Halttunen, Nathan Perl-Rosenthal, and Jacob Soll. Thank you also to Andrew Cashner, Cavan Concannon, and Pierrete Hondagneu-Sotelo. Thank you very much to the staff at the history department and EMSI.

Thank you to Marysa Navarro-Aranguren for introducing me long ago to the discipline of history and to Ann Taves for encouraging interventions spread across several decades. Thank you to the many historians who weighed in on this project at different points in its evolution. Thank you to Susan Juster and an anonymous reviewer at Yale University Press for sharp critiques. Thank you to the participants in the American Origins Seminar so ably convened at the Huntington Library by Carole Shammas. Thank you to Erik Seeman for a uniquely helpful and detailed review and to Christopher Grasso for wise counsel and especially for turning me on to George McKenna's *The Puritan Origins of American Patriotism*.

Thank you to Craig Brown and the people of the First United Methodist Church of San Diego for encouraging me to talk things through out loud. Thank you to Jessica Strysko, Melissa Spence, and the rest of the pastors and staff at the church for their solidarity with an oft distracted colleague. Thank you to Minerva Carcaño, Sandy Olewine, Adah Nutter, Nicole Reilley, and Jeff Luther for their hospitality. After a long day in the library, there was nothing quite like walking the tree-lined streets of Pasadena or eating a meal with friends.

Thank you to the docents at the Nathan Hale Schoolhouse in New London, Connecticut, to Conrad Edick Wright at the Massachusetts Historical Society, and to Richard Crocker at Dartmouth College. Thank you to Colin Calloway for pointing me to Archibald Loudon's remarkable collection of captivity narratives. Thank you to the staff and archivists at the Divinity Library at Yale University. The chance to browse the papers of Enoch Hale, who worked for some forty years as a pastor after his brother Nathan's execution, breathed new life into me and this book. And thank you to Jim Slaby for a spectacular night out on the town in Boston.

Thank you to John Loudon for his unwavering belief in this project. Thank you to others who read or worked on earlier versions: Adina Berk, Kevin Peterson, Simon Mayeski, Keith Peterson, and especially Paul Vogt for encouraging me not to bury the lede. Thank you to Emily King for a fabulous edit, to the editors at Scribe Inc. for the copyedit, and to the entire team at Fortress Press for seeing things through to publication.

Thank you to my family: to Jacob and Ellen and, most recently, the blessed and beautiful Asijah. Thank you to Jennifer, whose unfailing love and unwavering solidarity give me cause for rejoicing and thanksgiving. And thank you, Mom and Dad, for a lifetime of love.

Introduction

In early September 1776, Nathan Hale, a captain in the Continental Army under George Washington's command, volunteered to enter British-occupied New York as a spy. Hale had graduated from Yale College three summers earlier at the age of eighteen. After working for a year and a half as a schoolteacher, he had enlisted in Connecticut's colonial militia, which was incorporated into the Continental Army at the start of 1776. By September, Hale had been soldiering for some sixteen months but had seen no formal battlefield action. He was twenty-one years old and was ready to act. Hale entered New York on September 17 and was captured four days later. On September 22 he was executed by British troops under the command of General William Howe. His corpse hung for three days before being cut down.[1]

The precise locations of Nathan Hale's capture, execution, and burial cannot be confirmed.[2] Neither does evidence survive that Hale spoke the words for which he would be immortalized in the lore of the American Revolution: "I regret that I have but one life to lose [or 'one life to give'] for my country." The saying conjures Joseph Addison's *Cato*, one of the most popular plays of the eighteenth century, in which the play's title character, considering the corpse of Marcus, his soldier son, declares, "How beautiful is death when earned by virtue. Who would not be that youth? What pity it is that we can die but once to serve our country!"[3] While it is possible that Hale spoke these words—or words like them—at the time of his execution, they were probably attributed to him after the fact. After all, the story of Hale's death did not circulate widely, nor was he included regularly in the pantheon of Revolutionary heroes, until Jedidiah Morse included him in his popular 1824 *Annals of the American Revolution*.[4]

What we do know about Nathan Hale's execution, however, is intriguing. According to one British soldier who witnessed the event, Hale expressed regret that he "had not been able to serve my country better," and with "great composure and resolution," he encouraged his captors "to be at all times prepared to meet death in whatever shape it presented itself." Another recalled that Hale was "calm, and bore himself with gentle dignity, the consciousness of rectitude and high intentions." And yet another reported that "the frankness, the manly bearing, and the evident disinterested patriotism of the handsome young prisoner, sensibly touched a tender chord of General Howe's nature."[5] Clearly, in his final hours, Nathan Hale fulfilled expectations of bravery in the face of death that were revered among soldiers of his generation.

Which inspires the following question:

What animated so many young men—young men like Nathan Hale—to risk sacrificing their lives for the Revolutionary cause?

One Life to Give will answer this question by considering Nathan Hale's execution on September 22, 1776, as the culmination of a story that spans generations. This story will help explain why many young American men reached the intimate, personal decision to commit to the Revolutionary cause and why many chose to make this commitment a fight to the death. This story is rooted in a simple insight: as had their forebears, countless young revolutionaries like Nathan Hale were raised and trained to understand that divine approval attached to certain kinds of deaths, deaths of self-sacrifice for a sacred cause, the deaths of martyrs.

The Enduring Legacy of English Protestant Martyrdom

Although today the English word *martyrdom* may conjure thoughts of violent extremism, the constellation of ideas associated with the concept was constructed in the earliest unfolding of the Christian tradition.[6] Jewish antecedents presented varied counsel to those preparing to die, but the early Christian gospels, as these were passed down in oral and written forms, embraced Jesus's suffering, crucifixion, and resurrection as the undisputed template for an ideal death.[7] Tales of early Christian martyrdom typically reached their climax when the faithful refused to recant in final confrontations with ruthless tyrants, earning both the penalty of death and the prize of eternal salvation.[8] These stories built on ideals heralded in ancient Greece, where heroes secured their immortal fame by responding courageously when threatened with death. They were also shaped by Roman culture, which understood that the born male (*mas*) could become a true man (*vir*) through displays of masculine virtue (*virtus*) and that there was no more striking such display than in a dramatic confrontation with death.[9] During the first centuries of the Christian era, the Greek and Latin words for "witness" (*mártyras* and *martyris*, respectively) came to be linked inextricably to the ideal of proving willing to die for one's faith.

The durability and adaptability of this distinctly Christian ideal derived not just from acts of martyrdom themselves but from the narrative and commemorative traditions that were developed around these acts—that is, martyrology—and from the process by which the young were immersed in these traditions as part of their coming-of-age. This latter process can be called "indoctrination" or "grooming" or "radicalization," all of which have strong negative connotations in today's English. More neutrally, this process could be described as "training," or "education," but these misleadingly suggest a formal institutional process. Perhaps most accurately, this process can be described as "catechesis," the word derived from the Latin *catechismus*, meaning somewhat literally to teach by "word of mouth" but more generally instruction and formation of the young. People raised in today's Protestant churches might be most familiar with terms like *Christian formation* or *spiritual formation*. These practices of martyrdom, martyrology, and the spiritual formation of the young are not best understood as stand-alone parts that are blended by design—say, like water and lemon juice and sugar are mixed to make lemonade. Rather, they are best understood as existing naturally in their combined form such that only artificially can the component parts be separated out—say, the way that cells, platelets, and plasma can be separated out from human blood only by the application of centrifugal force.

As scholars of martyrdom have long understood, every act of martyrdom is both a death and a story about a death, and every story about a death holds the potential of inspiring the young to new acts of martyrdom.[10] The creative interplay of martyrdom, martyrology, and the spiritual formation of the young lends itself to continuous elaboration, composing an unfolding, always iterative cultural process, a self-perpetuating feedback loop that moves through time like a spiral. Across the long sweep of Western Christendom, this interplay has served to create and consolidate cultural identities across the span of generations. Vigorous demonstrations of courageous self-sacrifice have inspired the transmission, rehearsal, and celebration of stories about these deaths in oral, visual, and written (and, later, printed) forms. These deaths were also celebrated in public commemorations of many different kinds—none more important than the sacrament of the Eucharist, the ritualized rehearsal of Christ preparing for his own martyrdom on the cross. The transmission and commemoration of these stories, in turn, have inspired and strengthened the collective formation of communities and the spiritual formation of individuals, inciting and inspiring new acts of self-sacrifice.[11]

As we will see, the ideals and practices associated with martyrdom were especially important in giving shape to the many and varied Protestant movements in the English-speaking world. Martyrs remained important to English-speaking Protestants for centuries not because they represented statistically significant portions of specific generations or populations—they did not. Rather, they represented an ideal type of death that could shape the aspirations of all. As one historian has summarized, "The extremism of martyrdom should be understood not as the fanaticism of the fringe, but as exemplary action. Martyrs were exceptional in their behavior, but not in their beliefs or values."[12] Or as Isaac Watts, the composer of hymns that swept the English-speaking world in the eighteenth century, put it,

> How long shall death, the tyrant, reign,
> And triumph o'er the just,
> While the dear blood of martyrs slain
> Lies mingled with the dust?

. . .

O may my humble spirit stand
Amongst them clothed in white!
The meanest place at His right hand
Is infinite delight.[13]

No matter where they lived—and irrespective of whether they faced the prospect of actual martyrdom—generations of English-speaking Protestants embraced the spiritual inheritance of the martyrs, seeking to replicate their spiritual posture and demonstrate their fearlessness and virtuosity in the face of death.

The first waves of English Protestants to colonize North America brought with them across the Atlantic their ancestors' fanatical devotion to the ideal type of the martyr, and they bequeathed this devotion to their descendants. Leading Anglicans, Separatists, Baptists, and Quakers in early New England pointed routinely to their favorite martyrs as evidence that their own tradition represented the authentic Christian faith. In the eighteenth century, others would join this crowded field of contestation, including German Lutherans and Moravians, Anglican dissenters and Methodist itinerants, Anabaptists of many different kinds, French Huguenots and Scots-Irish Presbyterians. Even elites who were enthralled with ideas born from the Enlightenment found tales of martyrdom in their cherished "classics" of Greek and Roman antiquity. Every English speaker in colonial North America could trace their heritage to a long lineage of martyrs, and every one could see themselves in "the martyr's mirror."[14] For some, this may have been only a fleeting glance, but for others, it was a steady gaze born of deep spiritual devotion.

In *A Discourse concerning the Nature and Design of the Lord's-Supper*—first published in London in 1738 but so popular that in the following decades, it was distributed widely on both sides of the Atlantic and then printed in Boston in 1766—the dissenting Anglican minister Henry Grove laid this out with great concision. The death of Christ was "that of a Martyr," Grove explained, and so too was the death of any who "chooses rather to die for the truth, than to deny and forsake it." The essential task of every Christian was to "shew forth" in their own living and dying the kind of death they found exemplified in Christ's death, a death they rehearsed routinely in the Lord's Supper. As Grove exclaimed, "O Jesus, I now see what I have to do when I shew forth thy death in thy Supper! I am to contemplate the heavenly virtues and graces that then shone forth in thee . . . and to excite and oblige myself to imitate them." Pondering Christ's sacrifice on the cross, he encouraged his readers to join him in this prayer, addressed directly to Jesus: "I will endeavour to copy and describe the amiable virtues of thy soul upon my own! My aim shall be to be crucified to the world by thy Cross . . . to be actuated by the same spirit, and to live and die like thee."[15] Appeals, incitements, and encouragements like these—to live and die like Jesus, the first among a long line of martyrs—were common threads binding together the patchwork quilt of English Protestantism on both sides of the Atlantic through to the end of the eighteenth century and beyond.[16]

The Making of American Martyrdom

That the pan-Christian ideal of martyrdom retained enormous sway across the entire landscape of eighteenth-century British North America is evidenced by the surviving corpus of English-language print material from the period. In a vast and diverse array of publications—everything from childhood primers to tales of captivity, from hymnals and psalmbooks to sermons and essays and almanacs—authors and printers in colonial America celebrated martyrdom as an ideal type of death. Publications like these were more than reading material; they were used widely in devotional practices like singing, praying, worshiping, teaching, preaching, writing, meditating, and so on. They were also used in foundational ways to catechize the young.

Americans born in pre-Revolutionary America were encouraged to consider their mortality from cradle to grave, and in this consideration, the ideals of martyrdom were celebrated at every turn—in their learning to read and in the liturgies marking their coming-of-age, in their sacred texts and the preaching of their pastors, when they shared in the memorial feast of the Lord's Supper, as they prepared to go to sea or battle, and as they accompanied their friends and loved ones at their deathbeds and to their graves. Not just preachers but also poets, printers, engravers, and artists drew on a reservoir of famous stories and images of martyrdom in ways that were readily identifiable to Americans of diverse cultural backgrounds. In effect, English-speaking peoples in eighteenth-century America understood that deaths worthy of admiration could be scattered along a spectrum of right conduct, at the exemplary end of which could always be found deaths of self-sacrifice for a sacred cause, the deaths of martyrs. Thomas Mall summed up this view in the preface to his *The History of the Martyrs Epitomised*, an alphabetical compendium of martyrs published by Gamaliel Rogers and Daniel Fowle in Boston in 1747. Referring to the abiding preoccupation of English-speaking peoples with "last words," Mall concluded, "The Speeches of dying Men are remarkable; the Speeches of dying Christians are much more remarkable; How remarkable then are the Speeches of dying Witnesses for Christ?"[17]

One Life to Give chronicles how English colonists in North America appropriated this inherited tradition of English Protestant martyrdom and adapted it to their unique circumstances—and how this tradition came to play a critical role in the American Revolution. The ideals of English Protestant martyrdom found their first powerful expression in North America in the early print practices of New England's Puritans, who created what amounted to a "core curriculum" of martyrology for raising their young. Through the first decades of the eighteenth century, the materials composing this curriculum spread through the diverse colonial landscape, combining in varied ways with other traditions of martyrdom that were already established in other English-speaking communities in North America. Across several generations, conflicts between the English in North America and their colonial competitors, the French, facilitated the fusing of these various expressions. English-speaking peoples in North America were expert in producing narratives about noble deaths; in the arts of distributing these narratives in oral, written, and printed forms; and in catechizing their young to prepare them for the possibility that they might be called on to die self-sacrificing deaths. When the American Revolution came along, it presented an up-and-coming generation the perfect cause around which to rally and a perfect platform from which leaders of the cause could champion this spiritual ideal.

That the martyrdom embraced by the American revolutionaries was descended from the specific inheritance of English Protestant martyrdom can be seen in a few simple definitions that remained consistent across the span of generations:

- *Virtue* is a fully realized expression of true humanity, of true faith, and is exemplified most completely in the willingness to offer oneself in self-sacrifice for a sacred cause.
- A *tyrant* is an earthly ruler who seeks total domination of his subject, as exemplified most completely by his willingness to put the truly virtuous to death.

- A *martyr* is someone who proves entirely virtuous by embracing the immediate threat of death at the hands of a tyrant (or his agents) as an opportunity to bear witness to a cause deemed sacred.
- *Martyrdom* is a death deemed exemplary by others because the dying successfully demonstrated their willingness to die for the sacred cause and as a witness to the truth.[18]

The brand of martyrdom that fueled the American Revolution was organically related to variations that had come before, but it was also distinctly American. Beginning in the mid-1750s, as armed conflict played out in the North American theater of a near-global war, English-speaking colonists discovered new depths of solidarity with one another. As they prosecuted what they called the French and Indian War, leading colonists routinely and ongoingly conjured the ideals of martyrdom, celebrating the prospect of dying for the cause as holding out the martyrs' promise of divine approbation. They shared renderings of this tradition through an ever-thickening intercolonial network of print production and distribution and through the creation of a uniquely American pan-Protestant vernacular that took on oral, often lyrical, form. Along the way, they came to think of themselves as sharing both a racialized identity as the "white" people and what they called a "continental" destiny. True "patriots" were those who proved willing to die for this "American" cause, finally in a war to the death for "liberty" from the "tyrant" king George III. This tradition—call it "American martyrdom"—proved indispensable in the making of the American Revolution.

This understanding lies at the heart of *One Life to Give*. Colonists like Nathan Hale were trained from infancy to understand that there was no more important task in life than the task of confronting death. Likewise, they were raised to believe that the most dramatic expression of fully realized virtue was to offer one's life self-sacrificially in the pursuit of a sacred cause. Young boys especially were taught to expect that someday they might be called to fight and die for such a cause and that should this come to pass, their deaths could be meaningful in the eyes of others and meaningful in the eyes of God. As had centuries of English Protestants in their many wars with the agents of the popes of Rome—and as had earlier generations of English colonists in their many wars with the French and the Indians—young men like Nathan Hale took up arms in the American War of Independence because they were encouraged by their leading luminaries to consider that a tyrant represented a mortal threat to their liberty. They knew what this meant, for across the expanse of history as they had been taught it, the truly faithful had always resisted true tyrants unto death. Having concluded that the American Revolution was imbued with a sacred dimension—that the War of Independence was, in effect, a holy war—young men like Hale determined to support it completely, adding their own commitments of self-sacrifice to the commitments of those who had died similar deaths before.

The declaration attributed to Nathan Hale—"I regret that I have but one life to give for my country"—aptly encapsulates this tradition. The declaration is important to understand not because we can know with certainty that Hale spoke these specific words in the moments before his execution; we cannot. Rather, the declaration is important to understand because expressions of this sort were voiced by such a diverse cast of revolutionaries—from devout Congregationalists like the Connecticut-born Hale to Deists like the Scottish immigrant Thomas Paine, a devotee of Enlightenment thought; from passionate New Englanders like Samuel Adams and Paul Revere, always ready to go to war, to cautious and conservative Quakers like the Pennsylvanian John Dickinson, reluctant to resort to violence; from ruffian freethinkers like the Vermonter Ethan Allen to evangelically minded Anglicans like Virginia's Patrick Henry. Across this cultural landscape, and across this range of perspectives, people coming of age in pre-Revolutionary America held those who died self-sacrificing deaths in extraordinarily high esteem. Sharing this common view, they engaged with the onset of the War of Independence in ways that signaled to each other a deep spiritual solidarity, cementing their commitment to the Revolutionary cause.

Understanding this tradition allows us to make sense of what Abigail Adams wrote to her friend Mercy Otis Warren on December 5, 1773: "Such is the present Spirit that prevails, that if once they are made desperate Many, very Many of our Heroes will spend their lives in the cause, With the Speach of Cato in their Mouths, 'What a pitty it is, that we can dye but once to save our Country.'"[19]

John Adams shared this same sentiment, expressing it this way in a letter to Abigail on May 12, 1774: "We live my dear Soul, in an Age of Tryal. What will be the Consequence I know not. The Town of Boston, for ought I can see, must suffer Martyrdom: It must expire: And our principal Consolation is, that it dies in a noble Cause. The Cause of Truth, of Virtue, of Liberty and of Humanity: and that it will probably have a glorious Reformation, to greater Wealth, Splendor and Power than ever."[20]

This same tradition shaped what George Washington wrote in his general orders to the Continental Army on July 2, 1776, the same day his colleagues in the Continental Congress voted for independence: "Our cruel and unrelenting Enemy leaves us no choice but a brave resistance, or the most abject submission; this is all we can expect—We have therefore to resolve to conquer or die: Our own Country's Honor, all call upon us for a vigorous and manly exertion, and if we now shamefully fail, we shall become infamous to the whole world. Let us therefore rely upon the goodness of the Cause, and the aid of the supreme Being, in whose hands Victory is, to animate and encourage us to great and noble Actions."[21]

Evocative, spiritual language like this was not ethereal or incidental or inconsequential. It can be found at every turn in the historical record for generations leading up to the American Revolution. It is present in public orations and sermons and songs from the period, in the popular pamphlets and newspapers that rolled off printing presses with increasing efficiency in the middle decades of the eighteenth century, and in documents and declarations produced by members of the Continental Congresses as they birthed a new nation. This language is pervasively present because it reflected a spiritual inheritance that proved a galvanizing force in the lives of myriad people who committed themselves to the cause of the American Revolution.

Surely some of the Continental Army's rank and file fought and died for the high-minded ideals being hammered out contemporaneously by members of the Continental Congress. Surely some fought and died to defend the hard political and economic interests of the English colonies in North America, inspired by slogans like "No taxation without representation." Surely some were simply caught up in the moment, swept up in the larger cultural movements and communications networks that crisscrossed the colonies in the decades leading up to the outbreak of war. Surely some young men went to war, as some have from time immemorial, for the simple fight and adventure of it all. It is equally sure that all kinds of motives were projected onto the revolutionaries after the fact, through a process of romantic commemoration and myth making by which subsequent generations of Americans went about the work of constructing a national identity. Clearly, the origins of the American Revolution were many.[22]

But the tradition of American martyrdom described in this book animated countless personal commitments—including, as will be detailed in the final chapter, Nathan Hale's decision to risk his life on a volunteer mission behind enemy lines. Because this tradition evolved across many generations, a full understanding of it requires a deep historical perspective. Only by understanding the depth of this tradition can we begin to imagine how the full weight of it must have been felt by young men like Nathan Hale.

1

To Play the Man

English Protestant Martyrdom and the Core Curriculum of New England Martyrology

The first generations of English to colonize New England set out to establish communities grounded in the pure Christian faith. New England's Puritans traced their spiritual heritage back through a long line of martyrs to the self-sacrificing death of Jesus himself, and so they brought with them across the Atlantic—and then continued to import from London—print material drenched in the interrelated themes of mortality and martyrdom. Puritans considered these materials to be supplements and complements to the Bible, which they, like their Protestant forebears, embraced as containing the rule of everyday life. These materials reinforced a consistent message: the fundamental spiritual challenge confronting every individual was that of preparing to die, and in this challenge, Christian martyrs down through the ages were the quintessential guides.[1] As Michael Wigglesworth described in his *Day of Doom*, the spectacularly popular "poetical description of the great and last judgment," when the dead stood before the throne of the eternal kingdom, they would find seated at Christ's right hand the martyrs who most closely resembled him:

> *His holy Martyrs, who*
> *For his dear Name suffering shame,*
> *Calamity and woe.*
> *Like Champions stood, & with their Blood*
> *Their testimony sealed;*
> *Whose innocence without offence,*
> *To Christ their Judge appealed.*[2]

Rightly perceiving that the survival of their colonial experiments was fraught with peril, and eager to confirm that their loved ones had not died in vain, Puritan clergy in early New England anxiously cast their experience in light of this treasured spiritual inheritance, the inheritance of English Protestant martyrdom.[3]

Taught by bitter firsthand experience that death could come calling at any time, the early Puritans in New England were determined to teach their children to prepare for death at the earliest possible age.[4] Specifically, they taught them to read the Bible and a core group of supplemental texts through modes of repetition, recitation (reading aloud), and memorization.[5] On the one hand, this catechetical practice was content driven, the goal being for the young reader to learn by heart a core body of knowledge deemed necessary for salvation.[6] On the other hand, these texts were more than mere reading material. Through an unending cycle of lived experience, prayerful and improvisational reading, and oral and written reflection, devout Puritans sought to participate in what they conceived of as a divine action of incarnation.[7] They understood themselves to be partakers in what they called the "living Word," a transcendent power they experienced not just in the Bible but in many kinds of texts. In their persistent references to martyrdom, Puritans were not merely "writing about" or "reading about" the martyrs. Rather, they were engaged in catechetical and devotional practices that were foundational and formative to their identities. They were raising generation after generation of would-be martyrs.

The foundations of what would become the sweeping cultural tradition of American martyrdom were laid in New England, and Boston was its undisputed cornerstone.[8] While continuing to import Bibles and larger, more complex works from London, Bostonians began to produce locally a short list of steady sellers—psalmbooks, primers, catechisms, and almanacs.[9] These books also introduced readers, especially early readers and readers coming of age, to the spiritual trials of dying and to their inheritance of English Protestant martyrdom. Over time, as a colonial print enterprise was birthed, leading Boston clergy worked in collaboration with printers and booksellers to curate what would become a core curriculum for a distinctive New England brand of martyrology.[10] The works composing this core curriculum would remain among the most widely published books in colonial America, straight down through to the American Revolution. Familiarity with this core curriculum is as important to understanding the upbringing of America's Revolutionary generations as familiarity with the works of Disney media is to understanding the experience of American children today.

English Protestant Martyrdom and the Power of the Printed Word

Rightful claim to the ancient Christian tradition of martyrdom was hotly contested across early modern Europe, both Catholic and

Protestant. In England, even as the national church separated from Rome, Anglicans clung to the tradition, adding from their own number to the ever-unfolding lineage of Catholic saints and martyrs.[11] English Protestants, meanwhile, embraced the tradition of Christian martyrdom with distinct fervor, as they rejected the authority of the Roman Catholic Church, anathematized its prelate (the pope), and waged war against those English monarchs they perceived to be too loyal to Rome. Generations of English Protestant clergymen produced written works saturated in interrelated themes of mortality and martyrdom. As they sat at their desks—the Bible on one side and paper, pen, and ink on the other—they attempted to write themselves, their congregants, and their children into the story of God's salvation. All produced diaries, devotionals, sermons, and correspondence that touched routinely on questions of death. The more capable and connected among them, working collaboratively with printers, saw to it that the fruit of their pens reached larger audiences, addressing questions of death as a matter of course. They published accounts of deaths and other works memorializing their dead. They published essays and polemical works, arguing over the true meaning of death and disputing the best strategies for confronting it. They published catechisms, sermons, and works of liturgy, making clear that, in their view, the preparation for death was the fundamental spiritual challenge confronting every human being.

The way these English Protestant clergymen thought about it, their words connected them mysteriously, across a span of generations, to the lives and deaths of their Protestant forebears, to the lives and deaths of the early Christian martyrs, and to the life and death of Jesus himself. They understood themselves, as was articulated in their sacred Scripture, to be "compassed about with so great a cloud of witnesses," and so they set their sights on Jesus, "the author and finisher of our faith; who for the joy that was set before him endured the cross, despising the shame, and is set down at the right hand of the throne of God" (Heb 12:1–2). The word translated into English as "witnesses" was *martyrios* in the Greek of the New Testament, a language in which they were well schooled. The resulting corpus of print production communicated that the self-sacrificing deaths of the martyrs were the highest, and paradigmatic, expressions of true Christian faith and that following in their footsteps was the surest path to salvation from the overwhelming power of death.

Across these same centuries, English-speaking Protestants came to consider the medium of print as endowed with a certain transcendence—as suggested powerfully by the moniker they gave to the King James Bible, "the word of God." The first printing press was established in London in 1476, and the new technology quickly revolutionized the ways that English-speaking peoples thought about death and the way they engaged with their martyrs. As English Protestants came to understand it, the miracle of print and the witness of the martyrs combined to hold out the possibility that the truth contained in the Christian Scriptures could be made transparent and available to all. Especially as the Bible became more and more widely available in the seventeenth century, many began to use the Scriptures—and related materials like catechisms—to teach their children to read.[12] They also taught their very young that they might be called soon to their deaths and that if they were so called, theirs could prove important deaths, deaths that would be meaningful in the eyes of others and meaningful in the eyes of God.

As printing technologies improved and books became more widely available, Bibles, catechisms, psalters, and other books were reduced in size, eventually so much so that they could be held in the palm of a hand. Amazed at this technological miracle, English Protestants became transfixed by their cherished printed books, much as readers in the twenty-first century are transfixed by their handheld devices. Over time, the English became much more than mere readers of print—they came to use print material not just for reading silently and reading aloud, and not just for teaching and learning, but also for praying, singing, preaching, worshiping, writing, meditating, and so on. In this way, the tradition of English Protestant martyrdom came to involve much more than reading about or learning about the martyrs. Rather, this manifold use of print material became a foundational catechetical practice aimed at instructing especially the young in how to confront life's central challenge—that is, how to contend with the power of sin and death. All who participated in the production, distribution, and use of this kind of print material—authors, printers, people involved in the sale and distribution of printed material, and consumers—were engaged in a conscious, ritualized religious practice aimed at instructing and informing right conduct in individuals and maintaining right order in churches and other, including national, communities. At every level, there was no clearer measure of right conduct than the conduct of martyrs in the face of the prospect of death.[13]

The most enduring expression of English Protestant martyrdom is, without doubt, John Foxe's *Actes and Monuments of These Latter and Perilous Days, Touching Matters of the Church*.[14] First published in 1563, Foxe's monumental work chronicled over 280 instances of Protestants being burned at the stake during the brief, five-year rule of England's Catholic Queen Mary I (1553–58), a reign of terror for which her opponents nicknamed her "Bloody Mary."[15] In what came to be known simply as the *Book of Martyrs*, Foxe crafted his tales, many accompanied by woodcut illustrations, as substitutes for the Roman Catholic legends of the medieval saints, piling them one on top of the next, casting them always against a scriptural backdrop.[16] Among the most familiar profiles was that of William Tyndale, famously burned at the stake by King Henry VIII in 1536 for translating the Bible into English. Foxe attributed to Tyndale the dying words "Lord—open the King of England's eyes," conjuring countless stories from Scripture.[17]

The world portrayed by Foxe was an epic and all-encompassing struggle between good and evil, between life and death. Protestant martyrs like Tyndale were defenders of true Christian "liberty" against "tyranny of three kinds, viz., that which enslaves the person, that which seizes the property, and that which prescribes and dictates to the mind." Foxe labeled this third kind "ecclesiastical tyranny" and deemed it the "worst kind of tyranny, as it includes the other two sorts." The Catholic popes were the very epitome of this total tyranny, which was in turn the true desire of the "Romish clergy" who "not only do torture the bodies and seize the effects of those they persecute, but take the lives, torment the minds, and, if possible, would tyrannize over the souls of the unhappy victims."[18] Foxe lauded John Wycliffe, another translator of Scripture whose "observant mind penetrated into the constitution and policy of Rome." Before his martyrdom, Foxe explained, Wycliffe "inveighed in his lectures, against the pope—his usurpation—his infallibility—his pride—his avarice—and his tyranny": "He was the first who termed the pope Antichrist. From the pope, he would turn to the pomp, the luxury and trappings of the bishops, and compared them with the simplicity of primitive bishops. Their superstitions and deceptions were topics that he urged with energy of mind and logical precision."[19] In Foxe's understanding, true Christians embodied the essential Protestant claim that the Bible, not papal authority, was the essential rule of Christian faith. The "true Church of Christ," therefore, was an inherently oppositional body that resisted papal assaults on true Christian liberty. Although this true church was routinely "oppressed by tyranny" and suffered long periods of persecution, "some remnant always remained," personified by martyrs like Tyndale and Wycliffe who "stood in open defense of truth against the disordered Church of Rome."[20] Foxe's martyrs were usually men, but women, too, could realize the ideal. Whatever their personal histories, they became "witnesses to the truth," and Foxe drew explicit connection between them and the early Christian martyrs, who responded faithfully and at great personal cost to play a role in a divinely authored script.[21]

In one of the most famous of his accounts, Foxe portrayed the Protestant English bishop Hugh Latimer exhorting his colleague Nicholas Ridley, who had lived a life that was "a pattern of godliness and virtue, and such he endeavored to make men wherever he came." As the two men were burned on a pyre at the instruction of the Tudor queen Bloody Mary in 1555, Latimer proclaimed, "Be of good comfort Master Ridley, and play the man: we shall this day light such a candle by God's grace in England, as (I trust) shall never be put out."[22] The exhortation attributed to Latimer was a precise echo of the heavenly encouragement given to Polycarp, one of the early martyrs Foxe heralded in his "first Book containing the first persecutions of the Primitive Church": "And when there was such uproar in the place of execution, that he could not be heard but of a very few, there came a voice from heaven to Polycarpus as he was going into the appointed place of judgment, saying: be of good cheer Polycarpus and play the man. No man there was, which saw him that spoke but very many of us heard his voice."[23] Foxe's phrasing would find its way into the King James Bible, first published in 1611, where it appeared in multiple places, including in the second book of Samuel, where the warrior Joab challenged his fellow Israelites with these words as they prepared for battle against the Syrians: "Be of good courage, and let us play the men for our people, and for the cities of our God" (2 Sam 10:12).[24] The phrase *play the man* captured succinctly the ancient association of martyrdom and masculinity, communicating clearly that the preparedness to die was a signal marker of maturity for Englishmen coming of age. The equivalent of this phrase in today's vernacular might be "manning up" or perhaps even "taking it like a man."[25]

John Foxe's *Book of Martyrs* remained among the most widely printed books in the English language for over two centuries, its reach growing exponentially as it passed through the hands of generations of printers.[26] In multiple and ever-expanding editions, Foxe and the printers who abridged, appended, altered, and promulgated his work staked their claim that the Protestant martyrs, not the Roman Catholic saints, were the rightful inheritors of the true Christian faith. Generations of English Protestants on both sides of the Atlantic were raised on tales inspired by Foxe's *Book of Martyrs*, tales portraying an unending parade of new martyrs who witnessed to their faith by conforming themselves to this ancient archetype, whether through powerful demonstrations of patient long-suffering as they were tortured or through self-sacrificing bravery as they battled valiantly to their deaths.

Across generations, as they spread themselves along a spectrum of resistance to the established national church—variously refusing to conform to it, dissenting from it, seeking to purify it, and at times, separating from it—English-speaking Protestants retained John Foxe's core conviction that martyrdom represented the paradigmatic Christian death. Inspired by the Reformation principle that ordinary Christians could be true saints, they also embraced the parallel belief that even otherwise ordinary deaths could be rightly understood through this prism. In this way of thinking, even people not subjected to religious persecution would eventually face the greatest of all tyrants—death—and in this climactic encounter, as they were tested by the physical pain of dying and by the spiritual temptation to recant their faith, they would be presented the challenge of conforming themselves to the martyr's measure. English-speaking Protestants routinely compared deathbed performances to the trials of martyrdom, and they expected the truly faithful to witness openly to their faith so long as they could speak. They also took pains to ensure that their children were prepared to meet this inevitable challenge.

New England Children Primed for Martyrdom

No book beyond the Bible was more widely distributed in British North America than *The New-England Primer*, an early reader derived from Benjamin Harris's *Protestant Tutor*, first published in Boston sometime before 1686.[27] *The New-England Primer* featured a pictured alphabet, with each letter accompanied by an image and a simple rhyme, beginning with "In Adam's fall / We sinned all." With this alphabet, parents taught their young children to read while simultaneously challenging them to confront their own mortality with rhymes like these:

> G—*As runs the Glass, Man's life doth pass.* . . . .
> R—*Rachel doth mourn For her first born.* . . . .
> T—*Time cuts down all, Both great and small.* . . . .
> X—*Xerxes the great did die, And so must you and I.*
> Y—*Youth's forward slips, Death soonest nips.*[28]

The New-England Primer also included "Lessons and Verses for Children" like this:

Awake, arise, behold thou hast,
Thy Life a Leaf thy Breath a Blast;
At Night lay down prepar'd to have
Thy Sleep, thy Death, thy Bed, thy Grave.[29]

It also included this bedtime prayer, destined to become the most familiar prayer in the English language beyond the Lord's Prayer:

Now I lay me down to sleep,
I pray the Lord my soul to keep,
If I shall die before I wake,
I pray the Lord my soul to take.[30]

Generations of English-speaking children were taught to end their days with poems and prayers emphasizing that they might not live to see the next morning.

Almost all editions of *The New-England Primer* included standard catechetical material like the Lord's Prayer, the Ten Commandments, and the Westminster Short Catechism, and formal catechisms—most commonly the *Assembly of Divines Catechism* or some variation on John Cotton's *Spiritual Milk for Babes*—were routinely appended as a supplement. These catechisms offered older children a more detailed introduction to the essentials of the Christian faith. Taking their readers through a series of questions and answers in a format that encouraged memorization, they drove young readers relentlessly to the doctrine of the final judgment, as found, for instance, in the concluding questions of John Cotton's *Milk for Babes*, one of the earliest examples of the genre:

Q. What is the judgment, which is sealed up to you in the
   Lord's Supper?

A. At the last day we shall appear before the judgment seat of Christ, to give an account of our works, and receive our reward according to them.

Q. What is the reward that shall then be given?
A. The righteous shall go into life eternal, and the wicked shall be cast into everlasting fire with the Devil and his angels.[31]

This core doctrine of Protestant theology not only was found in *The New-England Primer* but was replicated with only slight variation in dozens of other catechetical works printed in eighteenth-century North America.[32]

But the capstone of *The New-England Primer*—functioning as a climax to the introductory material and as an introduction to the formal catechisms—was an adapted excerpt from Foxe's *Book of Martyrs*, often labeled simply *Martyrology*. The featured martyr was "Mr. John Rogers, Minister of the Gospel in *London* . . . the first Martyr in Queen *Mary's* Reign, and was burnt at *Smithfield, February 12th, 1552*." These renderings of Rogers's martyrdom invariably included details of his family, approximating the account rendered in the *Book of Martyrs*: "His Wife, with nine small children, and one at Her Breast, following Him to the Stake, with which sorrowful Sight He was not the least daunted, but with wonderful Patience died courageously for the Gospel of Jesus Christ."[33] That John Rogers was given a place of such prominence by publishers of *The New-England Primer* is no surprise. As the first to be martyred under the reign of the notorious Bloody Mary, Rogers had also been given special treatment in Foxe's *Book of Martyrs*, and the illustrations of his martyrdom were among the most elaborate in each edition of Foxe's martyrology. In Foxe's rendering, when he was confronted by one of the sheriffs, demanding that he recant his "abominable doctrine," Rogers replied, "That which I have preached I will seal with my blood." When he was set ablaze, Foxe reported, Rogers washed his hands in the flames of the fire as they consumed him.[34]

The New-England Primer, with its climactic story of Rogers's martyrdom, remained the most widely available children's book in colonial America, straight down through the period of the American Revolution.[35]

"Exemplary Children" and the Ideals of Martyrdom

As they were introduced to the inheritance of English Protestant martyrdom while learning to read, children in colonial New England were also taught they need not wait for adulthood to put the ideals of martyrdom into practice. Hence the extraordinary popularity of James Janeway's *A Token for Children*, a popular anthology affording children an age-appropriate martyrology akin to John Foxe's landmark *Book of Martyrs*. The first edition of the book, commonly referred to as *Janeway's Token*, was published in 1673 and subtitled *Being an Exact Account of the Conversion, Holy and Exemplary Lives, and Joyful Deaths, of Several Young Children*. In this first edition, the Anglican clergyman Janeway included six accounts organized in numbered paragraphs, each presenting an episode in the child's life and together composing a brief biography. The accounts, or "examples," moved quickly to the matter at hand—whatever their conduct before falling ill, the subjects became holy as they approached their deaths, died happily, and went on to heaven.

Janeway's very first account, entirely representative of the others, was "of one eminently converted between Eight and Nine years old, with an account of her Life and Death." A protracted illness at the age of fourteen took her repeatedly to the edge of death, giving

her ample opportunity to demonstrate her faith and her preparedness to die: "32. Upon Friday, after she had had such lively discoveries of Gods [*sic*] love, she was exceeding desirous to die, and
cryed out, Come Lord Jesus, come quickly conduct me to thy Tab-
ernacle; I am a poor creature without thee: but Lord Jesus, my soul
belongs to be with thee: O when shall it be? Why not now, dear
Jesus?" Her death "on the Lords Day" did the same: "34. . . . She
oft commended her spirit into the Lords hands, and the last words
she was heard to speak, were these, Lord help, Lord Jesus help,
Dear Jesus, Blessed Jesus—and thus upon the Lords Day, between
Nine and Ten of the Clock in the Forenoon, she slept sweetly in
Jesus, and began an everlasting Sabbath, February 19, 1670."[36]

In the preface to his collection of deathbed tales, Janeway
extended introductory advice "to all Parents, School-masters and
School-Mistresses, or any that have any hand in the Education of
Children." He also admonished young readers with "Directions
to Children," thirteen pages consisting principally of catechetical
questions like these:

> 8. Did you never hear of a little Child that died? And if
> other Children die, why may not you be sick and die? And
> what will you do then, Child, if you should have no grace in
> your heart and be found like other naughty children?
> 9. How do you know but that you may be the next Child
> that may die? And where are you then, if you be not God's
> Child?[37]

What to modern readers would seem a cruel mix of maudlin sentiment and scolding torment was embraced by Puritan families on
both sides of the Atlantic for its presentation to children of sound
advice connecting their earthly conduct to their eternal salvation:

"Resolve to continue in well-doing all your dayes," Rev. Janeway counseled his young readers, "then you shall be one of those sweet little ones that Christ will take into his Arms, and bless, and give a Kingdom, Crown and Glory."[38]

By the time the second and expanded edition of *A Token for Children* went to press in 1676, critics had called into question the veracity of Janeway's accounts.[39] In the preface to his supplemental material, he chose to address these doubts by conjuring once more the direct lineage of his subjects to the age-old tradition of English martyrology: "Doth not credible History acquaint us with a Martyr at seven years old, that was whipped almost to death, and never shed one tear nor complained, and at last had his Head struck off? I do not speak of these as common matters, but record them amongst those stupendious Acts of him that can easily work Wonders as not." And lest the reference be lost on his readers, the first supplemental account—"Of a child that was very serious at four years old, with an Account of his comfortable Death when he was twelve years and three weeks old"—included this telltale biographical detail: "7. He was hugely taken with the reading of the Book of Martyrs, and would be ready to leave his Dinner to go to his Book."[40]

Imported regularly to North America from the time of its original publication, *Janeway's Token* was first reprinted in Boston in 1700, when Cotton Mather collaborated with Timothy Green—who with his father, Bartholomew, launched what would become Boston's most prolific publishing dynasty—to produce a version supplemented by Mather's own collection of tales from the deathbed of New England children. As a first example proving that the faithfulness Janeway had documented in England was attainable also in New England, Mather offered an account of John Clap of Scituate, who was "little more than Thirteen years Old . . . when he Died . . . a Young Old Man, full of Grace, though not full of Days." Also among the exemplary children was Mather's own son Nathanael, who, upon his death at the age of nineteen, his father described as "an Instance of more than common learning and virtue."[41] Mather's innovation launched a publishing trend—*Janeway's Token* was printed over two dozen times in New England in the middle decades of the eighteenth century, and by the end of the century, it had been published not only in New England but in New Jersey, New York, and over a dozen times in Philadelphia. Like Foxe's *Book of Martyrs* before it, *Janeway's Token* became a living document, as English-speaking residents of England's North American colonies continued to reassure themselves that they and their children belonged to an uninterrupted tradition of English martyrdom that assured them of safe passage beyond the veil of death.

"Am I a Soldier of the Cross?"—the Spread of Metered Verse

If James Janeway rendered the tradition of English Protestant martyrdom in a literary format accessible to young American readers, Isaac Watts did the same in the format of metered verse.[42] Born in Southampton, England, in 1674; raised in a devout and nonconforming family; and educated at institutions established by Christians dissenting from Anglican orthodoxy, Isaac Watts was immersed from childhood in the musical tradition of English psalmody and became its most prolific innovator. Across the eighteenth century, Watts revolutionized the singing of psalms while also introducing a new genre of "spiritual songs" that were embraced across the entire spectrum of English-language Protestantism. Watts's brand of metered verse afforded people the opportunity to sing simple lyrics to simple tunes, including popular tunes that could therefore be sung with great passion in public spaces. In this way, Isaac Watts and his many imitators birthed a distinctive discourse of metered verse rooted in direct use of language and a core set of simple meters. This combination facilitated the practice of interchanging lyrics and tunes and inspired the creation of new lyrics that could be sung to a variety of tunes, in a variety of styles, and to a variety of instrumentations. Embedded in the catechesis of children, and in the spiritual formation of even modestly educated adults, the singing of metered verse appealed to people from a wide range of religious backgrounds and traditions.[43]

Isaac Watts retained his ancestors' preoccupation with preparing for death and so unceasingly exhorted the faithful to seek deaths that conformed to Christ's pattern of self-sacrifice. While persistently evoking ancient themes of suffering, persecution, and resistance, Watts challenged people not merely to sing "about Christ" but rather to embody the ideals of Christ's martyrdom in the very act of singing, to summon courage and confidence in the face of the prospect of death, and to bear witness to their personal conviction through song as they prepared for their own deaths.[44] Entirely representative is this hymn, which Watts first published as a supplement to his own sermon on 1 Corinthians 16:13 ("Watch ye, stand fast in the faith, quit you like men, be strong"):

Am I a soldier of the cross,
A follower of the Lamb,
And shall I fear to own His cause,
Or blush to speak His name?

Must I be carried to the skies
On flowery beds of ease,

While others fought to win the prize,
And sailed through bloody seas?

Are there no foes for me to face?
Must I not stem the flood?
Is this vile world a friend to grace,
To help me on to God?

Sure I must fight if I would reign;
Increase my courage, Lord.
I'll bear the toil, endure the pain,
Supported by Thy Word.

Thy saints in all this glorious war
Shall conquer, though they die;
They see the triumph from afar,
By faith's discerning eye.

When that illustrious day shall rise,
And all Thy armies shine
In robes of victory through the skies,
The glory shall be Thine.[45]

Watts was also a prolific promoter of the anti-Catholicism that bound Protestants together across theological and denominational dividing lines. As he did with countless others, Watts set "A Prospect of the Resurrection"—the lyric beginning with the line "How long shall death, the tyrant reign"—to the common meter of alternating eight- and six-syllable lines (8.6.8.6). And in it he also cast the plight of English Protestants as destined to triumph over corrupt earthly rulers, none greater than that "Great Babylon," the Catholic Church:

How will our joy and wonder rise,
When our returning king
Shall bear us homeward through the skies
On love's triumphant wing!
. . .

Great Babylon, that rules the Earth
Drunk with the Martyrs' blood
Her crimes shall speedily awake
The Fury of our God.[46]

In 1712, Timothy Green published Cotton Mather's sermon entitled *Seasonable Thoughts upon Mortality: A Sermon Occasioned by the Raging of a Mortal Sickness in the Colony of Connecticut, and the Many Deaths of Our Brethren There.* To this dreary publication, Green appended Watts's reflection on Revelation 14:13, which Green rendered, "The Dead which Dy in the Lord":

Hear, What the Voice from Heav'n proclaims
*   For all the Pious Dead.*
Sweet is the Savour of the Names,
*   And soft their Sleeping Bed.*

They Dy in JESUS and are Blest
*   How kind their Slumbers are!*
Fro Suff'rings and from Sins releast,
*   And freed from ev'ry Snare.*

Far from this world of Toyl and Strife,
*   They're present with the Lord;*
The Labours of their Mortal Life
*   End in a large Reward.*[47]

In this, Mather and Green were once again at the cutting edge. Cutting across parochial, geographic, and cultural boundaries, Watts's *Hymns and Spiritual Songs* was reprinted by at least seventeen North American publishers in Massachusetts, New York, Pennsylvania, Rhode Island, and Connecticut by the year 1787.[48] Watts's *Divine Songs Attempted in Easy Language for the Use of Children* was printed even more widely; its audience multiplied many times over by its popularity as a "hand-me-down."[49] By combining elements in ways that seemed to match perfectly emerging sensibilities—reason and passion, an enlightened wonder at the natural world, and affective pietistic expression—Watts became the undisputed leader of a tradition of corporate singing that was perfectly suited to the tumultuous context of eighteenth-century America, and the influence of Watts's style spread as others improvised on the pattern it set.[50]

To English Protestants in colonial North America, the lyrics of Watts stood out as a powerful, and scripturally grounded, endorsement of their resistance to tyrannical authority. Watts's lyrics, and those of his many imitators, would prove especially popular in the period of the American Revolution. In the first half of the century, though, most colonists presumed that the object of their resistance would be the "Romish" pope and his earthly agents, the French and Spanish and their Indian allies.

Tales of Indian Captivity—Preparing to Face Down Terror

Early generations of colonists in New England possessed a naive belief in the power of the printed word—and a racist assumption that the Christian gospel, if only it were properly disseminated, would naturally and peaceably convert the residents of what they conceived of as a natural and spiritual "wilderness."[51] Over time, as the gap between expectations and reality widened, the cultural misunderstanding deepened between the English colonists and Native peoples in New England.[52] Faced with incessant English aggression and expansion, Natives responded with their own traditional practices of war making.[53] Oblivious to the fact that their own practices of warfare were also culturally conditioned, the English routinely characterized Native practices as alien and barbaric. Self-justifying accounts of relations with "barbarous" and "savage" Native peoples would become a staple of the American press for generations.[54] Archibald Loudon summed things up when he published his 1808 compendium of eighteenth-century "outrages committed by the Indians in their wars with the white people": "All that is good and great in man, results from education; an uncivilized Indian is but a little way removed from a beast who, when incensed, can only tear and devour, but the savage applies the ingenuity of man to torture and inflict anguish."[55]

New Englanders' fears were not entirely unfounded, for their adversaries were indeed adept at the interrelated skills of raid making, captive taking, and cultural incorporation, skills honed across generations of intertribal warfare. Common Native practices including surprising enemy settlements and killing any who might compromise the arduous journey that captivity would invariably demand—those who could be expected to resist (adult males, for instance) were routinely killed during raids, but so too were those thought to lack mobility and endurance, such as the elderly and small children. Older children, by contrast, made for ideal captives—not only because they could travel readily with adults but also because they were naturally adept at acquiring new languages and customs and, with exceptions, established new relationships with peers readily and easily. Culturally mandated rites of incorporation, such as running the gauntlet and ritual washing, were effective in identifying young captives amenable (or susceptible) to these strategies of cultural accommodation.[56] As they came of age, moreover, young captives were likely to establish attachments of affection to members of the opposite sex that made for a powerful incentive to acculturate. In seeking to protect their children, women captives could be incorporated into the new tribe by force or accommodation, or a combination of the two. In this long-standing and highly patterned practice of warfare, captives routinely faced life-and-death decisions—or had these choices made for them—between execution, on the one hand, and conforming to their captors' expectations, on the other.[57]

If some young readers in early New England were inclined to consider the prospects of martyrdom remote, they would have been persuaded otherwise by tales of Indian captivity—enormously popular precursors, of sorts, to the tales of horror and suspense marketed so successfully to today's teens in movies and books. The authors of these tales improvised off the allegorical style of John Bunyan's landmark work *The Pilgrim's Progress*.[58] Formally entitled *The Pilgrim's Progress from This World to That Which Is to Come*, Bunyan's epic allegory tells the story of an ordinary man named Christian, who—convicted of his own sin by the book he carries with him on his journey—departs from his hometown, the City of Destruction, in search of a rumored Celestial City. In transit, Christian meets up with Faithful, another refugee from the City of Destruction, and soon the traveling companions are arrested and put on trial for their rebellion against Beelzebub, the ruler of a town called Vanity Fair. Interrogated by a duplicitous Judge, Faithful refuses to admit a crime, encouraged by an omniscient narrator:

> *Now, Faithful, play the Man, speak for thy God:*
> *Fear not the Wicked's Malice, nor their Rod:*
> *Speak boldly, Man, the Truth is on thy Side:*
> *Die for it, and to Life in Triumph Ride.*[59]

After entrusting Christian to the care of Hopeful, another sojourner, Faithful is executed at the stake, only to be whisked away in an angelic chariot, his martyrdom having earned him free passage to the Celestial City. Published in 1678 in London, the first part of *Pilgrim's Progress* met with immediate and widespread acclaim on both sides of the Atlantic, proving so popular in New England that it was reprinted in Boston by Samuel Green in 1681, an exceptional effort for a book of its size at this early stage of American print production.[60] Soon, though, its prolific publication in London made it readily available throughout New England by way of importation.[61] *Pilgrim's Progress* ran through more than twenty-five editions in its first quarter century of publication, and it remained among the most widely printed books in the English language straight through to the middle of the nineteenth century.[62] Among its immediate effects was to inspire New England authors—who had been looking for ways to counter the influence of compelling legends that French Catholic priests had been telling for generations—to recount their own tales of Indian captivity.[63]

Narratives of Indian captivity played a unique and powerful role in shaping the collective imagination of English colonists in early New England, far out of proportion to the number of actual experiences of captivity. English women taken captive were the central characters in the earliest examples of the form in New England, including the precedent-setting *A True History of the Captivity and Restoration of Mrs. Mary Rowlandson, a Minister's Wife in New-England*, which came to be known for a title attached to it in later editions, *The Sovereignty and Goodness of God*.[64] Rowlandson had been taken captive in 1676, but six years passed before her husband, the Reverend Joseph Rowlandson, brought her autobiographical account to press, with the assistance of his fellow minister, Increase Mather. Rowlandson's account resonated powerfully on both sides of the Atlantic, and other New England clergy quickly realized that tales of colonial women taken captive lent themselves naturally to the same kind of allegorical reading by which English readers were accustomed to interpreting their Bibles and Bunyan's epic *The Pilgrim's Progress*. Hannah Swarton of Maine was taken captive in 1690, and Cotton Mather appended her print account of it to his 1697 lecture "Humiliations Follow'd with Deliverances." Hannah Dunston was taken captive in 1697, and Mather, again, popularized her story, first in a fast sermon of 1697, then in *Decennium Luctuosum* of 1699 and *Magnalia Christi Americana*, published in 1702.[65]

For decades on both sides of the turn of the eighteenth century, English clergy produced captivity narratives sounding powerful themes of danger and bravery, loyalty and betrayal. The most common form of the narratives—naturally, given that most were written by survivors—revolved around the "redemption" of the captives by their own community, through acts of warfare or exchange, after having remained faithful to their God in the face of great suffering. But the narratives also celebrated another outcome as equal—in some ways superior—to human redemption: through acts of willing self-sacrifice, captives could also be redeemed by God through acts of martyrdom. Whatever the outcome, the fates of the captives reinforced a central message: the "continental" destiny of the English was divinely sanctioned, the collaboration of Native peoples with the French was diabolically inspired, and the English cause was therefore worthy of martyrdom.[66] They also reinforced the essential lesson taught by the more formal catechetical material of the New England curriculum: death could come calling at any time, allied with earthly enemies, and its appearance presented unparalleled opportunities for demonstrations of true faith.[67]

"O Welcome Day!"—the Promise of Dying a Faithful Death

While the overall life expectancy of English colonists in New England continued to grow through the early decades of the eighteenth century, the march of death provided a steady flow—and, intermittently, a torrent—of raw material for New England clergy to work with as they expounded on familiar themes of mortality and martyrdom. This common discourse was rooted in the spiritual formation and clerical training offered at Harvard and Yale, established to ensure a reliable flow of orthodox clergy for the church networks of North America. Both institutions retained this core mission through the early eighteenth century, ensuring that a coherent conceptual framework was shared across these networks, even as clergy attached to different traditions engaged in sometimes heated disputes over ecclesial turf and the finer points of Christian doctrine.[68]

The matter of preparing for death remained the source of greatest controversy—a great proportion of the astonishing literary production of early New England clergymen addressed this question head-on, often by examining the lives and deaths of relatives and other intimates.[69] Even deaths that might otherwise be characterized as ordinary were commonly attributed importance in other dimensions, depending on the conduct of the dying and the dispositions of those who witnessed the death. As summarized by the title of a sermon published in 1717, Cotton Mather and those who followed in his footsteps were perpetually committed to extracting *Instructions to the Living, from the Condition of the Dead.*[70]

In accounting for the dynamics of unpredictable—and, occasionally, catastrophic—mortality that swirled around them, English Puritans in New England found convenient reinforcement for their view that the experience of the continent's Native peoples was evidence of divine Providence. In a 1715 sermon, *Just Commemorations: The Death of Good Men, Considered*, Cotton Mather observed, "The number of *Indians* in this Land, is not comparable to what it was, in the middle of the former Century. The Wars which after an Offered and Rejected Gospel, they perfidiously began upon the English, above Thirty Years ago, brought a Quick Desolation upon whole Nations of them."[71] Mather also interpreted this outcome, matter-of-factly, as the inevitable outcome of Indian collaboration with the papist French: "At present, we can do nothing for those Bloody Salvages in the Easter Parts, who have been taught by the *French Priests*, That the Virgin Mary was a *French Lady*, and that our Great Saviour was a *French-man*, and that the *English* murdered Him and that He Rose from the Dead, and is taken up to the Heavens, but that all that would recommend themselves to His Favour, must Revenge His Quarrel on the English People."[72] In Mather's view, all this not only rendered the cause of the English colonists worth dying for but in fact rendered death in its service a glorious outcome. As he thought about it, the recognition of this divine dimension could, indeed ought to, change the way that the faithful in New England conceived of death altogether:

> The Lord sees how *Precious Death* is unto His Children. Death was terrible, was amazing, was confounding to them, while they were not sure of the Blessedness, which belongs to the *Children of God*. It was to them the *King of Terrors*. But now the Nature of *Death* is changed unto them. When they think of *Dying*, they soon fall into such Thoughts at these, "*Rejoyce not against me, O mine Enemy! My Saviour has turned this Enemy into a Friend. The Day of my Death will be better to me, than the Day of my Birth.* O Welcome Day!"[73]

Mather based his sermon on his rendering of Psalm 116:15—"Precious in the Sight of the Lord, is the Death of His Saints"—and counseled his readers: "The advice to the *Children of God* would now be, *O live in daily Expectation of Death.*"[74]

The typical funeral sermon delivered in eighteenth-century New England included an immense variety of material—poems, aphorisms, quotations, and allusions drawn from Scripture; devotional and liturgical material; and so on. By concluding their sermons with vivid chronicles of the now deceased's final confrontation with death—or by appending to their printed sermons separately labeled "accounts" of these confrontations—clergy from across New England connected their loved ones' deaths to a centuries-old tradition that celebrated martyrdom as the most exalted form of death. These tales from the deathbed presented clergy the opportunity to defend their doctrinal and ecclesial turf by celebrating individuals who exemplified Christian faithfulness, not just in their lives, but also in their deaths. They cast these celebrations, naturally, against the scriptural accounts of Jesus's crucifixion and resurrection, which served as the template for accounts of deaths of every imaginable kind.

* * * * *

The works composing the core curriculum of New England martyrology remained among the most widely distributed forms of locally produced print material in New England straight through to the end of the eighteenth century. *The New-England Primer* and other Puritan catechisms, Janeway's *Token for Children*, the psalms and hymns and spiritual songs of Isaac Watts, the tales of Indian captivity, and the often-combined forms of funeral sermons and deathbed accounts—New Englanders used these works to introduce their children and youth to what they considered divine mysteries. These print materials, produced collaboratively by clergymen like Cotton Mather and publishers like Timothy Green, are rightly understood as the distinctive New England fruit of the centuries-old tradition of English Protestant martyrdom, a tradition that involved the production, distribution, and manifold use of print material replete with talk of martyrdom and related themes.[75]

Devout parents in colonial New England taught their children to read using primers, poems, and stories offering instruction in the proper preparation for death, and they read aloud to their children, including bedtime stories of other little children who died happy and went to heaven. Young readers passed around tales of adventure and captivity, and they rehearsed in play their own bravery in the face of death. Young men and women shared with their siblings and friends printed accounts of women who died in pregnancy and men who died at sea or in battle, cementing in the popular understanding a powerful association between the rites of coming of age and the practices of confronting the power of death. At home and in corporate worship, the faithful employed books of prayer to profess their confidence that God could deliver them from the powers of sin and death, and they sang their way through collections of psalms and hymns elaborating on themes of life and death as these are treated in the Hebrew and Christian Scriptures. People heard their own pastors and elders extract from the Scriptures counsel for contending with death, and then they compared this counsel to that offered by famous preachers in sermons and essays in print. As they gathered around the deathbeds of their loved ones, they read the Scriptures and other devotional texts while looking upon the dying as translucent portals opening onto the dimension of the divine. And when their loved ones were gone, they wrote in longhand correspondence—and often published in print—deathbed accounts prompting readers to experience vicariously their own anticipated deaths.

This core curriculum of New England martyrology dominated the early spiritual formation of generations of New Englanders across the seventeenth and eighteenth centuries. Both the content of this curriculum and the way it was delivered communicated clearly to children and young readers coming of age that the fundamental spiritual challenge they would face in this life was the challenge of preparing to die. This curriculum also communicated clearly that the martyr's death, esteemed above any other, could be emulated by all, even those whose specific circumstances did not compel them to undertake formal acts of martyrdom. Anyone, after all, could look to the martyrs as exemplars of faith in the face of the prospect of death. In preparing to die, in facing down threats of death, and in the acts of dying themselves, anyone could put into practice the ideals of martyrdom and demonstrate their virtue and faithfulness. In these convictions, New Englanders were not alone.

2

The Spirit of the Martyrs Revived

The Varied Spread of English Protestant Martyrdom in Colonial America

Through the middle decades of the eighteenth century, print materials composing the core curriculum of New England martyrology reached a wider and wider audience, their distribution facilitated by the expansive geographic dispersal of the New England population and by the concomitant spread of print technology. Beginning with the multiplication of printing presses in Boston in the 1720s and continuing with the pioneering of print in New York and Philadelphia, the practices of print production spread dramatically through the colonies. Following the growth of colonial populations along the riverways of eastern North America, printing presses, or "houses," as they were commonly called, were established in the first half of the century at Portsmouth in New Hampshire; Salem, Worcester, and Newbury in Massachusetts; Newport and Providence in Rhode Island; New London, New Haven, Hartford, and Norwich in Connecticut; Albany in New York; Trenton in New Jersey; Annapolis in Maryland; Wilmington in Delaware; Williamsburg in Virginia; Halifax in North Carolina; and Charleston in South Carolina.[1] In almost every instance, new printers attempted to establish or break into a local market at least in part by printing or selling works that formed part of the core curriculum of New England martyrology—*The New-England Primer* and the martyrology of John Rogers that concluded it; James Janeway's *A Token for Children* and its multiple American expansions; the metered lyrics of Isaac Watts and their evocations of inspiring deaths; the harrowing and awe-inspiring narratives of Indian captivity; and the related forms of the elegy, the funeral sermon and the deathbed account. Steady sellers like these remained a staple of the early American literary diet through much of the eighteenth century. The popularity of these print materials can be partly attributed to their availability and affordability. But they were made available and affordable by printers because they proved enduringly popular across many lines of division—ecclesial, theological, regional, and generational.[2]

As was true of the tradition of English Protestant martyrdom from which it descended, the tradition of New England martyrology was a living and malleable one, lending itself to continuous innovation and elaboration. It did not spread uniformly through the colonies of British North America but rather interacted in varied ways with diverse local cultures. These local cultures often included their own traditions of martyrdom—as in the case of Quakerism in colonial Pennsylvania and the Anglican traditions of colonial Virginia, to name just two examples. The experiences of four prominent men—Jonathan Edwards, Benjamin Franklin, George Whitefield, and Samuel Davies—illustrate how English speakers in other parts of colonial America elaborated their own expressions of English Protestant martyrdom, appropriating materials from the New England curriculum along the way and adapting them to their varied contexts. Familiarity with just a few of these many and varied expressions will prove helpful because—through the experience of protracted war with the Native peoples of North America and with their colonial competitors, the French—the English colonists would later combine these varied expressions as they constructed a "continental," or "American," identity. And the resulting synthesis, a distinctly American brand of English Protestant martyrdom, would play a critical role in shaping America's Revolutionary generation.

"Watchman of the Soul"—Jonathan Edwards and the Necessity of the New Birth

Jonathan Edwards was born in 1703 in East Windsor, Connecticut, into a family tree stock full of Congregational pastors. His father, Timothy, was a pastor, and his mother, Esther, was the daughter of the Reverend Solomon Stoddard, pastor of the Congregational Church in Northampton, Massachusetts, and a towering figure among New England's Congregational churches.[3] Edwards was trained to read using traditional New England catechetical material like *The New-England Primer* and Janeway's *Token for Children*, and he grew up with an especially powerful sense of connection to tales of Indian captivity. In February 1704, a raid of Deerfield, Massachusetts, resulted in the deaths of thirty-nine of the town's some three hundred residents and the capture of dozens more. Among the victims was the family of Edwards's uncle, the Reverend John Williams. The Williamses' captivity loomed large in the extended family, including in the household of Timothy and Esther Edwards, during the two and half years of their captivity. And upon their release, John Williams wrote *The Redeemed Captive, Returning to Zion*, which went on to become among the most popular tales of Indian captivity in early American history. As suggested by its title, Williams's account celebrated his own redemption and that of several sons as signs of God's Providence. At the same time, he sought to reconcile himself, and his readers, to less favorable outcomes. Williams's wife and two children were killed in transit, for instance, as was one "Mary Brooks, a pious young woman," who, after suffering an abortion, recognized that her weakness, by rendering her unsuitable for continued travel, meant that she was almost certain to be killed. Williams lauded Brooks for her exemplary posture in the face of her impending demise: "'And,' says she, 'I am not afraid of death; I can, through the grace of God, cheerfully submit to the will of God.' 'Pray for me,' said she at parting, 'that God would take me to Himself.' Accordingly, she was killed that day. I mention it to the end I may stir up all in their young days to improve the death of Christ by faith to a giving them a holy boldness in the day of death."[4] Among Edwards's earliest memories were memories of his own family praying for his uncle's captive family, and among his earliest reading materials was his uncle's account of their harrowing spiritual trial.[5]

Prepared for the ministry from childhood by his father and grandfather, Edwards enrolled at Yale at the age of twelve in 1715 and so came to share with other mid-eighteenth-century New England clergy a common discourse grounded in shared experiences of spiritual formation and academic training. Having mastered the ancient languages in their preparatory studies, "Yalensies" were trained to read what they called the Old Testament in the original Hebrew, the New Testament in the original Greek, and the works of Roman antiquity in Latin. Students at Yale in the early decades of the eighteenth century were introduced to the latest discoveries of the Copernican and Newtonian revolutions and to the latest literature of the British Enlightenment. Still, they were taught not to seek contradiction and conflict between the exercise of reason and the Christian gospel—rather, they were taught to expect to discover a reconciliation and harmonization of the two.[6] They were also immersed, as had been earlier generations, in the practices of devotion that would prepare them, should they choose, for careers as preachers and teachers.

Edwards graduated from Yale in 1720, but he remained attached to the college in the ensuing years, first while pastoring churches in New York and Connecticut and then, in 1724, when he returned to New Haven as a tutor. Across this decade of his coming-of-age, Edwards experienced a personal spiritual crisis born from a profound encounter with the reality of death. New England had suffered outbreaks of smallpox perpetually from the time of its founding in 1630, and in 1721 Boston suffered a devastating smallpox epidemic. Between April and December 1721, half of all Bostonians—5,889 out of an estimated total population of 12,000—contracted smallpox, and 844 died from the disease, representing more than three-quarters of the total number of deaths in the city that year.[7] Through the summer months, Bostonians scattered throughout the colonies, carrying with them both the disease and a virulent fear of it. Edwards joined with other devout Puritans in taking the epidemic as a sign of God's judgment and disfavor and experienced great anguish over the future of the Puritan experiment in New England. In the ensuing years, Edwards himself suffered a sustained series of dramatic illnesses that repeatedly brought him close to death. After emerging from one such illness in 1725, Edwards moved to Northampton, where he succeeded to the prestigious Northampton pulpit after Solomon Stoddard's death in 1729.

Across his more than two decades in Northampton, Edwards oversaw a series of spiritual revivals that would become notorious through his accounting of them, most famously in his *A Faithful Narrative of the Surprising Work of God in the Conversion of Many Hundred Souls in Northampton, and the Neighbouring Towns and Villages of New-Hampshire and New-England,* first published in 1737 and then widely reprinted for years to come.[8]

Fundamental to Edwards's conceptual frame was the notion of God's absolute sovereignty and the associated notion that every individual would, at the time of their death, face a momentous confrontation with divine and righteous judgment. As Edwards put it in his *Faithful Narrative,*

> The drift of the Spirit of God in His legal strivings with persons, has seemed most evidently to be, to bring to a conviction of their absolute dependence on His sovereign power and grace, and an universal necessity of a mediator. This has been effected by leading them more and more to a sense of their exceeding wickedness and guiltiness in His sight; their pollution, and the insufficiency of their own righteousness; that they can in no wise help themselves, and that God would be wholly just and righteous in rejecting them and all that they do, and in casting them off for ever.[9]

Because death could come calling at any time, Edwards believed, the faithful pastor would call on those within his charge to prepare for this confrontation throughout the life cycle. For Edwards, the pastor was a "watchman of the soul," and "the Work of the Ministry is about the Soul, that Part of Man that is immortal, and made and designed for a State of inconceivable Blessedness, or extreme and unutterable Torments throughout all Eternity, and therefore infinitely Precious."[10]

Like his fellow Congregational clergymen in eighteenth-century New England, Edwards understood his principal responsibility to be that of expounding on the Scriptures and proclaiming the gospel of Jesus Christ.[11] Following in the path laid out by his forebears, Edwards's sermonizing was preoccupied, even tormented, by a simple yet fundamental question: What were the visible or "sensible" signs of a saving faith?[12] Seeking to illustrate the enduring power of true conversion while condemning what were considered excessive expressions of spiritual pride, Edwards turned to the tradition of English Protestant martyrdom that was his spiritual inheritance. Lacking specific instances of martyrdom close at hand, he turned instead to those he most admired, connecting their lives and deaths to the legends of the Protestant martyrs. In his 1742 *Some Thoughts concerning the Present Revival of Religion*, he offered a glowing portrait of his own wife, Sarah Pierpont Edwards, though he did not identify her by name at the time. In his accounting, Sarah's fullness of faith was demonstrated most powerfully by her preparedness to die. When, beginning in January 1742, she was overcome for two weeks in spiritual rapture that caused her frequently to collapse, she assured those who cared for her, "I should be willing to die in darkness and horror, if it was most for the glory of God." Subsequently, Sarah would remark that she would often "feel impatient at the thought of living" and was willing to die whatever death God might prescribe, even "on the rack or at the stake."[13] And then when a former student, David Brainerd, died from tuberculosis at the Edwards' home in 1747, Jonathan Edwards determined to lift Brainerd up as a paragon of faith, a martyr in all but the most narrow definition, first in a funeral sermon and later in a more extended account of Brainerd's life and death.

Born in 1718, David Brainerd enrolled in Yale in 1739 after a powerful experience of conversion. At Yale, he became an early adopter of the "New Light" philosophies that, much to the consternation of "Old Light" faculty, swept through the school's student populations in the 1720s and 1730s. Dismissed from Yale for accusing a faculty member of having "no more grace than a chair," Brainerd was already something of a hero among his peers when, in 1743, he embarked on a solitary mission to Mahican tribes in New York and then to the Delaware in New Jersey. As portrayed by Edwards, Brainerd's willing submission to spiritual trial, physical suffering, and Indian captivity demonstrated clearly that a powerful experience of true conversion could issue forth in a Christlike life. In God's hands, he "was the Instrument of bringing to pass the most remarkable Things among the poor Salvages, in enlightning, awakening, reforming and changing their Dispositions and Manners, and wonderfully transforming them." He was also a spectacular witness against the charges most often leveled at New Light proponents of palpable conversion. He "detested Enthusiasm in all its Forms and Operations; and abhor'd whatever in Opinion or Experience seem'd to verged towards Antinomianism." He "greatly nauseated a Disposition in Person to much Noise and Show in Religion" but did not shy of speaking of his Christian experience "on some Occasions, and to some Persons, with Modesty, Discretion and Reserve." As would be expected of a true saint, Brainerd "never was more full in condemning these Things than in his last Illness, and after he ceased to have any Expectation of Life."[14]

Brainerd's earthly trials and travails were dress rehearsals for dying, Edwards explained, and his dying was both the culmination of the life faithfully lived and the beginning of a new life in the hoped-for spiritual state of eternal salvation. Brainerd's performance on his deathbed was his crowning achievement and provided the most compelling evidence imaginable of the faith that issued forth from true Christian conversion. Brainerd's preparedness for death,

Edwards explained, was not "an ignoble mean Kind of Willingness to die, to be willing only to get rid of Pain, or to go to Heaven only to get Honour and Advancement there." Rather, "His own Longings for Death seemed to be quite of different kind. . . . At one Time and another, in the latter Part of his Illness, he uttered these Expressions. 'My Heaven is, to please God, and glorify him, and give all to him, and to be wholly devoted to his Glory: That is the Heaven I long for: That is my Religion; and that is my Happiness. . . . I don't go to Heaven to be advanced, but to give Honour to God."[15] Brainerd's dying example marked Edwards indelibly, and so, in concluding his sermon, he invited his listeners and readers to share in his experience of it:

> O that the Things that were seen and heard in this extraordinary Person, his Holiness, Heavenliness, Labour and Self-denial in Life, his so remarkable devoting himself and his All, in Heart and Practice, to the Glory of God, and the wonderful Frame of Mind manifested, in so stedfast a Manner, under the Expectation of Death, and the Pains and Agonies that brought it on, may excite in us all, both Ministers and People, a due Sense of the Greatness of the Work we have to do in the World, the Excellency and Amiableness of thorough Religion in Experience and Practice, and the Blessedness of the End of such, whose Death finishes such a Life, and the infinite Value of their eternal Reward, when absent from the Body and present with the LORD; and effectually stir us up to Endeavours that in the Way of such an holy Life, we may at last come to a blessed End. Amen.[16]

The death of Brainerd marked the first in a long series of traumatic events that dominated the final decade of Edwards's life.[17]

Through it all, Edwards continued to look to his fallen student, Brainerd, as a source of inspiration, publishing a carefully edited version of Brainerd's diary, which he framed with his own preface and concluding remarks. In the preface to *An Account of the Life of the Late Reverend Mr. David Brainerd, Minister of the Gospel*, Edwards wrote, "There are two Ways of representing and recommending true Religion and Virtue to the World, which God hath made Use of: The one is by Doctrine and Precept; the other is by Instance and Example: Both are abundantly used in the holy Scriptures."[18] After presenting extended excerpts from Brainerd's diary, Edwards returned once more in the conclusion to recount "the special and remarkable Disposal of divine Providence, with Regard to the Circumstances of his last Sickness and Death." Brainerd's diary had been providentially delivered to him by Brainerd's brother "a little before his death," Edwards argued, making it possible that "he being dead, yet speaketh, in these Memoirs of his Life." And so, even now, "he may still be as it were the Instrument of much promoting the Interest of Religion in this World." He would serve this purpose through Edward's accounting of it, the published account making it possible for readers to "see his dying Behaviour, to hear his dying Speeches, to receive his dying Counsels, and to have the benefit of his dying Prayers." Edwards concluded, "May God in his infinite Mercy grant, that we may ever retain a proper Remembrance of these Things, and make a due Improvement of the Advantages we have had, in these Respects! The Lord grant also, that the foregoing Account of Mr. Brainerd's Life and Death may be for the spiritual Benefit of all that shall read it, and prove a happy Means of promoting the Revival of true Religion in these Parts of the World."[19]

"Chronology of Things Remarkable"—Benjamin Franklin and the Spread of the Protestant Vernacular

The colony of Pennsylvania was founded in 1681 by William Penn and other leading Quakers, a seventeenth-century movement of people who believed that only by opening themselves fully to the "inshinings" of the divine light could the faithful inherit the essential promise of the gospel.[20] This controversial view of Christian faith and practice earned the early Quakers persecution in both England and New England, causing them to fashion an identity summed up this way by the early Quaker Edward Burrough in 1658: the "kingdom whereof Christ is King . . . shall be set up and advanced in the earth . . . through the suffering and patience of his people."[21] By the time William Penn and other leading Quakers established the Pennsylvania colony in 1681 as a "holy experiment" in religious liberty, the self-understanding of Quakers in North America was firmly grounded in stories of martyrs like Mary Dyer.[22] Threatened with hanging in 1659 for contesting the authority of the Puritan leaders of the Boston Bay Colony, Dyer ascended the ladder of her executioner with "great Cheerfulness" and proclaimed, "It is the greatest Joy, and Honour, I can enjoy in this World. . . . No Eye can see, no Ear can hear, no Tongue can speak, no Heart can understand the sweet Incomes and Refreshings of the Spirit of the Lord which I now enjoy." When a family member negotiated her release, Dyer had to be dragged down from the scaffold and promptly set herself once more to the task of witnessing, ensuring her eventual martyrdom the next year.[23]

Through the early decades of the eighteenth century, rapid population growth and an institutional environment allowing unprecedented liberty of expression turned the Quaker colony into a hothouse of religious pluralism and cultural contestation. Over time, the Pennsylvania colony's principal port, Philadelphia, overtook New York and Boston as the leading destination for disembarking immigrants to North America, those drawn in search of both economic and religious opportunities and those trafficked forcibly through the Atlantic slave trade.[24] Afflicted routinely by outbreaks of the bubonic plague and yellow fever, Philadelphia became known as a cauldron of communicable disease, a "contagious city."[25] Profound encounters with death and firsthand experiences of loss were pervasive and inescapable parts of life in eighteenth-century Philadelphia, and they naturally shaped the way people thought not just about death but also about the meaning of life. Forced continually to confront the prospect of immediate and unpredictable death, Philadelphians from different cultural and ecclesial backgrounds tapped ancient traditions of martyrdom in search of succor and inspiration. They tapped these same traditions as they gave birth to a competitive book trade that played a critical role in Philadelphia's emergence across the century's middle decades as a cultural hub not just for English colonists but for peoples of all kinds living on the Eastern Seaboard of North America.[26]

Born in Boston on January 17, 1706, Benjamin Franklin would become the unparalleled titan of this expansive intercolonial market in print material centered in Philadelphia.[27] Raised in Boston and catechized in the core curriculum of New England martyrology, Franklin began his career in print at the age of twelve as an apprentice to his older brother James. After a falling out, the brothers parted ways, and Benjamin moved to Philadelphia in 1723 at the age of seventeen. After working in several Philadelphia print shops, Franklin traveled to London with the Quaker businessman Thomas Denham at year-end 1724 with the intent of acquiring the type to start his own press. His plans foiled at first by lack of finances, Franklin again went to work for others, apprenticing with the accomplished London printers Samuel Palmer and John Watts. Denham convinced him to return to Philadelphia at year-end 1726, a momentous decision in that both men fell ill upon their return, Denham dying in February 1727 and Franklin barely surviving.[28] The ingenious and industrious Franklin went on to establish his own thriving publishing house, but his early brush with death, and the loss of someone who had been as a father to him, marked him permanently. In 1735, Franklin's perception of human mortality was torn further from its theoretical frame when his brother James died in Boston. And the year after that, his first child, a son named Francis, died at the age of four from smallpox. Over three decades later, in 1772, Franklin would write to his sister Jane Franklin Mecom that the birth of his grandsons to his daughter, Sarah Franklin Bache, "brings often afresh to my mind the idea of my son Franky, though now dead thirty-six years, whom I have seldom since seemed equaled in everything, and whom to this day I cannot think of without a sigh."[29] In these early encounters with death, as in so many other ways, Franklin was quintessentially a man of his times.

Among the first items to roll off Franklin's Philadelphia press were Joseph Brientnall's handbill *The Death of King George Lamented in Pennsylvania* and a string of tracts by prominent Pennsylvania Quakers addressing a range of topics.[30] As did Philadelphia's other most successful publishers, however, Franklin soon realized that the most reliable profits were to be found in securing the contract to publish official colonial business and in the publication of newspapers and almanacs.[31] In 1729, Franklin joined with Hugh Gaine to buy *The Universal Instructor in All Arts and Sciences: And Pennsylvania Gazette*, which Samuel Keiner had begun printing the previous year.[32] Franklin shortened the paper's title to the *Pennsylvania Gazette*, emblazoned its banner with a slogan promising the "freshest advices foreign and domestick," and filled its first pages with dispatches of news from both sides of the Atlantic. The last pages, meanwhile, featured paid advertisements, dominated by announcements of runaway slaves, books for sale, and services rendered. Punctuating these standard offerings were occasional poems about death, and announcements of deaths, elegies, and epitaphs, the forerunners of the modern obituary. Typically, these announcements, elegies, and epitaphs were reserved for persons of some fame or repute, from queens and governors to poets and priests.[33] On occasion, however, an otherwise ordinary death was heralded for some unique and remarkable characteristic, as was the case in the 1740 death of a "soldier that was unhappily drowned in crossing the River on the Ice on Sunday last." The soldier was found with his rifle "clinch'd in his hand," causing Franklin to imagine his dying words, spoken defiantly to the person of Death:

> *Know Tyrant, know, tho' I my Life resign,*
> *My Honour and my Arms shall still be mine.*
> *And by the Sequel plainly prov'd it true,*
> *That Death may kill the Brave, but can't subdue.*[34]

In 1732—just two years after he became the official printer of the colony of Pennsylvania—Franklin struck another vein of publishing gold when he launched his phenomenally successful almanac, which he published under the pseudonym of Richard Saunders, or simply, Poor Richard.[35] From the outset, Franklin made clear to his readers that questions related to human mortality were among Poor Richard's prime concerns. In the preface to the inaugural issue of the almanac for the year 1733, Poor Richard forecast for his readers the death of his "good Friend and Fellow-Student, Mr. Titan Leeds." The following year, in the almanac for the year 1734, Poor Richard professed ignorance as to whether his prediction from the previous year had been realized, but in the almanac for 1735, Franklin had Poor Richard regale his readers by confirming the death of Titan Leeds, lamenting, however, that his foe's ghost continued to haunt him. In the edition for 1736, Poor Richard reported that his earlier editions had "excited the Envy of some, and drawn upon me the Malice of others" because of "the great Reputation I gain'd by exactly predicting another Man's Death."[36]

As it was for other early American almanacs, the backbone of *Poor Richard's* was a series of monthly calendars guiding the reader through the year with the days of the month listed in a first vertical column and successive columns containing related information such as the day of the week, the rising and setting of the sun and moon, the location of planets and stars, and their implications for the tides and weather. Franklin also included in his calendars a column indicating the "days observ'd by the Church," including the days of saints and martyrs, and the image of the human anatomy, or the "man of signs," meant to connect the health of various parts of the body to the movement of celestial bodies. The poems Franklin printed atop the monthly calendars of his almanac routinely addressed the subject matter of death in tones ranging from sanctimonious to saccharine to sardonic, as in this poem from the September calendar for the year 1733:

> *Death is a Fisherman, the world we see*
> *His Fish pond is, and we the Fishes be:*
> *His Net some general Sickness; however he*
> *Is not so kind as other Fishers be;*
> *For if they take one of the smaller Fry,*
> *They throw him in again, and he shall not die:*

But Death is sure to kill all he can
And all is Fish with him that comes to Net.[37]

Across these early years of publishing *Poor Richard's*, Franklin advanced to a fine art the practice of filling what otherwise would have been white space atop, between, and amid the monthly calendars with poems, aphorisms, epitaphs, phrases drawn from Scripture, excerpts from hymns, and other miscellany.[38] As suggested by this mashing together of such varied information, the popular astrology of the almanacs was not understood to conflict with the revelation of the Christian Scriptures—the designs of Providence were believed to make all these data points align, even if this alignment evaded the precise calculation of human beings.[39]

The early editions of *Poor Richard's* also included a "Chronology of Things Remarkable," in which Franklin listed the years that had passed since each of a long string of events, beginning with the number of "years past since the birth of Jesus Christ." The ensuing list chronicled notable human events and accomplishments . . . and also extraordinary human deaths, such as "the great Plague of London, whereof died 100,000" and "the seven Bishops sent to the Tower" in the reign of King James II, the last of England's Catholic monarchs.[40] With fantastical chronologies like these, American almanacs in the eighteenth century taught their readers that the history of the English in North America was best understood as a natural extension of a larger sweep of human history. By nesting these timelines within each other as he did, Franklin endorsed the popular view that God was at work in human history and preferentially so in Christian history. Even more specifically, he made clear, God was providentially at work in the history of the English and their colonial experiment in North America. Through his mastery of this generic pan-Protestant vernacular, Franklin built a print empire so successful that in the 1750s, he could pass it off to his apprentice David Hall, allowing him to dedicate his best energies to his work as an inventor, scientist, and man of letters.[41]

From the outset of his career in Philadelphia, Franklin sought to establish himself not just as a printer but also as an importer and seller of books.[42] He also sought to exploit the opportunity when demand for some popular titles regularly imported from London nonetheless ran so high that there was additional profit to be made by a local print run. In 1729, in just his second year in business, Franklin determined that this was the case for Isaac Watts's *The Psalms of David, Imitated in the Language of the New Testament.* Franklin followed up with another print run of Watts's *Psalms of David* in 1740, and in 1744 he printed Watts's catechism *A Preservative from the Sins and Follies of Childhood and Youth, Written by Way of Question and Answer.* In 1760 Franklin and his apprentice David Hall published Watts's *Divine Songs Attempted in Easy Language for the Use of Children.* And in 1764 Hall, now running Franklin's publishing house with William Sellers, released a first Philadelphia imprint of Watts's *Hymns and Spiritual Songs.*[43]

Through the middle decades of the eighteenth century, the publishing strategy popularized by Franklin—combining the periodic newspaper and the annual almanac with repeated print runs of proven bestsellers like the works of Isaac Watts—came to dominate local print production in every colony of British North America. So, too, did Franklin's pan-Protestant style of discourse, grounded in ideals of masculine virtue, rooted in a distinctively American brand of moralism, and flowering in a posture of spiritual confidence in the face of death. Leading colonists in Pennsylvania embraced this sense of moral right and divinely sanctioned purpose as they pioneered for themselves a new identity as "white people," profoundly informed by the residual Quaker self-understanding as a suffering and victimized community. Philadelphians like Franklin embraced this identity wholeheartedly, contrasting themselves not just with their growing slave populations, over whom they exercised evermore brutal methods of control, and not just with the Native peoples of the mid-Atlantic region, against whom they waged near-perpetual war, but also with immigrants from Germany, Scotland, Ireland, and other parts of Europe.[44] This self-understanding—an aspiring and expansive colonial enterprise, imbued with a sense of divine destiny, cast in racialized terms, empowered by a living legacy of martyrdom—would soon be embraced by English-speaking Protestants from across colonial British North America. In championing this new pan-Protestant discourse, Franklin would not be alone.

"Ah! Lovely Appearance of Death"—George Whitefield and the Spread of Revival

Born in Gloucester, England, in 1714, George Whitefield "came up" to Oxford University in 1735, a prodigious step up for the son of innkeepers. At Oxford, he fell in with the brothers John and Charles Wesley, leaders of a small group devoted to fomenting spiritual renewal within the Church of England. Mocked by their peers for their fanaticism, the young men took names intended as insults and embraced them as badges of honor—the "Holy Club," for their Pietism, and "Methodists," for their rigorous discipline.[45] As a fitting expression for their zeal, the Wesley brothers and George Whitefield began their work as Anglican priests by traveling to the English colony of Georgia as missionaries for the Society for the Propagation of the Gospel (SPG), the Church of England's initiative designed to revitalize the American church.[46] There, the Wesley brothers met with failure and frustration—Charles failed to win over both Indians and settlers at Fort Frederica, where he was appointed chaplain, and John's contentious stay as the pastor of Savannah's Anglican parish was scarred by a broken romance, which he handled badly. Upon their return to England, John and Charles shared dramatic spiritual experiences that they came to describe as "conversions." Newly inspired, they went on to launch a grassroots movement of renewal that would dramatically alter England's ecclesial landscape, Charles producing a vast corpus of compelling spiritual hymns in the style of Isaac Watts and John creating an ever-expanding network of lay preachers, organized in what they called "circuits."

By contrast, Whitefield met with great enthusiasm during his first missionary sojourn in Georgia. In the summer of 1738, shortly before returning to England, he established an orphanage in Savannah, a charitable cause that became a lifelong passion. And when he returned to America in the late fall of 1739, Whitefield was embraced as a bona fide celebrity, preaching in the open air to enormous gatherings that included Blacks and whites, men and women, European colonists and Native Americans.[47] Whitefield's fame derived not just from his savvy in exploiting transatlantic networks of print communication, which he used to advertise advance notice of his preaching itinerary, and not just from his conjuring the legacy of Christian martyrdom, but also from his mastery of what some scholars now describe as a new American "soundscape." Commonly lacking the infrastructure of church bells, organs, and the like, English colonists in North America marked public events of diverse kinds not just by ringing bells but by shooting guns, sounding instruments, banging pots and pans, raising cheers, and so on. Open-air preaching fit nicely into this soundscape, and by the 1740s Philadelphia had become a preferred launching pad for itinerant evangelists who busied themselves organizing societies, meetings, fellowships, and classes, both in growing urban settlements and in the ever-unfolding western territories that English colonists continued to claim, often forcibly, from Native peoples.[48] Emphasizing the necessity of a spiritual new birth, these preachers often worked independently of any strict denominational affiliation or theological program, and they promoted—in varying combination—a wide range of controversial doctrines and practices.

Whitefield loomed as a giant over this patchwork ecclesial terrain, and Benjamin Franklin was one among countless Americans who would never forget the first time they heard Whitefield speak.[49] On November 8, 1739, Whitefield opened what would become his legendary second visit to America, delivering a sermon to a Philadelphia crowd that Franklin estimated as six thousand, a number approximating half of the city's settled population. Above all, what Franklin remembered was *hearing* something altogether startling and unique. Whitefield's delivery, Franklin observed, was "so improved by frequent repetition, that every accent, every emphasis, every modulation of voice, was so perfectly well-tuned, and perfectly placed, that without being interested in the subject, one could not help being pleased with the discourse."[50] And in his year-end edition of the *Pennsylvania Gazette*, Franklin reprinted this poem, entitled "To the Rev. Mr. Whitefield," from the *London Gazette*:

> *SWEET is thy voice, and manly is thy strain,*
> *Nor does thy wak'ng trumpet sound in vain.*
> *Then still go on, proclaim thy Master's laws.*
> *Warm'd with the promise of thy Lord's applause,*
> *In that important, that tremendous day,*
> *When seas shall vanish, rocks shall melt away;*
> *When the great Judge impartially shall trace*
> *The various actions of the human race.*[51]

In the ensuing years, Franklin forged a vital partnership with Whitefield, even as Franklin himself built his own reputation as America's foremost skeptic and iconoclast.[52] Whitefield's extraordinarily successful preaching tours of the American colonies were facilitated by the popularity of his printed sermons and tracts, and his collaboration with Franklin ushered in a new era of mass-market American print. Whitefield's tours were a bookseller's dream, a self-perpetuating feedback loop of print. Sermons preached previously in remote locations could be sold in advance of Whitefield's arrival in new destinations, along with his controversial tracts, and then the sermons he preached at the new destination could be sold prolifically on-site after the fact as well as sent ahead to his future destinations.[53]

Like so many other expressions of popular culture in eighteenth-century British North America, the music of Whitefield's oratory was born from a constant awareness of his own mortality. According to his friend John Wesley, Whitefield's health as a young man was "much impaired," such that he did not envision living a long life.[54] After returning to England from his second preaching tour in 1741, Whitefield and his wife, Elizabeth Burnell James, lost their first and only child to death in infancy. In grief, Whitefield threw himself entirely into his vocation as an itinerant evangelist and soon became renowned for working himself routinely to the point of exhaustion. After collapsing while preaching in Virginia in the summer of 1747, Whitefield (and many others) thought he was close to death, prompting him to declare, "I hope to yet die in the pulpit, or soon after I come out of it. Dying is exceedingly pleasant to me; for though my body is so weak, the Lord causes my soul to rejoice exceedingly."[55]

In all this, Whitefield was no outlier. He grounded his appeal in the ancient understanding that the culmination of the spiritual journey was the confrontation with death, which could come at any moment. Whitefield considered with great confidence that encounters with death represented unparalleled opportunities to experience firsthand—and simultaneously bear witness to—the true glories of the Christian faith. Deaths that bore such witness were deemed "noble" or "glorious" or "holy" or "happy" or "lovely" or even, to use Whitefield's vernacular, "exceedingly pleasant."[56] For the Methodists and Quakers alike, these deaths were expressions of a fully realized faith, akin to the expressions that were realized by the early Christian martyrs.[57] As he traveled through the American colonies, Whitefield assembled congregations small and large, composed of people from every cultural background and religious persuasion. As they joined their voices with that of their maestro, Whitefield, these congregations worked themselves into states of spiritual ecstasy, and in the very practices of worship—praying and preaching and singing—they experienced little foretastes of heaven.

Whitefield's embrace of this paradoxically joyful and triumphant spirit when confronted with the prospect of death placed him squarely in the tradition of English martyrology, as was made clear at the outset of his public ministry. Whitefield's brand of Methodism was widely taken as a new brand of Quakerism when he first appeared on the scene in North America. As one Philadelphian wrote, "It must . . . manifestly appear to every candid and unprejudiced Reader of these Abstracts, that George Fox, the Father of the Quakers, and the Reverend Mr. George Whitefield, one of the Apostles of the Methodists, in many Respects resemble each other; and that, notwithstanding they may possibly differ in some particular Points and Sentiments, they are both fond of the same Phrase and Diction; and their Pretences to Inspiration, to a very intimate Familiarity with the Deity, and the Power of working Miracles, are of the same Stamp and Authority."[58] When he came under attack while on his second tour of America, White-field collaborated with his friend and colleague Jonathan Warne to publish a defense of his ministry on precisely these grounds with a 1740 publication entitled *The Spirit of the Martyrs Revived in the Doctrines of the Reverend Mr. George Whitefield, and the Judicious, and Faithful Methodists.*[59] Whitefield and Warne drew the title from Quakerism's most celebrated martyrology, Ellis Hookes's *The Spirit of the Martyrs Revived, in a Brief Compendious Collection of the Most Remarkable Passages, and Living Testimonies of the True Church, Seed of God, and Faithful Martyrs in All Ages.*[60] The focus of the new work was a defense of Whitefield's distinctive teachings on the question of "regeneration" or the "new birth," and the prepon-derance of the text, as was made clear in the book's extended title, was dedicated to elaborating "Nine most Excellent, and Infallible, Signs" that Whitefield and "the faithful Methodists" were in fact "true MINISTERS OF JESUS CHRIST." The fact that White-field was met with opposition was itself taken as a sign of authentic Christian ministry, as Warne explained in his prefatory note "to the Reader": "It has been the Lot of all the faithful Followers of our Dear Lord Jesus Christ, to be hated, and reviled for preaching his Holy Gospel, and maintaining and defending his Holy Truths: And sure I am, that pious Soul, the Reverend Mr. Whitefield, was not one of the least Instances of it."[61]

Across the middle decades of the eighteenth century, White-field met with continued opposition as he expanded his preaching empire on both sides of the Atlantic. In response, he defended him-self in terms distinctly derived from the tradition of English Prot-estant martyrdom, even as he was accused of evoking the tradition too much. When an accusatory pamphlet called *The Enthusiasm of Methodists and Papists Compare'd* received wide circulation, for instance, Whitefield responded in print, retracting "whatever can be produced out of any of my Writings, to prove that I have desired, or pray'd for ill Usage, Persecution, Martyrdom, Death, &c." and acknowledging that "imagination" may have "mixed itself" with his preaching. Nonetheless, he insisted, "Sufferings for the Cause and Cross of Christ will come fast enough of themselves without praying for them." And this was especially true for those, such as his followers, who adhered to "the great Doctrines of the Reformation. . . . 'That Man is very far gone from original Righteousness'—'That he cannot turn and prepare himself by his own natural Strength and good Works to Faith and calling upon God'—'That we are accounted righteous before God, ONLY for the Merit of our Lord and Saviour Jesus Christ, by Faith, and not for our own Works or Deservings.'" And should they be put to the ultimate test, Whitefield ensured, they would remain stead-fast: "Should the Methodists be called even to die for the Cause in which they are embarked, as I am verily persuaded it is the Cause of God, so I doubt not but suffering Grace will be given for Suffering Times, and the Spirit of Christ and of Glory rest upon the Sufferers Souls." His ministry and preaching, he insisted, were descended directly from the most impeachable of all sources, the martyrdom of Nicholas Ridley and Hugh Latimer as portrayed in John Foxe's *Book of Martyrs*: "But, that the Work itself is of God; and, as good Bishop Latimer said, when the Papists laid a lighted Faggot at Dr. Ridley's Feet, so we may venture to affirm, a Candle is lighted in England (through the Instrumentality of the Method-ists) which will not easily be put out."[62]

A man who transcended country, Whitefield considered that dying, if done rightly, could be a beautiful experience, both for the dying and for those who survived. In fact, he was so enthralled with the prospect of death that he composed this hymn, exhorting those who would sing it to imagine themselves over an open casket:

Ah! lovely Appearance of Death!
No Sight upon Earth is so fair;
Not all the gay Pageants that breathe;
Can with a dead Body compare.

With solemn Delight I survey
The Corpse when the Spirit is fled,
In Love with the beautiful Clay,
And longing to lie in his Stead.[63]

The hymn was sung at his own funeral in 1770, by which time Whitefield was arguably the most famous figure on both sides of the Atlantic. He had become so, in large measure, by inspiring generations of English Protestants to dream of dying holy deaths, beautiful deaths, deaths that conjured the spiritual mastery of their beloved martyrs.

An Impartial Trial of the Spirit—Samuel Davies and the Spread of Anglican Dissent

The practice of print production was slow to take root in colonial Virginia, the oldest of England's North American colonies, and for many reasons. The dispersal of Virginia's population among farmsteads, plantations, and small towns made the distribution of ephemeral print material—newspapers, almanacs, broadsides, pamphlets—less practical and profitable than it proved in the smaller northern colonies and in the first American cities of Boston, New York, and Philadelphia. Lower rates of literacy among early Virginia colonists coupled with the less exalted place of sermonizing in the liturgical tradition of the Church of England, the colony's established church, meant that print materials produced by clergy—catechisms, captivity narratives, sermons, essays, accounts of death, and the like—played a less decisive role in Virginians' spiritual foundation. Finally, and perhaps most decisively, from the outset the colony's governing elite considered the production of print an inherently subversive activity. Virginia's royal governors outlawed printing of any kind up through the year 1690, and even then, they retained the right to license—and, conversely, forbid—all manner of publication. William Berkeley, the longest tenured of Virginia's seventeenth-century governors, expressed succinctly the prevailing suspicions: "I thank God, there are no free schools nor printing, and I hope we shall not have these for an hundred years; for learning has brought disobedience, and heresy, and sects into the world, and printing has divulged them, and libels against the best government. God keep us from both." Berkeley's wish would be fulfilled in part—until 1766, the officially sanctioned *Virginia Gazette* remained the colony's only regularly published newspaper.[64]

For all these reasons, it is easy to draw a sharp contrast between the "New England way," a catechetical tradition dominated by print production and consumption, and the oral culture of colonial Virginia, dominated by public settings where the spoken word reigned supreme—the church, the courtroom, the town square, the marketplace, the battlefield. But this contrast obscures important points of continuity. Like their northern neighbors, and like those they left behind in the British Isles, Virginia's colonists understood themselves to be strung, albeit in different proportion, along a spectrum of dissent. They also shared with their peers in England and New England an inherited understanding that a demonstrated preparedness to die was the hallmark of a fully realized Christian faith . . . and that death could come calling at any minute.

* * * * *

The colony of Virginia was founded in 1607, just one year after the London Company was awarded a royal charter to establish colonial settlements in North America. In his landmark 1982 *The Transformation of Virginia*, Rhys Isaac identified some of the ways loyal Britons sought to establish the colony as an outpost of the Church of England: "the delimitation of parishes, the building of handsome brick churches, and the maintenance of beneficed clergy, all at public expense."[65] With the Book of Common Prayer, they attempted to shape the colony's spiritual landscape too. First produced in 1549 under King Edward VI, and then substantially revised in 1662, the prayer books known collectively as the Common Prayer rooted the Anglican faithful in the tradition of Christian martyrdom by providing liturgical resources replete with tales of self-sacrificing deaths. Monthly calendars at the front of the Common Prayer included a steady supply of holy days and festivals and featured martyrs prominently: January's calendar, for instance, marked the martyrdoms of Lucian (eighth), Prisca (eighteenth), Fabian (twentieth), Agnes (twenty-first), Vincent (twenty-second), and King Charles I (thirtieth). The last week of each year presented a special occasion for all to reflect on their mortality—and the opportunity for witness that the prospect of death represented—by commemorating the slaughter of the innocents as reported in the Gospel of Matthew (Matt 2) and by honoring Saint Stephen, the first of the early Christians to be martyred as reported in the seventh chapter of the book of Acts. An alphabetical listing of "Notes on Festivals" concluded the calendar section in most editions, reminding the faithful of how those included in the calendars came to be honored. These notes make clear that for Anglicans true martyrdom encompassed various kinds of conduct, ranging from pacifistic defiance to martial valor. So Saint Stephen was memorialized for having loved and blessed his persecutors and even praying for them as he died.

But on November 20 of each year, "Edmund, King and Martyr, a Saxon Saint, King of East Anglia (855–870)" was also honored for having been "taken prisoner by the Danes after a brave struggle, and, refusing life on condition of apostasy and vassalage, shot to death with arrows."[66]

After a brutal decade of civil war came to an end in 1651, the Church of England's martyrological inheritance became grounded in the memory of King Charles I, whose execution on January 30, 1649, inspired his followers to memorialize their fallen hero as "King Charles the Martyr." Charles's legacy was kept powerfully alive by the Anglican cleric Jeremy Taylor, who, in the wake of Charles's death, sought to extract from his example the "means and instruments of obtaining every vertue."[67] This quest resulted in the publication—in 1650 and 1651, respectively—of his twin volumes *The Rule and Exercises of Holy Living* and *The Rule and Exercises of Holy Dying*.[68] In Taylor's view, God had intended for human life to be "long and happy, without sickness, sorrow or infelicity," but because of Adam's fall, "man . . . fell from that state to a contrary." Taylor believed that the essence of human life was therefore a preparation to die and that the truly faithful would pursue holiness, such that by the time they died they would be spiritually equipped to share life with God for eternity. As exemplified by the saints and martyrs, fearlessness in the face of death, inspired by the promise of heaven, was, for Taylor, the truest sign of a fully realized Christian faith: "God could not chuse but be pleased with the delicious accents of martyrs, when in their tortures they cried out nothing, but Holy Jesus, and, Blessed be God. And they also themselves, who with a hearty designation to the divine pleasure, can delight in God's severe dispensation, will have the transports of Cherubims, when they enter into the joys of God."[69] Printed separately but often bound within a single cover, Taylor's *Holy Living* and *Holy*

Dying went through twenty-five London editions by 1739 and were imported in large numbers to Virginia.[70]

This spiritual infrastructure of Anglican martyrdom proved indispensable to the first generations of English colonists in Virginia, who experienced death on a monumental scale.[71] The high death rate required a continual replenishment of the Virginia workforce from England's laboring classes, and the concentration of productive coastal land in the hands of the colony's gentry cast into Virginia's backcountry a combustible mix of peoples—displaced Indians; freedmen, both Black and white, who had worked their way out of indentured servanthood; and small-time landholders who cleared land and farmed side by side with their household slaves. In 1675, a discontented freedman named Nathaniel Bacon assembled a multiracial revolt against the colonial government, succeeding even in burning the colony's Jamestown capitol building to the ground. The next year, after Bacon's rebellion had been suppressed, Virginia's Natives—organized in tribal chiefdoms that were principally Algonquin but also Iroquois and Sioux—were completely displaced from their ancestral lands along the fertile shores of the Chesapeake. By the turn of the eighteenth century, their removal was so complete that colonial authorities were able largely to control their ever-expanding perimeter with a series of interconnected forts.[72]

As Virginia's increasingly diverse colonial population spread from settlements surrounding the Chesapeake Bay; up the Potomac, Rappahannock, and James Rivers; and into the piedmont of Virginia's Blue Ridge Mountains, the Church of England's hold on the spiritual life of the colony grew less and less complete.[73] Expressions of dissent ranged from simple absenteeism to outright contestations of established authority, and these expressions were encouraged by a self-perpetuating feedback loop that produced persistent clerical vacancies in the colony's Anglican parishes. Many Anglican clergy considered the colony to be a provincial backwater where priests were given neither the respect nor the compensation their vocation warranted. Many Virginians, meanwhile, believed that only the least able of England's priests would seek to fulfill their vocations in American parishes.[74]

In 1724, local authorities in one of the colony's westerly counties, Hanover County, made an unprecedented concession: hoping to prevent the spirit of dissent from simply running amok, they constructed a chapel for a group of dissenters led by Samuel Morris and Isaac Winston, who had been repeatedly fined for absenting themselves from parish observances. Within a few years, the governors even agreed to fund a salary for the group to hire a dissenting minister.[75] This strategy of accommodation did not put a stop to the growth of dissent, however; in fact, it seemed to foment this spirit, turning Hanover County into a virtual laboratory for religious experimentation. Years later, the Anglican priest Patrick Henry—the namesake uncle of the American Revolutionary—wrote to William Dawson, the colony's commissary for the bishop of London, lamenting that the itinerant preachers who routinely "invaded" his parish were nothing short of a menace:

> They thunder out words and new coind phrases what they call the terrors of the law, & scolding, calling the old people, Grey headed Devils, and all promiscuously Damn'd, double damn'd whose souls are in hell, though they are alive on earth, Lumps of hellfire, incarnate Devils, 1000 times worse than Devils &c and all the while the Preacher elates his voice puts himself into a violent agitation stamping & beating scar'd, cry out fall down & work like people in convulsion fits to the amazement of Spectators, and if a few only

are thus brought down, the Preacher gets into a violent passion again, Calling out Will no more of you come to Christ?[76]

Summarizing the doctrinal claim of these "younger Preachers," Henry wrote that they insisted an experience of personal conversion should be "sensible . . . as would be of a wound or a stab" and that they were "great boasters of their assurance of salvation."[77] For traditionalists like the Reverend Henry, declarations like these, pretending to know the mind of God when it came to the fundamental matter of life after death, represented the ultimate presumption.

In the face of increasingly exuberant contestations of their authority, Virginia's Anglican clerics worked assiduously to defend their turf, both geographic and spiritual. Among the ways they attempted to do so was to make their case in print. In 1740, they commissioned William Parks—the colony's official printer since 1730 and possessor of an exclusive license to print the colony's only newspaper, the *Virginia Gazette*—to make more widely available two landmark Anglican pamphlets, the first reasserting the Church of England's place of ecclesial privilege and the second defending traditional Anglican views of death and the afterlife.[78] In *The Sacrament of the Lord's Supper Explain'd*, Edmund Gibson, the bishop of London, staked out the Anglican Church's case as proper administrators of the sacrament, elaborated the "obligations upon Christians to come frequently to it," and then sought "to remove out of the Way whatever Scruples or Excuses may either hinder Men from complying with these Obligations, or be made a Cloak to hide the Shame and Scandal of neglecting them." To Gibson's treatise, Parks appended a listing of "the Holy-Days, or the Feasts and Fasts, as they are observed in the Church of England, Explained, and the Reasons why they are yearly celebrated."[79]

The second treatise Parks published for the Virginia clerics was *A Practical Discourse concerning Death*, authored by William Sherlock, the former dean of St. Paul's Cathedral in London, who from his retirement had determined to "make the Press supply the Place of the Pulpit." Reminding his readers of the "certainty of Death," Sherlock shared instructions "concerning the Time of our Death, and the proper Improvement of it," again and again rooting his argument in England's martyrological inheritance:

> Since we must certainly die, it makes it extremely reasonable to sacrifice our Lives to God, whenever he calls for them.

> There are Arguments indeed enough to encourage Christians to Martyrdom, when God calls them to suffer for his Sake: The Love of Christ in dying for us, is a sufficient Reason why we should cheerfully die for him.

> The great Rewards of Martyrdom, that glorious Crown which is reserved for such Conquerors, made the primitive Christians ambitious of it.

> And what Man then, who knows he must die, and believes the Rewards of Martyrdom, can think it so terrible to die a Martyr?[80]

With their promulgation of classic works like Gibson's and Sherlock's, Virginia's Anglican clergy in the 1740s expressed their clear concern for maintaining good order within the body of Christ, which they understood to be singularly represented by the Anglican parish. In their view, the most fundamental threat posed to this good order was the misconduct of individuals in their observances of the sacraments and in their spiritual posture when confronted with death.

While struggling to assert their spiritual authority over these primal matters, Virginia's colonial governors continued to waver between strategies of coercion and accommodation in their attempts to contend with colonists who refused to conform to the expectations of the clergy assigned responsibility for the spiritual supervision of their Anglican parishes. In 1744, Virginia's colonial legislature, the House of Burgesses, finally surrendered to the facts on the ground and abolished the law requiring that colonists participate in their parish's Anglican observances. This formal sanction accelerated the spread of what was already common practice: local leaders continued to invite itinerant (traveling) and upstart (lay) preachers into their meetinghouses and communities, affording people from across not just ecclesial but also racial lines of division.

Samuel Davies was not the only dissenting minister to move into this fluid spiritual and social environment of Virginia's backcountry, but across his twelve years in the colony, he would prove the most successful and leave the most enduring legacy. Born in Delaware in 1723 to parents of Welsh ancestry, Davies had been trained for ministry at Samuel Blair's classical academy at Faggs Manor in Chester County, Pennsylvania. Blair's academy was a hothouse for the "New Side" philosophy that split the burgeoning Presbyterian movement in North America in the 1730s, and there Blair prepared his preachers to drive their listeners unwaveringly to consider their mortality.[81] By all accounts, Davies—who was commissioned in 1747 by the New Castle Presbytery of neighboring Delaware to establish a network of preaching points in Virginia—was an exceptionally effective practitioner of this homiletical method. Davies often cast God as a judge, presiding over a "Supreme Tribunal." Understanding themselves to be guilty of gross sin, and confronted with their own very deserved damnation, the truly faithful, he taught, would throw themselves at the mercy of the court. One of Davies's listeners likened him to "a skillful pleader before a jury," except that the members of the jury found themselves inevitably seated in the defendant's chair by the end of his sermons.[82] In a 1753 sermon to his fellow clergy from the New Castle Presbytery, Davies described their "important End" as "to snatch perishing Sinners from everlasting Misery, and bring them to a happy Immortality." Describing those who had died in this pursuit as "martyrs of the Pulpit," he reminded his colleagues that they, too, could be connected to a vast lineage of those who had sought to save the unconverted.[83] And in correspondence with his colleague Thomas Gibbons, Davies reflected on "the difficulty of the ministerial work," lamenting,

Perhaps once in three or four months I preach in some measure as I could wish; that is, I preach as in the fight of God, and as if I were to step from the pulpit to the supreme tribunal. I *feel* my subject. I melt into tears, and I shudder with horror, when I denounce the terrors of the Lord. I glow, I soar in sacred extasies, when the love of Jesus is my theme, and, as Mr. Baxter was wont to express it, in lines more striking to me than all the fine poetry in the world:

> *"I preach as if I ne'er should preach again;*
> *And as a dying man to dying men."*[84]

But Davies did not have to engage in flights of imagination to preach "as a dying man." Just one month after his arrival in Virginia in the summer of 1747, Davies returned to Delaware suffering from symptoms consistent with tuberculosis. While there, his wife, Sarah, died in childbirth. In his own Bible, beside Sarah's name, Davies wrote, "Sept. 15, 1747, separated by death, and bereaved of an abortive son." He returned to Virginia the following spring, secured a license to build meetinghouses in the Virginia backcountry, and in his biographer William Bland Whitley's estimation, "threw himself into preaching, convinced that he, too, was about to die." Or as the nineteenth-century Civil War historian William Henry Foote put it in the overwrought language characteristic of his era, "In his domestic afflictions and bodily weakness, Davies felt the sentence of death gone out and already in execution. His soul burned with the desire of usefulness, and his tongue uttered the earnest persuasions of a spirit that would reconcile man to God, and lay some trophies at the Redeemer's feet before his lips should be locked up in the grave."[85]

Among Davies's initial, and most dramatic, accomplishments in Virginia was to successfully challenge the exclusion of dissent from William Parks's official colonial press. In 1747, the year of Davies's arrival in Hanover County, the colony's Anglican clergy published and distributed widely a pamphlet entitled *An Impartial Trial of the Spirit*, attacking dissident preachers as "pretenders" and "teachers of error and false doctrines" who "were either themselves deceived, or intended to deceive others."[86] Arguing that he and other dissenters had the right to defend themselves, and "to the Liberties allowed to Protestant Dissenters, by the Act of Toleration" of 1689, Davies convinced Parks to publish his response, *The Impartial Trial, Impartially Tried, and Convicted of Partiality.*[87] Building on this success, Davies won other concessions from the Anglican vestrymen who staffed the Virginia courts, securing licenses to build meetinghouses in seven Virginia counties. Davies oversaw the establishment of the Hanover Presbytery in 1755, rendering Presbyterianism a permanent feature of Virginia's public landscape.[88]

The Church of England's surrender of monopoly power in colonial Virginia was as much the by-product of cultural change as it was the cause of it. As more and more Virginians distanced themselves from their Anglican roots, they were not all becoming more spiritually isolated, as their parish priests imagined. Rather, many were becoming more actively engaged with their own slaves, who continued to know catastrophic rates of mortality as the defining feature of life. Gathering together with African slaves and their descendants, many white Virginians of the lower and middling sort began to embrace a range of ritualized expressions that were explicit affronts to the colony's Anglican elite. The experience of conversion—dramatized as the death of an old self and a "new birth" as one of God's elect—functioned for both Blacks and whites as a dress rehearsal of sorts for the actual death and promised resurrection of the converted. Conversions were marked by the ritual of baptism by immersion, in which the one being baptized was lowered into and then pulled from "a watery grave," or by the approximate ritual of fainting (or falling down) and getting back up.[89] White Virginians also found common ground with their neighbors of African descent in the notion that demonstrations of fearlessness in the face of death represented a kind of fully realized masculinity.[90]

Beginning sometime in the early 1750s, just a few years into his tenure in Virginia, Davies began to include African and African American slaves in his religious instruction and services of worship. Arguing that true faith was best cultivated by both hearing and reading the Word, he secured permission from several slave owners to teach their slaves to read and to admit them for formal membership in his Presbyterian congregations. In 1754, Davies summarized his recent success as having been "chiefly among the extremes of Gentlemen and Negroes. Indeed, God has been remarkably working among the latter. I have baptized about 150 adults; and at the last sacramental solemnity, I had the pleasure of seeing the table graced with about 60 black faces."[91] And in a 1757 sermon entitled *The Duty of Christians to Propagate Their Religion among Heathens*, Davies addressed "the Masters of Negroes in Virginia" commending that "sundry of you not only consent that your Negroes should receive instruction from me, but also zealously concur with me, and make conscience of your own duty to them, in this respect."[92] Davies's rationale for this was clear enough, as he explained in opening the sermon:

> A creature formed for immortality, and that must be happy or miserable through an everlasting duration, is certainly a being of vast importance, however mean and insignificant he may be in other respects. His immortality gives him a kind of infinite value. Let him be white or black, bond or free, a native or a foreigner, it is of no moment in this view: he is to live forever, to be forever happy, or forever miserable! Happy or miserable in the highest degree! This places him upon a kind of equality with Kings and Princes; nay, with Angels and Arch-Angels.[93]

In the body of the sermon, Davies addressed objections one by one, making clear that his practice remained controversial and bitterly opposed by most Virginia slave owners. Appealing to the paternal instincts of these slave owners, Davies concluded by challenging them to consider "how vast, how awful the trust! To be instrumental to render such a being happy, through its immortal duration! To 'SAVE A SOUL FROM DEATH.' . . . How benevolent, how noble an exploit, how glorious a salvation is this!"[94]

Davies departed Virginia in 1759 to succeed Jonathan Edwards as president of the College of New Jersey, later to become Princeton

University. He took with him the fundamental preoccupation that dominated his life—the question of what the individual Christian must do to be saved from the powers of sin and death.[95] Davies died on February 4, 1761, and so did not live to see the victory of the English in what he and many others, as we will see, so passionately championed as a holy war. Neither did he live to see how this passionate quest to advance "a holy and happy eternity" would help galvanize a new, "continental" identity among a next generation of Americans, nor how this identity would eventually advance the cause of the American Revolution.

* * * * *

Like other variations of the form, traditions of martyrdom in colonial America are best understood as amalgams of three parts—practices of self-sacrificing deaths (martyrdoms), practices of commemorating these deaths (martyrology), and practices of instructing and preparing the young to offer themselves in self-sacrifice (catechesis). As evidenced by the lives of Jonathan Edwards, Benjamin Franklin, George Whitefield, and Samuel Davies, English-speaking peoples in eighteenth-century British North America remained devoted to these core practices. Creatively appropriating the core curriculum of New England martyrology and adapting it to their distinctive circumstances, they continued to immerse their young in the ideals of martyrdom, even as instances of sectarian persecution became less and less frequent. In short, the tradition of English Protestant martyrdom proved an immensely malleable one, amenable to continuous innovation and elaboration. This meant that just as surely as they could branch and splinter, the various strands of English Protestant martyrdom that survived in North America held the potential of being grafted back together.

3

Join or Die

The Birthing of an American Brand of Martyrdom in the French and Indian War

Across the first half of the eighteenth century, the English colonies in North America were drawn closer together by varied means, sometimes by happenstance, sometimes by design, but in ways that were mutually reinforcing. Dramatic flows of emigration, both from England and from other European nations, led to rapid population growth and an ever-expanding geographic footprint. Aggressive policies of forcible expansion into what the English called "Indian country" and the rapid growth and racialized hardening of the system of chattel slavery compelled English colonists at various times and places to seek common cause with one another over and against their erstwhile neighbors. Improved roads and more routinized networks of transportation facilitated a more efficient intercolonial exchange of goods and material of every kind. Ties between the colonies were also strengthened by the continued extension of intercolonial networks of correspondence and print production and distribution. The practices of itineracy and revivalism, embraced by preachers refusing to conform to established boundaries of parish and denomination, birthed intercolonial networks both supporting and opposing new forms of religious expression. A new ideological synthesis—described by the historian Bernard Bailyn as a "surprising mix" of "Enlightenment abstractions, and common law precedents, covenant theology and classical analogy"—began to bridge gaps between the colonies' elites.[1] So, too, did new moral philosophies that were giving birth to new expressions of the inner life, using categories like "sensibility" and "passion" and "spirit."[2] Jointly, these developments helped leading colonists discover common ground and "common cause" with one another.[3]

Perhaps most importantly, leading colonists in British North America forged a deep sympathy with their counterparts in sister colonies through near-perpetual armed conflict with the Native peoples whose lands they were forcibly occupying.[4] Most commonly, wars in eighteenth-century North America are listed using the names and dates for which they came to be known in retrospect by English colonists—King William's War (1689–97), Queen Anne's War (1702–13), Dummer's War (1722–25), King George's War (1744–48), and so on. But listings like these do the experience only partial justice, for they represent only those occasions when conflict between colonists and Native peoples in North America intersected with larger wars between the English Crown and its colonial competitors, the French and the Spanish. In fact, armed conflict in England's North American colonies was never fully disengaged.

Whether directly, vicariously, or in some combination, every generation of English colonists in North America—and almost every colonial household—experienced warfare as an ongoing fact of life. For young American men, the experience of preparing to go to war—even if they would never fight in battle—was a foundational part of their coming-of-age. Catechized in the varied expressions of English Protestantism, most understood this rite of passage to be a matter of faith. As it had to their forefathers, the prospect of war presented to these young men an opportunity to demonstrate their masculine virtue and honor and their fidelity to what most considered to be an intrinsically Protestant struggle against the French, who the English took to be essentially diabolical, and against the Indians, who they viewed as at once inherently savage and at the same time capable of extraordinary courage.

By the midpoint of the eighteenth century, English colonists in North America understood that their generations-long struggle was coming to a head. As they mobilized for the war that would come to be known in Europe as the Seven Years' War and in North America as the French and Indian War, leading colonists forged their own alliances with each other and with the member tribes of the Iroquois Nation. They also tapped their shared cultural inheritance—the tradition of English Protestant martyrdom. In newspapers, almanacs, captivity narratives, and sermons, leading colonists routinely and ongoingly celebrated the prospect of dying for the cause as holding out the martyrs' promise of divine approbation.

"Your Country Is in Danger"—the Emergence of a Continental Print Network

In May 1754, delegates from seven British colonies in North America arrived in Albany, New York, for a gathering that would come to be known as the Albany Congress. Alarmed that the French in North America had forged a broad and well-coordinated alliance with tribes from the Pottawattamie, Winnebago, Ojibwe, Mississauga, and Huron peoples, Benjamin Franklin had been championing for years the idea that the English colonies should fashion a coordinated response. In 1752, inspired in part by the Iroquois Confederacy, with whom colonists in Virginia and Pennsylvania had formed a temporary alliance, Franklin published in his *Pennsylvania Gazette* his own woodcut image of a segmented snake, each segment labeled as one of England's nine northern colonies, under the caption "JOIN, OR DIE." The delegates to what would become known as the Albany Congress were unable to broker a formal plan of mutual defense, but the image of Franklin's snake—inherently vulnerable to dismemberment and death—proved a hit. Often recaptioned with the slogan "UNITE OR DIE," the image circulated widely through the colonies in the ensuing war. After the war concluded in 1763, the image was picked up by champions of intercolonial opposition to Britain's postwar policies of trade and taxation. And beginning in 1774, colonial newspapers from Isaiah Thomas's the *Massachusetts Spy* to William Bradford's the *Pennsylvania Journal* emblazoned Paul Revere's version of the snake on their mastheads in support of the Revolutionary cause.[5]

The wide circulation of Franklin's snake in the aftermath of the Albany conference of 1754 reflected a larger explosion of print capacity and print distribution in the English colonies.[6] Continuing in almost every instance to follow Franklin's model, a new generation of printers attempted to break into existing markets, or open new ones, by publishing newspapers and almanacs. Working sometimes in collaboration, and sometimes in competition, with each other, these printers joined with Franklin and other established printers to create a network of intercolonial communication.[7] As war between the French and the English (and their respective Indian allies) spread across the Eastern Seaboard and western backcountry of the colonies, colonial newspapers began to exchange news in the form of excerpts and reprints in local newspapers.[8] These included not just battlefield accounts and other reports from the ever-shifting front lines but also calls to arms, commonly cast in the generalized Protestant vernacular that had already proven so popular. In 1756, for instance, the writings of an anonymous author, "the Virginia Centinel," were first published in the *Virginia Gazette* and then quickly and widely excerpted throughout the colonies:

FRIENDS! COUNTRYMEN! . . . AWAKE! ARISE!
. . . When our Country, and all that is included in that important Word, is in most threatening Danger; when our Enemies are busy and unwearied in planning and executing their Schemes of Encroachments and Barbarity . . . when in short our All is at Stake . . . the Patriot Passions must be roused in every Breast capable of such generous Sensations.

Countrymen! Fellow-Subjects! Fellow-Protestants! To engage your Attention, I need only repeat, YOUR COUNTRY IS IN DANGER.

Countrymen and Fellow-Subjects! At length the Matters are come to a Crisis. The Controversy that was long in Suspence, has issued in a Declaration of War. . . . Therefore COURAGE! My Countrymen COURAGE! Our Affairs are in a promising Posture; and we live under the Administration of a just Almighty Ruler, who is not wont to abandon the Cause of Truth and Righteousness. . . . And this may encourage us to hope, that these Commotions may terminate in our Favour.

Let every Man breathe an heroic Spirit, to diffuse it around him. Let the Clergy especially, shock their Hearers with the

Horrors of Popery; animate them with publick Spirit, and the ardent love of Liberty; and rouse them from their Lethargy with just Representations of Danger. . . . Let the Love of our Country be incorporated with our Religion; be cultivated as an important Duty towards God and Man; and become the universal ruling Passion. This is the Way to obtain a speedy and well-established Peace, the most desirable Blessing of human Life; and then we may repose in her downy Lap.[9]

As appeals like these crisscrossed the colonies, the cause of specific colonies became transformed increasingly into the "continental" cause of the English in North America.[10] Again and again, this cause was celebrated as worthy of the price of martial martyrdom. To cite just one among countless examples, in the September 16, 1756, issue of the *Pennsylvania Gazette*, Franklin reprinted yet another of the Virginia Centinel's appeals and appended these lines from Shakespeare:

> *In Peace, there's nothing so becomes a Man*
> *As modest Stilness and Humility:*
> *But when the Blast of War blows in our Ears,*
> *Then imitate the Action of the Tyger;*
> *Stiffen the Sinews, summon up the Blood,*
> *Disguise fair Nature with hard-favour'd Rage;*
> *Now lend the Eye a terrible Aspect.*
> *Now set the Teeth, and stretch the Nostrils wide;*
> *Hold hard the Breath, and bend up every Spirit*
> *To his full Height. Now on, you noblest* English.[11]

Newspapers were not the only print material to conjure ancient themes of martyrdom in support of the midcentury war. A new raft of captivity narratives was published, even as traditional favorites were reprinted continually throughout the period. These narratives reinforced the same essential composite narrative: the continental destiny of the (Protestant) English was divinely sanctioned, and the aspirations of the (Catholic) French were diabolically inspired. First published in Boston in 1758, Robert Eastburn's *A Faithful Narrative, of the Many Dangers and Sufferings, as Well as Wonderful and Surprizing Deliverances of Robert Eastburn* is entirely representative. Chronicling his captivity in Canada, Eastburn observed that "our Enemies leave no Stone unturned to compass our ruin; they pray, work, and travel to bring it about, and are unwearied in the Pursuit." The alliance of the Indians and French, he argued, had "laid a good Part of our Country desolate, and threatens the Whole with Destruction." Eastburn concluded with a familiar appeal: "O may the Almighty awake us, cause us to see our Danger, before it be too late, and grant us Salvation! O that we may *be of good Courage, and play the Man, for our People, and the Cities of God!*"[12]

New narratives like Eastburn's—including those of James Smith, William Fleming, Thomas Brown, Isaac Hollister, and others—conjured a paradox: the colonists' primal fear of their Native neighbors was often imbued with a certain respect. At the most immediate level, this respect derived from what many English recognized as Indian discipline and ferocity. As James Smith concluded, after being taken from his Bourbon County, Kentucky, home and living as a captive for five years beginning in 1755, "I have often heard the British officers call the Indians undisciplined savages, which is a capital mistake—as they have all the essentials of discipline. They are under good command, and punctual in obeying orders: they can act in concert, and when their officers lay a plan and give orders, they will cheerfully unite in putting all their directions into immediate execution."[13] At a yet more fundamental level, the English came to respect Native warriors because cultural expectations of Indian males taken captive were analogous to expectations the English attached to performances of martyrdom. Indian warriors were taught to see dying courageously as a final opportunity to put one over on their enemies, to prove victorious even if they were being tortured as part of ritual execution at the hands of an enemy. Within long-standing practices of tribal warfare, performances of death like these were considered the highest expressions of masculinity—the opposite of showing weakness, the last thing a male would want to do. In some instances, they were things that a warrior would almost relish.[14]

As far as the English could discern, Indian warriors—"braves," the English called them—could summon this kind of courage on either side of any conflict, something that made them both valuable allies and fearsome enemies. This also pointed inevitably to the conclusion that the manipulative French were the ultimate source of the threat to the English in North America. In the August 19, 1756, issue of the *Pennsylvania Gazette*, Benjamin Franklin included an extended excerpt from an article first published in the *Gentleman's Magazine* that served the dual purpose of demonstrating the inhumanity of the French and the bravery of the Iroquois, with whom the English were then allied. The author crafted the account to discount rumors that French cruelty in the present war was being overblown, asserting that "however pious and laudable . . . a charitable Opinion of our Enemies may be in general, yet the *French*, as a Nation, are by no means intitled to such a favourable Judgment from us." In support of this claim, the author recounted how the Frenchman Louis de Buade de Frontenac, then governor of Canada, had "condemned two Prisoners of the Five Nations to be publickly burnt alive" at the end of the seventeenth century, in King William's War. After refusing to assent to the Catholic faith, as presented by Jesuit priests assigned that task, the two condemned Iroquois "began to prepare for Death in their own Country Manner, by singing their Death Song." While one of the Indians chose suicide after "some charitable Person threw a Knife into the Prison," the other was "carried out to the Place of Execution . . . to which he walked seemingly with as much Indifference as ever a Martyr did to the Stake." And then, "while they tortured him, he continued singing, that he as a Warrior, brave and without Fear; that the most cruel Death should not shake his Courage; that the most cruel Torments should not draw an indecent Expression from him; . . . He fully verified his Words, for the most violent Torments could not force the least Complaint from him, tho' his Executioners tried their utmost Skill to do it." The author concluded by expressing confidence that "by this time the Reader is convinced, that the *French* are not at all inferior to the most savage of the *Indians*, in their inhuman Treatment of such of their Fellow Creatures as have the Misfortune to fall under their Power; and that a Man may believe what is set forth in our *American* Accounts."[15]

The Curse of Cowardice—Sermons in Support of the War

As the perpetual conflict with the French and the Indians erupted into full-scale war in the mid-1750s, Protestant clergy in British North America came to think of themselves as fighting on the front lines of a cosmological battle. As Samuel Finley argued before the Synod of New York at the onset of war in September 1754, "Ministers may expect a formidable Opposition, in the Discharge of their Office. . . . He that rushes among hostile Swords, needs not more Courage, than he who opposes himself to the Corruption of Mankind."[16] Hundreds of sermons were preached as "muster sermons" to mobilize local militia, as "battle cry" sermons to send troops into battle, and as "memorial sermons" to commemorate the fallen. Dozens of such sermons made their way into print—here are just a few examples from a single year, 1755: in Newport, Rhode Island, James Franklin Jr. published Jonathan Ellis's sermon *The Justice of the Present War against the French in America*; in Boston, John Draper published John Lowell's *The Advantages of God's Presence with His People in an Expedition against Their Enemies* and Isaac Morrill's *The Soldier Exhorted to Courage in the Service of His King and Country, from a Sense of God and Religion*; in New Haven, Connecticut, James Parker published Isaac Stiles's *The Character and Duty of Soldiers Illustrated*; in Philadelphia, Benjamin Franklin and David Hall published Philip Reading's *The Protestant's Danger, and the Protestant's Duty. A Sermon on Occasion of the Present Encroachments of the French*; in New York, Hugh Gaine published Theodorus Frelinghuysen's *Wars and Rumors of Wars, Heaven's Decree over the World*.[17]

Beginning in 1755 and continuing through 1759, his last year in the Virginia colony, Samuel Davies preached rabidly in support of the war—and his printed sermons spread through the burgeoning network of colonial print production. Davies had spent nearly a decade building dissenting congregations in Hanover and surrounding counties, and the war presented him the rare opportunity to demonstrate to Virginia's Anglican elite his virtue and patriotism.[18] He justified his fervor in a 1756 sermon entitled *The Meditorial Kingdom and the Glories of Jesus Christ* elaborating on the nature of the enemy confronting the British:

This is the great mystical Babylon which was represented to St. John as drunken with the blood of the saints, and with the martyrs of Jesus, Rev. xvii.6. In her was found the blood of the prophets, and of the saints, and of all that were slain upon the earth, Ch. Xviii.24. And these scenes of blood are still perpetrated in France, that plague of Europe, that has of late stretched her murderous arm across the wide ocean to disturb us in these regions of peace. There the Protestants are still plundered, chained to the gallies, broken alive upon the torturing wheel, denied the poor favor of abandoning their country and their all, and flying naked to beg their bread of other nations.[19]

Most of Davies's sermons were more practical, if no less fervent, aimed at recruiting and inspiring young men to go to war. In August 1755, preaching to a volunteer company of the Hanover County militia, Davies delivered a sermon entitled *Religion and Patriotism the Constituents of a Good Soldier* based on the verse with roots buried deep in centuries of English martyrology, 2 Samuel 10:12, which he rendered, "Be of good Courage, and let us play the Men, for our People, and for the Cities of our God: And the Lord do that which seemeth him good." Grossly misrepresenting the early history of Virginia as "an Hundred Years of Peace and Liberty," Davies declared that "now the Scene is changed. . . . Our Territories are invaded by the Power and Perfidy of *France*; our Frontiers ravaged by merciless Savages, and our Fellow-Subjects there murdered with all the horrid Arts of Indian and Popish Torture."[20] Lest his listeners and readers remain uncertain about the nature of the threat confronting them, he went on to characterize Virginians as innocent victims and their Indian enemies as demons:

The bloody Barbarians have exercised on some of the most unnatural and leisurely Tortures; and others they have butchered in their Beds, or in some unguarded Hour. Can human Nature bear the Horror of the Sight! See yonder! The hair

Scalps, clotted with Gore! The mangled Lims! The ript-up Women! The Heart and Bowels, still palpitating with life, smoking the Ground! See the Savages swilling their Blood, and imbibing a more outragious Fury with the inhuman Draught! Sure these are not Men; they are not Beasts of Prey; they are something worse; they must be infernal Furies in human shape.[21]

Enjoining the Hanover militiamen to join the cause not for provincial concerns but as an expression of their faith, Davies asked rhetorically, "Shall Virginia incur the guilt, and the everlasting shame, of tamely exchanging her liberty, British liberty, her religion, and her all, for arbitrary Gallic power, and for Popish slavery, tyranny and massacre?"[22]

Three years later, on May 8, 1758, Davies delivered *The Curse of Cowardice*, a sermon aimed at raising a company of militiamen for the Virginian captain Samuel Meredith. Once again, Davies based his appeal on a verse from the Hebrew prophets, this time Jeremiah 48:10, which he rendered, "Cursed be he that doth the Work of the Lord deceitfully; and cursed be he that keepeth back his Sword from Blood." Reminding his listeners yet again of the "barbarities and depredations a mongrel race of Indian savages and French papists have perpetrated upon our frontiers," Davies declared the present generation to be living in such a "corrupt [and] disordered state of things" that "even the God of Peace proclaims by His providence, 'To arms!' The sword is, as it were, consecrated to God, and the art of war becomes part of our religion." After rehearsing a list of motives for enlisting—love of country, love of religion, love of family, even love of money—Davies concluded by inviting his listeners and readers to "mingle with the assembled Universe before the supreme Tribunal." Addressing them as "*sinners* and as *Candidates for Eternity*," he assured them that his invitation to enlist was a win-win proposition: "God grant you may return in Safety and Honour, and that we may yet welcome you Home, crowned with Laurels of Victory! Or if any of you should lose your Lives in so good a Cause, may you enjoy a glorious and blessed Immortality in the Region of everlasting Peace and Tranquility!" Davies appealed to Hanover's young men to enlist: "Can Protestant Christianity expect quarters from heathen savages and French Papists? Sure in such an alliance, the power of hell makes a third party! . . . SOMETHING MUST BE DONE! Must be done BY YOU! Therefore, instead of assuming the state of patriots and heroes at home, TO ARMS! and away to the field and prove your pretensions sincere. Let the thunder of this imprecaution rouse you out of your ease and security—'Cursed be he that doth the work of the Lord deceitfully; and cursed be he that keepeth back his sword from blood.'"[23] Within the year, Davies's "curse of cowardice" sermon was reprinted in Boston, New York, and Woodbridge, New Jersey.[24]

George Whitefield's martial preaching also received a wide audience as the war played itself out in theaters on both sides of the Atlantic. In *A Short Address to Persons of All Denominations*, Whitefield encouraged the faithful to put aside any reservations about the war, first citing precedents from "antient History," then "those heroic Worthies" cited in Scripture "who by Faith subdued Kingdoms, and put to Flight the Armies of Aliens." Finally, he grounded his appeal in the spiritual inheritance of English martyrdom: "And if our Researches descend forwards down to our own Annals, we shall be soon satisfied, that the British Arms were never more formidable than when our Soldiers went forth in the Strength of the Lord, and with a Bible in one Hand, and a Sword in the other, cheerfully fought under his Banner, who hath condescended to stile himself a Man of War." Placing his own generation in this long tradition,

Whitefield argued that "if God himself is pleased to stile himself a Man of War, surely a just and righteous Cause (such as the British War at present is) we may as lawfully draw our Swords, in order to defend ourselves against our common and public Enemy, as a civil Magistrate may sit on a Bench, and condemn a public Robber to Death." King George, Whitefield continued, had displayed "a fatal Scrupulosity against bearing Arms, even in a defensive War," but was now in "danger of losing that lately most flourishing Province of Pennsylvania, the very Centre and Garden of North America." He continued, "Far be it from me, who profess myself a Disciple and Minister of the Prince of Peace, to sound a Trumpet for War: But when the Trumpet is already sounded by a perfidious Enemy, and our King, our Country, our civil and religious Liberties are all, as it were, lying at Stake, did we not at such a Season lend our Purses, our Tongues, our Arms, as well as our Prayers, in Defence of them?" Describing himself as "fully convinced of the Justice of the British Cause," Whitefield declared the outbreak of war a "happy misfortune," arguing, "For, surely, it is far more preferable to die, tho' by a Popish Sword, and be carried from the Din and Noise of War by Angels into Abraham's Bosom, than to be suffered to survive, only to drag on a wearisome Life, and to be a mournful Spectator, and daily Bewailer, of one's Country's Ruin." After citing a proclamation from the king of France that all Protestant "preachers, who shall call Assemblies, preach in them, or discharge any other Function, be put to Death," Whitefield exhorted his fellow preachers to prepare themselves to die for the cause, conjuring first the heritage of early Protestant martyrs—at Smithfield in London and in Ireland—and then connecting this heritage to the recent reported execution of Protestants at Languedoc in France: "Speak, Smithfield, speak, and . . . declare to all . . . how many English Protestant Martyrs thou hast seen burnt to Death, in the Reign of a cruel Popish Queen. . . . Speak, Ireland, speak and tell if Thou canst, how many Thousands, and Tens of Thousands of innocent unprovoking Protestants were massacred in cold Blood by the Hands of cruel Papists within thy Borders, about a Century ago. . . . But why go we back to such distant Aeras? Speak, Languedoc, speak and tell, if thou canst, how many Protestant ministers have been lately executed."[25] Whitefield's sermon ran through six editions in London, Philadelphia, New York, and Boston in the year of its release, 1756.[26]

Through to the conclusion of the great midcentury war, English preachers on both sides of the Atlantic joined Davies and Whitefield, lending their homiletical support to what they uniformly portrayed as a Protestant cause worthy of martyrdom.

* * * * *

Benjamin Franklin's all-or-nothing appeal to his fellow English colonists in 1754—"JOIN, OR DIE"—did not produce the formal union that he had hoped to forge in advance of the colonists' great midcentury war with the French and the Indians. As was so often the case, however, Franklin was simply ahead of history's curve. At the time the war began, most English colonists still thought of their respective colonies, not of England, when referring to their "country." By the end of the war in 1763, more and more considered the "American" struggle to be a shared struggle of continental dimension. In this, they were encouraged by news accounts of the war, by a new raft of captivity narratives, and by the sermons of celebrated preachers like Samuel Davies and George Whitefield. All these print materials promoted a kind of spiritual bond of distinctly Protestant hue.[27] This emerging pan-Protestant American identity was firmly tethered to the spiritual inheritance of English Protestant martyrdom. Through the early decades of the eighteenth century, the martial dimensions of this tradition had proven invaluable to colonists in diverse settings as they engaged almost perpetually in small-scale conflict with their neighbors. During the French and Indian War, a new generation of leaders picked up these strands and wove them into a distinctly American tapestry.

When the signing of the Treaty of Paris in February 1763 brought an end to the great war, English colonists in North America were ready to sound a triumphant note. Later that year, when Benjamin Franklin's protégé David Hall prepared *Poor Richard's* for the year 1764, he inserted a "beautiful historical Summary" amid the monthly calendars, pithy sayings, and practical information that readers of the almanac had come to expect. The summary, authored anonymously but probably by Franklin himself, offered a "picture of the rapid and irresistible Progress of the Christian Religion":

> Our Saviour passed Thirty Years of his Life in Obscurity and Poverty; then preached, and confirmed his Doctrine with Prodigies, gave Health to the Sick, Light to the Blind, Life to the Dead: He died by Mens Malice, and rose again by his own Power, sent twelve Fishermen to subdue the World; Success waited on their Labours, and crowned their Endeavours; so that, in a few Years, the Christian Religion spread its Conquests beyond the Bounds of the Roman Empire. Prejudice, Libertinism, and Atheism, conspired its Ruin, Philosophers opposed Arguments; Emperors, Torments, and Libertines Sensuality: Yet Christianity broke through the Violence of the Opposition; it multiplied by Disputes, and increased by Persecution; Millions of Martyrs lost their lives in the Quarrel; they demonstrated the Truth of their Creed, by the Constancy of their invincible Valour, though their Torments were inexpressible. So that,

notwithstanding the Christian Religion has been so furiously attacked by Impiety and Prophaneness, it has always appeared holy, always victorious, and always triumphant; it has been proved by Miracles, sealed with the Blood of Martyrs, testified by the Apostles, confirmed by Reason, published by the very Elements, and confessed even by Devils.[28]

While they would have found any number of reasons to quibble with this synopsis, leaders from across the colonies—and from across the ecclesial spectrum of British North America—would have approved of its broad and highly idealized outline of Christian history. They would have also embraced its clear implication: the true Christian religion, "sealed with the Blood of Martyrs," had prevailed once more, this time in North America. In the war's aftermath, Benjamin Franklin and others would raise high the banner of English Protestant martyrdom newly embroidered in an American style. A new generation of Americans would come of age beneath this banner, and soon enough they would hang it over a new platform, a platform of revolution.

4

An Aggravated Tyranny

American Martyrdom and the Raising of a Revolutionary Generation

The English victory in the Seven Years' War provoked a crisis in relations between the mother country and her colonies in North America. The war had nearly doubled Britain's national debt, and as far as authorities in London were concerned, much of it had been accumulated defending English interests abroad. In the war's aftermath, Parliament adopted the Sugar Act and Currency Act in 1764, the Stamp Act in 1765, the Townshend Duties beginning in 1767, and other measures intended to raise revenue from the colonies. As British authorities rolled out these postwar policies in North America, leading colonists seethed in suspicion and frustration. These leaders resented that the new taxes were imposed by a political body, the English Parliament, in which they had no direct representation. They also chafed at Parliament's continuation—and in some cases, expansion—of long-standing restrictions on trade. Parliament was not the only English institution the colonists targeted for postwar resistance. Those with expansionist aspirations—in Pennsylvania and Virginia, especially—were outraged when the Royal Proclamation of 1763 forbid the issuance of new land grants beyond a line drawn along the Appalachian Mountains. The expanded presence of British troops in North America—sent to enforce the controversial postwar regime of taxation and to keep the postwar peace between colonists and Indians—became the source of widespread controversy. In much the same fashion, leaders from across the increasingly diverse American ecclesial landscape perceived authorities from within the Church of England to be exercising too much power in postwar North America.[1]

These distinctly American resentments were given early voice by three prominent spokesmen—by Patrick Henry in Virginia, where dissent from the established authority of the Church of England was woven into the very fabric of the colony's life; by Samuel Adams in Massachusetts, where Bostonians in particular had a long history of protesting against restrictions imposed by British magistrates; and by John Dickinson in Philadelphia, where Quaker-inspired resistance to perceived threats to religious liberty still ran deep. These men were part of a larger rhetorical movement that saw the transformation of the early American "soundscape," exposing Americans to a new brand of oratory and propaganda and lyrical improvisation. This movement embraced both the rising tide of republican philosophy and the oppositional spirit of English Protestantism. It also embraced the ancient inheritance of English Protestant martyrdom, framed in new terms. More and more the term *patriot* served as a functional equivalent for the term *martyr* in the American vernacular. The time was nearing, this upstart generation began to declare, when true patriots would be called to offer themselves in self-sacrifice to the American cause.

"Treason! Treason!"—the Early Oratory of Patrick Henry

Joannes "John" Henry immigrated to Virginia in 1727, after abandoning his course of study at King's College in Aberdeen, Scotland. Henry settled in one of the colony's newest counties, Hanover County, and in 1733 married Sarah Winston Syme, a young widow wealthy both from her own family's inheritance and from that of her deceased husband. Over time, Henry came to occupy every key position in Hanover County's overlapping institutions: a vestryman in the county parish of the Anglican Church, a judge in the county court, a colonel in the county's regiment of the Virginia militia, a land surveyor for the county government. His social standing was further enhanced when his brother, the Reverend Patrick Henry, arrived from Scotland in 1735 to become the priest of St. Paul's Church, the seat of the Church of England's principal Hanover County parish. When their first son was born the following year, on May 29, 1736, John and Sarah Henry named him Patrick Henry after his uncle.

The Hanover County parish had long been one of the unruliest in the Virginia colony, and by the time Rev. Patrick Henry arrived to oversee it, it was home to a well-organized group of dissenters that included Isaac Winston, the father of Sarah Winston Syme, John Henry's new bride. The domestic life of the Henry family was set in turmoil when—after the October 1745 visit of George Whitefield to Hanover County—Sarah Henry began to join her father in his open dissent. This dramatic change cut close to the hearts of both Henry brothers. To Rev. Patrick Henry, Sarah was not just any old sheep of his flock—she was his sister-in-law and the mother of his namesake nephew. As a member of the parish vestry, John Henry's embarrassment and inconvenience had to be enormous—his own wife was now in open religious rebellion against his own authority, the authority of his brother, and the authority of the church.[2] John Henry's embarrassment was destined to grow yet more profound—when the Presbyterian Samuel Davies began to organize a set of preaching points in Hanover County beginning in 1747, Sarah Henry became a fan. As far as the Henry brothers were concerned, Davies represented a far greater threat than did Whitfield and lesser itinerant evangelists. Davies was seeking to establish enduring congregations in the Virginia backcountry, he admitted Black slaves to his preaching services, and he embraced extemporaneous prayer and preaching as a gift of the Holy Spirit—each practice an explicit rebuke of the colony's established Anglican Church.

One of Davies's preaching points was at Fork Church, just a short distance and easy carriage ride from John and Sarah Henry's residence. In his 1991 *Son of Thunder*, Henry Mayer shared the same story recorded in almost every biography of the Revolutionary Patrick Henry: "Sarah Henry, like everyone else, found Davies' preaching close to sublime. She took her little girls with her to the services and had their older brother Patrick, now entering his teens, drive the carriage. On the way home, she would make Patrick repeat aloud the substance of the sermon."[3]

There is no indication that the young Patrick Henry considered following Davies into the ministry. Instead, he chose the law, another esteemed profession requiring the exercise of oratorical prowess. In 1759, at the age of twenty-three, Henry hung his shingle from the rafters of Shelton Tavern, conveniently located across the street from the Hanover Court. By 1765, he had argued over 1,300 cases not just in Hanover but also in the neighboring counties of Goochland, Cumberland, Louisa, Albemarle, and Chesterfield, which staggered their schedules to allow for lawyers like Henry to travel from one county to the next. Just as Davies had spent the preceding decade of the 1750s establishing an ecclesiastical circuit of Presbyterian preaching houses in the Virginia Piedmont, Henry worked this same territory as a lawyer through the 1760s, traveling from courthouse to courthouse, arguing cases before juries composed of male landholding Virginians.[4] From this foundation, Henry would build, as had Davies before him, a colony-wide, and eventually continental, reputation.

On December 1, 1763, a controversial case to limit the pay of the colony's Anglican clergy came before the Hanover County Court. On the surface the case was simple enough: the question was whether back pay was owed to James Maury, a clergyman from neighboring Louisa County—and, if so, how much. When it came before the Hanover County Court in December 1763, James Maury's was the third such suit to be tried in Virginia that year. The earlier suits had not produced clear outcomes, however, rendering Maury's the source of great public notoriety and controversy. On the first day of the trial, the Hanover Court ruled in Maury's favor, setting a precedent that held the potential to require the collection of taxes, parish by parish, to cover the cost of several years of back pay for every clergyman in the colony. The court's ruling did not truly settle the matter, however, for the question of how much back pay should be awarded the Reverend Maury had not been a part of the ruling. The penalty phase of the trial gave both sides the chance effectively to argue the case anew, and this time—on the matter of damages to be paid—the reputation of the Anglican establishment would be put to a jury. What came to be known in Virginian lore as "the Parson's Cause" had taken on the feel of a referendum over the public authority of the Church of England.[5]

The next day, in what would prove a great miscalculation, Peter Lyons, Rev. Maury's counsel, concluded that his client would best be served by presenting his case as simple and matter-of-fact and so presented to the jury the simple math of what he calculated to be owed in back pay.[6] While the entire content of Patrick Henry's closing argument in the Parson's Cause cannot be known with precision, several firsthand accounts survive to give an honest rendering of events. Henry opened his remarks with extensive reference to what he called "the original compact between king and people," arguing that the English Crown and Church had violated this compact with their peoples in the American colonies. Painting the picture in vivid and highly personal terms, Henry called the Anglican clergy "rapacious harpies" who were bound to take from their humble parishioners "their last hoe-cake." He also condemned King George's support of the Anglican clergy, arguing that the English monarch risked being "degenerated" from his status as "father of his people" into "a tyrant [who] forfeits all right to his subjects' obedience." At this point, according to Maury, "the more sober part of the audience were struck with horror," and a number were heard to murmur, "Treason! Treason!" Although Maury's lawyer, Mr. Lyons, "called out aloud, and with an honest warmth, to the Bench, 'that the gentleman had spoken treason,'" Henry was allowed to carry on "in the same treasonable and licentious strain, without interruption." The jury awarded damages of a single penny, a stunning rebuke of the colony's Anglican establishment.[7]

With his attack on the Anglican clergy in the Parson's Cause, Patrick Henry launched what would become a legendary career in Virginia politics. The next year, Henry moved to neighboring Louisa County, where he joined the vestry of the very Anglican parish he had defended from having to offer back pay to the Reverend Maury. The following year, he was elected from Louisa County to the colonial legislature, the House of Burgesses, in which he served through to its dissolution in 1776.

On May 29, 1765, Henry made a thunderous debut before the Burgesses, speaking against the Stamp Act, Parliament's tax on colonial commerce requiring that goods for sale and administrative documents be affixed with prepaid stamps. Working with a group of younger delegates, Henry drafted resolutions asserting that "the General Assembly of this Colony have the only and sole exclusive Right and Power to lay Taxes and Impositions upon the Inhabitants of this Colony."[8] On the one hand, this assertion was a simple reaffirmation of long-standing precedent in Virginia. In the tense atmosphere that prevailed in the wake of the French and Indian War, however, this assertion carried with it a powerful whiff of rebellion, and when he rose to speak in support of the resolutions that followed from it, Henry once again mustered a brazen challenge to the king's authority.

Unlike his speech in the Parson's Cause of 1763, the content of Henry's 1765 speech in support of the Stamp Act Resolves is not so easy to detail with confidence. According to legend, as he reached the climax of his speech, Henry declared, "Caesar had his Brutus, Charles the First his Cromwell, and George the Third . . ." and then—after being interrupted by cries of "Treason! Treason!" from other Burgesses—concluded, "may profit by their example!"[9] Whatever words Henry actually spoke, their impact was lasting—as Thomas Jefferson, then a student at the College of William and Mary, would write many years later, "I well remember the cry of treason, the pause of Mr. Henry at the name of George III, and the presence of mind with which he closed his sentence, and baffled the charge vociferated."[10] Patrick Henry's Stamp Act Resolves were not passed by the House of Burgesses, but they were distributed widely through the colonial press, along with reports of Henry's oratorical prowess.[11]

That Patrick Henry modeled his oratory after that of Davies was self-evident to his contemporaries. In his 1817 *Patrick Henry*—the first complete biography of Henry, which by the end of the nineteenth century found its way through twenty-five printings—William Wirt testified to the sheer marvel with which his contemporaries beheld the power of Patrick Henry's oratory. Of Henry's 1763 speech in the Parson's Cause, Wirt wrote, "I have tried much to procure a sketch of this celebrated speech. But those of Mr. Henry's hearers who survive, seem to have been bereft of their senses. They can only tell you in general, that they were taken captive; and so delighted with their captivity, that they followed implicitly, whithersoever he led them. That, at his bidding, their tears flowed from pity, and their cheeks flushed with indignation. That when it was over, they felt as if they had just awaked from some ecstatic dream, of which they were unable to recall or connect the particulars."[12] Accounts like these of Henry's oratorical prowess read remarkably like accounts of Davies's preaching in Virginia, or of Whitefield's preaching on both sides of the Atlantic. Again and again, hearers are reported to "gasp" or "gape in awe," to be "struck as if by lightning," and to "stand in amazement" at what they heard, or even fall to the ground.[13] For much of the nineteenth and twentieth centuries, Henry's biographers would retain this essential focus on the stylistic similarities that Henry shared with Davies, even as they moderated Wirt's effusive prose.[14]

But the power of Patrick Henry's oratory was derived from more than stylistic mastery and from more than some vague sense of spiritual ecstasy. In the aftermath of the French and Indian War, Patrick Henry took the oppositional spirit that was an essential part of the English heritage of dissent and applied it powerfully to the cause of the continental experiment being birthed in America. Enthusiasts of this heritage were always prone to see themselves as victims of tyrannical authorities. These authorities, they believed, were inherently susceptible to corruption, by virtue of their proximity to power, both ecclesial and civil. Little wonder that lurking in the back of Patrick Henry's mind—and at the margins of the explosive oratory that helped launch his political career—was the English monarch, the head of both Church and Crown.

Edmund Randolph—who, after the Revolution, would succeed Henry as governor of the new state of Virginia—understood clearly why Patrick Henry's oratory packed such a powerful punch. As Randolph remembered it, Henry's enthusiasm "was nourished by his partiality for the dissenters from the established church. He often listened to them, while they were waging their steady and finally effectual war against the burdens of that church, and from a repetition of his sympathy with the history of their sufferings, he unlocked the human heart and transferred into civil discussions many of the bold licenses which prevailed in their religions." This enthusiasm was most powerfully on display, Randolph observed, when Henry was "descanting with particular emphasis on the martyrs in the cause of liberty."[15]

"An Aggravated Tyranny"—the Propaganda of Samuel Adams

On August 14, 1765—just a few weeks after Virginia's House of Burgesses approved their Stamp Act Resolves—a protest of the Stamp Act was organized at the Port of Boston, the protest consisting, according to one observer, of "two or three hundred little boys with a Flagg marching in a Procession." It would have come as no surprise to Bostonians that resistance to the Stamp Act originated among laboring youth near the city's harbor or that this resistance culminated eventually in violence and public controversy. Boston's working class was young; the census of 1765 showed that of the city's 15,520 inhabitants, 8,119—or 52 percent—were white children under the age of sixteen. These Boston youth fought among themselves so frequently that one boy who emigrated from Ireland at the age of nine could later recall of his life working along Boston Harbor, "My life was one continued State of warfare."[16] But Boston's youth did not just fight among themselves—they also routinely banded together to contest the authorities that governed their lives, sometimes focusing their ire on Boston's local merchant class and at other times on the British authorities who managed the colony's maritime commerce. One historian has counted "at least twenty-eight riots and illegal actions" along the Boston waterfront between 1689 and 1765.[17]

What distinguished the protests that emerged in the aftermath of the French and Indian War was the unprecedented coalition that mobilized behind them. In the years following the initial Stamp Act protests, an array of clubs and organizations that had often been in competition with one another lit up with common currents of resentment. Under the banner of the "Sons of Liberty," and using the "Liberty Tree" as a rallying point, Bostonians protested the Stamp Act of 1765 and the Townshend Acts of 1767, policies of taxation named after their principal architect, Charles Townshend, then chancellor of the Exchequer. Bostonians were especially outraged by the Quartering Act of 1765, requiring colonists to collaborate in the quartering of occasional British troops, and their outrage grew in 1767, when the British sent additional troops to the city to support the magistrates and officials who were attempting to enforce the new policies of taxation. The decision the following year, in 1768, to establish four British regiments as a permanent military presence in the city provoked yet more bitter protest. As chronicled by the historian Eric Hinderaker, "Three newspapers—the *Boston Evening-Post*, edited by Thomas Fleet Jr. and John Fleet; the *Boston-Gazette and Evening Journal*, under the joint editorship of John Gill and Benjamin Edes; and John

Green and Joseph Russel's *Massachusetts Gazette and Boston Weekly News-Letter*—served as mouth-pieces for the movement, giving coherent and sustained attention to radical concerns." Providing the content for these newspapers, and ideological coherence to the movement, was a small network of radicals from within Boston's elite. Aligning themselves with disaffected merchants and building on long-standing resentments of working-class artisans, laborers, and apprentices, these men galvanized an increasingly coordinated resistance to the new postwar regime.[18]

No one embodied this network of resistance more completely than Samuel Adams.

Born on September 16, 1722, Samuel Adams was the son of Mary Fifield Adams and Samuel Adams Sr., a devout Congregationalist known most familiarly as "Deacon Adams." His nickname notwithstanding, Deacon Adams was not uniquely devoted to the church. A brewer by trade and a member of the "Boston Caucus"—"a club of small shopkeepers, mechanics, and North End shipyard workers . . . that held a tight grip on local offices," according to John C. Miller—Deacon Adams's crisscrossing relationships in church, commerce, and politics provided a firm foundation for his son's career in the public life of the city. In response to an economic crisis in the early 1740s, Deacon Adams joined with other Boston merchants to organize a "Land Bank," a fanciful initiative that, in Miller's summation, promised "a Utopia of paper money backed by real estate." As did dozens of other merchants, Deacon Adams lost his shirt in the failed enterprise, and because of his involvement in the scheme, his election to the Massachusetts assembly was vetoed by the colonial governor—an extraordinary process known as "negativizing."[19] Together with his wife, Mary, Deacon Adams transferred his dreams for the future to his namesake son and invested in his education in hopes that he would go into the ministry. Eight years at the preparatory school Boston Latin did not persuade Samuel Jr., however, and by the time he graduated from Harvard in 1743, his passion for business and politics had prevailed.

Adams is rightly remembered as an innovative propagandist, but his propaganda was steeped in generations of pathos. One of twelve siblings, Samuel was one of only three to survive the decades of the 1730s and 1740s. Adams's parents died within weeks of each other in 1748, and across the next decade, this train of death was replicated in his own offspring. In 1749, Adams married Elizabeth Checkley, who gave birth every year but one between 1750 and 1757. In 1750, a child named Samuel, after his father and grandfather, survived just one day. The next year, the Adams gave another son the same name, and this Samuel lived to the age of thirty-six before dying in 1788. In 1752 and 1753, two more children, Elizabeth and Joseph, were lost at birth. In 1754, a daughter, Mary, survived three months. Hannah, born in 1756, would become the only child to outlive her father, dying in 1821 at the age of sixty-four. In 1757, Elizabeth Adams gave birth once more, and this time, at the age of thirty-two, she joined the infant in death at the time of birth. There is no record that Samuel Adams gave this last child a name. No self-reflective correspondence or journal entries survive to help us know exactly how all this affected Adams's consideration of life and death and life after death. But his devotion to family is reflected in the memorial he wrote in his Bible after Elizabeth's death: "To her husband she was as sincere a friend as she was a faithful wife. Her exact economy in all her relative capacities, her kindred on his side as well as her own admire. She ran her Christian race with remarkable steadiness, and finished in triumph! She left two small children. God grant they may inherit her graces!"[20] Seven years later, in 1764, Adams married Elizabeth Wells, with whom he had no children, and the cause of American independence became his life's passion.

Adams's political views were profoundly shaped by those of John Locke, the English moral philosopher so frequently cited by leading Americans in the buildup to revolution that his name functioned almost as a ritual incantation.[21] But Adams's acquaintance with Locke was more than passing. While at Harvard, Adams had earned a master's degree by writing on the question of "whether it be lawful to resist the Supreme Magistrate, if the Commonwealth cannot be otherwise preserved."[22] Following Locke, Adams answered this question in the affirmative, and he took this spirit of resistance with him into public life. In 1748 Adams joined with several classmates to launch a newspaper called the *Independent Advertiser*, which mixed nostalgia for earlier generations of New England Puritanism with Locke's mistrust of government, directed toward Massachusetts's colonial authorities.[23] As articulated in his *Two Treatises of Government*, first published in 1690, Locke considered that the "natural law" of reason "teaches all Mankind, who would but consult it, that being all equal and independent, no one ought to harm another in his Life, Health, Liberty, or Possessions." Elsewhere Locke reduced the list to three: "life, liberty, or possession." In Locke's view, the right of "every man" to property represented an absolute, and good government should be founded only to protect and preserve these rights and the right to property most proximately: "The great and chief end therefore, of men uniting into Commonwealths, and putting themselves under Government, is the preservation of their property." In this view, the rights of individuals are inherently jeopardized by the formation of governments, no matter their form. According to Locke, "Wherever the power that is put in any hands for the government of the people and the preservation of their properties is applied to other ends, and made use of to impoverish, harass, or subdue them to the arbitrary and irregular commands of those that have it, there it presently becomes tyranny, whether those that thus use it are one or many."[24]

Locke's preoccupation with this inherent tension between individual liberty and governmental power—and his conviction that the failure to defend the former against the latter led inevitably to absolute tyranny—does much to account for Samuel Adams's virulent opposition to British colonial policy in the aftermath of the French and Indian War. In 1764, in response to the very first of the postwar taxes imposed by the British Parliament, Adams drafted the "Instructions of the Town of Boston to Its Representatives in the General Court": "If our Trade may be taxed why not our Lands? Why not the Produce of our Lands? Why not the Produce of our Lands & every thing we possess or make use of? This we apprehend annihilates our Charter Right to govern & tax ourselves. . . . If Taxes are laid upon us in any shape without having a legal Representation where they are laid, are we not reduced from the Character of free Subjects to the miserable State of tributary Slaves?"[25] But for Adams, taxation without representation not only "annihilated" the rights of Americans as British subjects; it also struck at the very foundation of their spiritual inheritance. Conjuring not John Locke but John Foxe, Adams asserted that New England had been established by people who were "persecuted in England at a Time when the Nation was intoxicated with Bigotry & the Ideas of Ecclesiastical Tyranny." As articulated by Adams, this inheritance inspired in Bostonians a deep reverence:

When we recollect the ardent love of Religion and Liberty, which inspired the Breasts of those Worthys; which induced them at the Time when Tyranny had laid its oppressive Hand on Church and State in their Native Country, to forsake their fair Possessions and seek a Retreat in the distant

Part of the Earth—When we reflect upon their early care to lay a solled Foundation for Learning, even in a Wilderness, as the surest means of preserving and cherishing the Principles of Liberty and Virtue, and transmitting them to us their Posterity, our Mind is filled with deep Veneration and we bless and revere their Memory.[26]

As British postwar policy unfolded across the latter half of the 1760s, Adams saw confirmation of his worst fears at every turn. As he became a key leader in the Boston Sons of Liberty, he championed the American cause, in large part through prolific publication in the *Boston-Gazette*, for which he wrote under a variety of pseudonyms. In a series of December 1768 articles submitted to Edes and Gill, the editors of the *Boston-Gazette*, Adams argued that the quartering of British troops in Boston confirmed Locke's saying "Where Law ends, TYRANNY begins, if the Law be transgress'd to another's harm."[27] The spirits of Bostonians, however, were "as yet unsubdued by tyranny" and were "unaw'd by the menaces of arbitrary power" and would never "submit to be govern'd by military force."[28] But Adams also published articles in this same year that he signed "A Puritan," pretending to have unearthed evidence that Catholic treachery lay behind England's monarchical claims: "The more I know of the circumstances of America, I am sorry to say it, the more reason I find to be apprehensive of POPERY."[29]

Beginning in 1768, Adams and others began to publish the *Journal of Occurrences*, which was excerpted in nearly every newspaper in colonial America. The journal portrayed the suffering of Bostonians at the hands of British troops not just as a provincial but rather as a uniquely "American" predicament.[30] In October 1769, his optimism was waning. He submitted once again to Edes and Gill an article for publication in the *Boston Gazette*, and once again he conjured the potent mix of Lockean political thought and New England's sacred memory: "Let any one imagine the distress of this people—a free city, I mean once free and still entitled to its freedom, reduc'd to the worst of tyranny—an aggravated tyranny! Was not an army of placemen and pensioners sufficient, who would eat us up as they eat bread, but an array of soldiers must be stationed in our very bowels—Where is the bill of rights, magna charta and the blood of our venerable forefathers! In this dilemma to what a dreadful alternative were we reduc'd! To resist this tyranny, or, submit to chains."[31] For Adams and others, the choice was obvious.

"United We Stand or Divided We Fall"—the Lyrical Encapsulations of John Dickinson

Opposition to the Stamp Act galvanized an unprecedented network of intercolonial opposition, and in October 1765, delegates from nine colonies gathered in New York for what would come to be known as the Stamp Act Congress. Among those representing Pennsylvania was John Dickinson, who earned a reputation among his fellow delegates as a fine writer by drafting the Congress's summary resolutions. Only at the end of the nineteenth century would historians dub Dickinson "the Penman of the Revolution," but as his biographer Jane Calvert has noted, the rationale for the nickname is easy to understand. Dickinson would go on to draft more formal declarations of the Continental Congresses than any other single individual. Having secured his reputation at the Stamp Act Congress, Dickinson would author four of the six documents produced by the First Continental Congress in the fall of 1774—*To the Inhabitants of the British Colonies, The Bill of Rights and a List of Grievances, Petition to the King*, and *A Letter to the Inhabitants of the Province of Quebec*. As a delegate to the Second Continental

Congress, he authored two more foundational documents, attempting yet again to reconcile these same competing impulses: the so-called *Olive Branch Petition*, which Congress adopted on July 5, 1775, professing their continuing loyalty to King George III, and the *Declaration of the Causes and Necessity of Taking Up Arms*, which Congress approved the very next day. In 1776, Dickinson led the committee that produced the first draft of the Articles of Confederation.[32]

John Dickinson was born on November 8, 1732, in Talbot County, Maryland, into a lineage of one of Pennsylvania's earliest Quaker families. Raised for much of his youth in Kent, near Dover, Delaware, Dickinson trained as a lawyer in London, and by the time he returned in 1757 to establish what would become a successful law practice in Philadelphia, he was as cultured and cosmopolitan—if not nearly so famous—as his fellow Philadelphian Benjamin Franklin. Dickinson's elite upbringing, and his rise to prominence in Pennsylvania politics, gave him a unique vantage on the process by which a continental identity was fashioned across colonial lines in North America. As this same process drove a wedge between the colonists and their king in the aftermath of the French and Indian War, Dickinson would give early voice to the growing American resentment. Having abandoned the absolute pacifism of his Quaker heritage, he nonetheless remained, throughout his life, a reluctant Revolutionary.[33]

For all his production of formal petitions and declarations, the most widely circulated fruit of Dickinson's pen were more accessible encapsulations of the American cause. In a series of *Letters from a Farmer in Pennsylvania*, Dickinson laid out in simple language the rationale for American opposition to the Townshend Acts, the series of revenue-enhancing measures the English Parliament had approved as an intended compromise after Americans had so loudly protested the Stamp Act. Dickinson's *Letters from a Farmer* spoke to the essential concern shared across the colonies, employing terms familiar to even the modest readers on both sides of the Atlantic: "Let these truths be indelibly impressed on our minds—that we cannot be HAPPY, without being FREE—that we cannot be free, without being secure in our property—that we cannot be secure in our property, if, without our consent, others may, as by right, take it away." Supremely well educated himself, Dickinson addressed his *Letters from a Farmer* to those less philosophically inclined, providing a concise articulation of the peculiarly American view that taxation without representation was the equivalent of slavery. "*Those* who are *taxed* without their own consent, expressed by themselves or their representatives, are *slaves*," he wrote. "We are taxed without our consent, expressed by ourselves or our representatives. We are therefore—SLAVES."[34] Dickinson's *Letters from a Farmer* were first published anonymously and serially in several colonial newspapers beginning in 1767. The next year, however, Benjamin Franklin's business partners, David Hall and William Sellers, printed Dickinson's *Letters from a Farmer* in a compendium, and printers in Boston and New York soon followed suit, producing one of the first truly intercolonial articulations of the American cause.[35]

Like the compendium of his *Letters from a Farmer*, Dickinson's "A New Song" was first published anonymously in early 1768. The broadside published by Benjamin Franklin and David Hall proved so successful that it was soon rebranded the "Liberty Song." An anthem of resistance to British policy in the colonies, Dickinson's composition gained such wide circulation that within a few months of its release, it was being described in newspapers as far-flung as the *Connecticut Journal* and the *Virginia Gazette* as "so justly admired thro' all North-America."[36]

Come join hand in hand, brave Americans all,
And rouse your bold hearts at fair Liberty's call;
No tyrannous acts, shall suppress your just claim,
Or stain with dishonor America's name.

. . .

Our worthy forefathers—let's give them a cheer—
To climates unknown did courageously steer;
Thro' oceans to deserts, for freedom they came,
And, dying, bequeath'd us their freedom and fame.

. . .

Then join hand in hand brave Americans all,
By uniting we stand, by dividing we fall
In so righteous a cause let us hope to succeed,
For Heaven approves of each generous deed.

. . .

All ages shall speak with amaze and applause,
Of the courage we'll show in support of our laws;
To die we can bear,—but to serve we disdain,
For shame is to freedom more dreadful than pain.[37]

As indicated on the original broadside, Dickinson wrote the lyrics to be sung to the tune of "Hearts of Oak," an explicit counter to the anthem of the British Royal Navy. With its repeating eleven-syllable lines, one of the most familiar meters in the eighteenth-century English repertoire (11.11.11.11), the "Liberty Song" could have been memorized easily by almost any American. And with its pledge of willingness to die for the rightness of the cause, it struck a resounding and familiar note.[38]

It is no coincidence that Dickinson's *Letters from a Farmer* captured the imagination of such a wide audience—they represented a masterful articulation of the American cause in the generic

Protestant vernacular that Benjamin Franklin and his many imitators had already proven so popular through their publication of almanacs, hymnals, newspapers, and the like. Neither is it coincidental that the signature line of Dickinson's "Liberty Song" would become one of the most enduring slogans of the American Revolution. Its rhythmic eleven syllables could be shorthanded easily as "United we stand or divided we fall." Across the preceding generations, this meter had come to sound natural in the ears of English speakers on both sides of the Atlantic, making it easy for people to memorize rhymes and lyrics composed for them.[39] The origins of Revolutionary lyrics like those of the "Liberty Song" can be traced directly to this English tradition of metrical rhyming and singing, as it was appropriated and adapted in the diverse settings of colonial North America. Political ballads were more than propaganda—they were part of a popular movement that circulated Revolutionary thought and sentiment through the emerging body politic in the buildup to the American Revolution. They also reinforced consistently the notion that preparing to die was the essential spiritual task confronting every human being.

In the years leading up to the outbreak of the Revolutionary War, these lyrical expressions of popular American sentiment leaped off the page, onto well-prepared American tongues, and into receptive American ears. Across a public sphere shaped profoundly by the singing of psalms and sacred hymns, the practice of rhyming and singing lent itself naturally to every kind of cause.[40] One expression of this widespread practice was to parody the favorite songs of people championing an opposing cause. Sometimes the parody was given a new title, composing a play on words, but more commonly, the parody was labeled as such and new lyrics were written to the familiar meter and easy-to-sing tune. So after Franklin and Hall first published Dickinson's "Liberty Song" in 1768, a back-and-forth in verse broke out in response to its brazen contestation of British authority. A September 1768 issue of the *Boston-Gazette* included a "Parody on the Liberty Song," written by one of its loyalist readers.[41] The next month, another Bostonian fired back in the *Boston Evening-Post* with "The Parody Parodized."[42] This kind of rhyming back-and-forth was both cause and consequence of the ever-increasing tension that built continually through the 1760s and 1770s between independence-minded American colonists and loyalists to the English Crown.

* * * * *

Across the 1760s, colonial frustrations with Britain's postwar regime of taxation and governance—and with the British magistrates in North America who were charged with enforcing it—continued to widen and expand. Over time this frustration birthed an unprecedented network of intercolonial communication and collaboration, expressed through membership associations like the Sons of Liberty and through ever-thickening networks of intercolonial correspondence and print exchange. This much has long been well understood.[43]

But the emerging nation was also being bathed in a sonic environment that did as much to bind together the soon-to-be revolutionaries as did the network of intercolonial print exchange. This environment was shaped by the oratory of Patrick Henry and others who modeled themselves after the midcentury revivalists; by the strident rhetoric of Samuel Adams and others who were raised in the argumentative culture of Puritan New England; by the lyrical Protestant vernacular of John Dickinson and others who came of age in America's "First City," Philadelphia; and by the genre of metered verse that proved so popular across the entire cultural landscape of English-speaking North America. Through these practices, revolution-minded Americans were immersed in the tradition of

English martyrdom as this had been appropriated and adapted to the American context. Through an ever-expanding network of communication and collaboration, key leaders from across England's North American colonies came to a shared conclusion that British impositions had set them on a slippery slope to what Samuel Adams called "an aggravated tyranny."

All this confounded and maddened the British, who considered this way of thinking ethereal, at best, and self-serving and hypocritical, at worst. In a 1775 essay entitled *Taxation No Tyranny*, Samuel Johnson famously summed up the English view: "How is it that we hear the loudest yelps for liberty among the drivers of negroes?"[44] But these "yelps" represented a potent mix—they were bold expressions of a new American identity that was grounded in the oppositional spirit that had characterized Protestant movements for centuries. Across the 1760s, growing numbers of American colonists embraced this new identity as they contested ecclesial and civil turf. As they went speaking and shouting, rhyming and singing, preaching and proclaiming their resistance to colonial rule, more and more concluded that the American cause was a sacred cause, stamped with divine approval. The essential measure of commitment to the American cause became a willingness to sacrifice one's life for it, and more and more Americans declared with gusto their willingness to do exactly that.

This way of thinking reflected the ancient spiritual inheritance of English Protestant martyrdom appropriated to the context of pre-Revolutionary America. It can aptly be called "American martyrdom." To those who embraced this frame of mind, it made sense to expect that corrupt earthly rulers would mount greater and greater threats to individual rights and liberty, eventually becoming full-fledged tyrants. It also made sense to assume that these earthly tyrants would team up with demonic forces, including that transcendent tyrant that Isaac Watts had famously called "the tyrant Death."[45]

5

Patriotism, This Noble Affection

American Martyrdom and the Revolutionaries' Coming-of-Age

On February 20, 1770, an angry crowd of Boston youth gathered outside the shop of Theophilus Lillie, a Boston merchant accused of violating the Nonimportation Agreement, a boycott protesting British taxes of imports to the American colonies. When Ebenezer Richardson, a British customs official, came to Lillie's defense, the mob turned their ire on him and followed him home. There, Richardson fired on the crowd, injuring one and mortally wounding another, Christopher Seider, age eleven. The next week, the publishers Benjamin Edes and John Gill announced a funeral procession for Seider in the February 26 edition of their *Boston-Gazette*, the city's oldest newspaper: "He will be buried from his Father's House in Frogg

Lane, opposite Liberty-Tree, on Monday next, when all the Friends of Liberty may have an Opportunity of paying their last Respects to the Remains of this little Hero and first Martyr to the noble Cause."[1] Seider's "manly Spirit," they reported, was evident in his final encounters with his parents and "the Clergymen who prayed with him" and in "the Firmness of Mind . . . with which he met the King of Terrors." In the *Boston-Gazette*'s next weekly edition, dated March 5, 1770, Edes and Gill included a detailed account of Seider's burial, including a funeral procession led by "five Hundred School Boys" and a "train of Citizens" totaling an "estimation of . . . at least Two Thousand of all Ranks, amidst a Crowd of Spectators; who discover'd in their Countenances and Deportment the evident Marks of true Sorrow." Edes and Gill reminded their readers that "in the gayest Season of Life amidst the most flattering Scenes, and without the least Apprehensions of an evil Hour, we are continually expos'd to the *unseen* Arrows of Death: *The Serpent is lurking in the Grass*, ready to infuse his deadly Poison!"[2]

On the very same day that this account appeared in the *Boston-Gazette*, March 5, 1770, British troops headquartered in Boston opened fire on a protesting crowd, killing three young men on-site and mortally wounding two more. Edes and Gill dedicated the entire second page of the March 12 edition of the *Boston-Gazette* to this second incident, lamenting the "melancholy Demonstration of the destructive Consequences of quartering Troops among Citizens in a Time of Peace, under a Pretence of supporting the Laws and Aiding Civil Authority." On the third page, they celebrated the promised withdrawal of British troops from Boston and marked the burial of the first four victims—Samuel Gray, Samuel Maverick, James Caldwell, and Crispus Attucks—with an account of the funeral procession, concluding that the "aggravated Circumstances of their Death, the Distress and Sorrow visible in every countenance, together with the peculiar Solemnity with which the whole funeral was conducted, surpass Description." The account was accompanied by images of four coffins, each marked with a victim's initials and the image of skull and crossbones. The following week, in the March 19 edition, the *Boston-Gazette* featured a fifth coffin, marking the passing of Patrick Carr, and reported, "His Remains were attended on Saturday last from Faneuil-Hall by a numerous and respectable Train of Mourners, to the same Grave, in which those who fell by the same Hands of Violence were interred the last Week."[3]

The March 5, 1770, incident that would become known as the Boston Massacre is routinely—and rightly—portrayed as launching a sequence of events that would culminate five years later in the outbreak of formal hostilities between colonial militia and British troops at the Massachusetts towns of Lexington and Concord.[4] Rarely is the massacre remembered, however, for the elaborate and sustained response of Bostonians to these very public deaths *as deaths*, beginning with the accounts of how the victims comported themselves in their dying hours.

In the first years of the 1770s, open expressions of resistance to British policy spread through the colonies with increasing velocity and ferocity in oral, visual, and printed forms. These expressions resonated with powerful political sentiments like "No taxation without representation." But they also routinely conjured the high ideals of English Protestant martyrdom, as these had been appropriated and adapted across English-speaking North America. These expressions of resistance resounded with a crystal clear message that came ringing down across the ages: when young men lost their lives in support of this resistance, their deaths were not in vain. To the contrary, they were martyrs to the patriot cause.

"The Bloody Massacre"—Paul Revere's Engraving of the Boston Massacre

On March 26, 1770, the week after Patrick Carr's funeral was reported in the *Boston-Gazette*, the newspaper's editors, Edes and Gill, included an advertisement announcing the sale of "a PRINT containing a Representation of the late horrid Massacre in King-Street." The print was from an engraving made by Paul Revere, who had copied the image from a young Boston artist, Henry Pelham. Revere made very few changes to Pelham's original. He labeled the Boston Customs House (the building behind the line of soldiers) the "Butcher's House," and in the sky, he added storm clouds stirring over the soldiers' side of the frame. He altered and abbreviated the title, from Pelham's "THE FRUITS OF ARBITRARY POWER, OR THE BLOODY MASSACRE," to "THE BLOODY MAS-SACRE perpetrated in King Street."[5] And at the foot of the image, where Pelham had quoted verses from the ninety-fourth Psalm as they were found in the King James Version of the Bible, Revere placed a more strident poem of unknown origin, perhaps of his own composition. The poem closed with lines declaring that if the British Crown's colonial courts ("the venal C——ts") did not deliver the soldiers their just penalty, fate would summon them eventually to stand before "a JUDGE who never can be brib'd."[6] Pelham accused Revere of reproducing his work without permission and made prints from his own engraving available to the public one week later, but it was too late.[7] The first to hit the market, Revere's engraving was widely circulated—first throughout Boston, then throughout the colonies. Over time, it became one of the most famous images from the period of the American Revolution. Revere and Pelham would chart entirely different courses through the coming revolution. Revere would continue as a champion of American independence, his ultimate fame as a patriot hero secured in 1860, when the poet Henry Wadsworth Longfellow penned the poem "Paul Revere's Ride," taking literary license to dramatize the role played by Revere in spreading word through the Massachusetts countryside on the eve of the April 19, 1775, battles of Lexington and Concord. Pelham would remain loyal to the British Crown, abandoning Boston for England in 1776 and dying in Ireland thirty years later.[8] Upon learning that young men had died at the hands of British soldiers in March 1770, however, Pelham and Revere reacted in much the same way. They shared a spiritual conviction: whatever the outcome of the coming public trial, the judgment in the matter of the tragedy on King Street would ultimately belong to God, and this judgment would be right and true.[9]

In the ensuing months, Bostonians followed the unfolding of parallel trials, one of Ebenezer Richardson for the murder of Christopher Seider and the other of Captain Thomas Preston and the British soldiers responsible for the deaths of Gray, Maverick, Caldwell, Attucks, and Carr. Represented in court by John Adams, Captain Preston was acquitted in a jury trial, and just two of the soldiers, from among the several who fired on the crowd on March 5, were found guilty of the lesser charge of manslaughter, verdicts generating enormous controversy in the conflicted city. Richardson, meanwhile, was convicted of murder, but Boston's judges, appointed by the English Crown, delayed his sentencing in anticipation of a royal pardon. When Richardson's pardon finally came in early 1772, Revere pounced, collaborating with the Boston printer Isaiah Thomas to publish a handbill entitled *A Monumental Inscription on the Fifth of March*. The handbill linked the two events, and the two trials, to larger questions of justice, calling on Americans to "BEAR IN REMEMBRANCE the HORRID MASSACRE! perpetrated in King-street, Boston, New England On the Evening of March the Fifth, 1770" and to "also, BEAR IN REMEMBRANCE That on the 22d Day of February,

1770, The infamous EBENEZER RICHARDSON, Informer, and tool to Ministerial hirelings, Most *barbarously* MURDERED CHRISTOPHER SEIDER, An innocent youth!"[10] The handbill decried Richardson's pardon in a poem, presumably of Revere's or Thomas's own composition, that read in part,

> *O MURD'RER! RICHARDSON! With their latest breath*
> *Millions will curse you when you sleep in death!*
> *Infernal horrors sure will shake your soul*
> *When o'er your head the awful thunders roll.*
> *Earth cannot hide you, always will the cry*
> *Of Murder! Murder! Haunt you 'till you die!*
> *To yonder grave! With trembling joines repair,*
> *Remember, SEIDER's corps lies mould'ring there;*
> *There drop a tear, and think what you have done!*
> *Then judge how you can live beneath the Sun.*
> *A PARDON may arrive! You laws defy,*
> *But Heaven's laws will stand when KINGS shall die.*[11]

The handbill also featured a simplified woodcut version of the now familiar image that Revere had copied from Pelham's original engraving.

The iconic engraving of the Boston Massacre produced by Paul Revere conjured clearly images of John Rogers's martyrdom rendered across several generations in various editions of John Foxe's *Book of Martyrs*. (See figures 1 and 2.) Similarly, the simplified woodcut that Revere included in his 1772 handbill conjured clearly images of Rogers's martyrdom rendered in *The New-England Primer*. (See figures 3 and 4.) In both instances, Revere retained a basic composition — executioners on the right, victims on the left, plumes of smoke in the center of the frame echoed in stormy skies.

Figure 1. Paul Revere's engraving *The Bloody Massacre* [. . .] (1770)

The Bloody Massacre Perpetrated in King Street Boston on March 5th, 1770 by a Party of the 29th Regt (Boston: Paul Revere, 1770). Reprinted with permission of the Massachusetts Historical Society.

Compare to figure 2.

Figure 2. *The burning of Master John Rogers, Vicar of St Sepulchers & Reader of St Pauls in London*, illustration from 'Foxes Martyrs' c.1703 (litho)

The Stapleton Collection / Bridgeman Images

Compare to figure 1.

Figure 3. Paul Revere's woodcut of the Boston Massacre as reproduced in
Isaiah Thomas's handbill (1772)

Detail from Paul Revere's woodcut, Isaiah Thomas, *A Monumental Inscription on the
Fifth of March. Together with a Few Lines on the Enlargement of Ebenezer Richardson,
Convicted of Murder* (Boston: printed by Isaiah Thomas, 1772), https://tinyurl.com/
sz82nhtm. Reprinted with permission of the Massachusetts Historical Society.

Compare to figure 4.

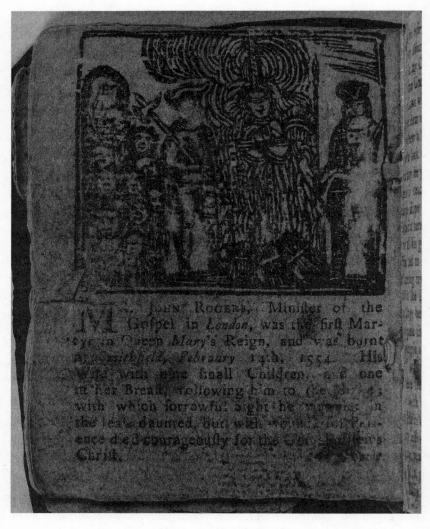

Figure 4. The martyrdom of John Rogers as portrayed in
The New-England Primer (1762)

The New-England Primer Improved (Boston: printed and sold by S. Adams, 1762). Used
by permission of the American Antiquarian Society, Worcester, Massachusetts.

Compare to figure 3.

Consider the Revere engraving, *The Bloody Massacre Perpetrated in King Street*, to the representation of Rogers's martyrdom in the lithograph from the 1703 "Foxe's Martyrs." (Compare figures 1 and 2.) Each image is presented in a bordered frame and beneath a banner headline. In Foxe's image, the scene of Rogers being burned at the pyre is framed against the backdrop of a three-story courtyard, the stately buildings conveying the significance of the venue and adding to an air of solemnity, and so in Revere's engraving, the scene of the massacre is framed by a view of King Street, with Boston's State House in the background, the dome and steeple of Boston's historic First Church looming over it. In Foxe's representation, a uniformed soldier lights the fire of Rogers's pyre at the command of his superiors, and so in Revere's engraving, red-coated British soldiers are portrayed as firing on the order of a commanding officer at innocent and unarmed Bostonians. In each instance, the "attack" comes from the right side of the scene, and the respective weapons are extended horizontally and angled slightly downward, making clear the position of dominance of the men portrayed as executioners. In each composition, the commanding officers stand erect and behind their soldiers, their own weapons pointing vertically toward the sky. The center of each frame is dominated by billows of smoke, rising from the fire of Rogers's pyre in the image from Foxe and from the rifles of the British soldiers in Revere's engraving. In each, a crowd of onlookers or bystanders surrounds the scene. In each, the indisputably innocent occupy the ground near the bottom of the frame—lamenting women in Foxe's image, the bleeding victims and a loyal dog in the Revere engraving. Each image is accompanied by a narrative in verse, promising that the perpetrators will be finally judged, and the victims finally vindicated, by God in heaven.

The composition of Revere's simpler image of the massacre also bears striking resemblance to that of the block woodcuts representing Rogers's martyrdom as these had appeared across generations in *The New-England Primer*. (Compare figures 3 and 4.) In each of these images, the dominant and central plumes of smoke are echoed in storm clouds that hover only over the executioners, standing erect on the right side of the frame. In each, the clearly innocent are portrayed as children or youth, clustered to the lower or left of the frame, where they are watched over by would-be custodial adults.

Woodcut images of Rogers's martyrdom were featured in almost every edition of *The New-England Primer*, their sophistication and artistry varying over time, reflecting the resources and skills brought to bear by different printers at various times and places. The characters included in the portrayal remained largely constant, however—Rogers, his wife and children, and the executioner or executioners. But different editions of *The New-England Primer* featured different scenes from Rogers's martyrdom as it was recounted in Foxe's *Book of Martyrs* and presented the characters in slightly different configurations. In some, Rogers was portrayed as standing between the executioners and his family, refusing to recant.[12] In others, Rogers was portrayed as offering a farewell blessing to his wife and children.[13] A third variation portrayed Rogers as engulfed in flames, with the executioners standing tall and proud as his family huddled humbly to the side, powerless to intervene. The scene in this third variation is the one that Revere chose to conjure in his 1772 woodcut of the Boston Massacre.

Rogers was also typically presented as having left advice "to his children," which *The New-England Primer* presented to its young readers in the form of a poem often spanning several pages. The poem, composed in the "common meter" of alternating eight- and six-syllable lines, made clear to New England children that the essential challenge they would face in life was that of preparing for death. It concluded,

> When I am chained to the Stake,
> And Faggots gird me round,
> Then pray the LORD by Soul in Heav'n
> May be with Glory Crown'd,
> Come welcome Death, the end of Fears,
> I am prepared to die,
> Those earthly Flames will send my Soul
> Up to the LORD on high.
> Farewel my Children to the World,
> Where you must yet remain,
> The LORD of Hosts be your Defence,
> till we do meet again.
> Farewel my true and loving Wife,
> My Children and my Friends.
> I hope in Heaven to see you all,
> When all Things have their Ends,
> If you go on to serve the Lord,
> As you have now begun,
> You shall walk safely all your Days,
> Until your Life be done.
> God grant you so to end your Days,
> As he shall think it best,
> That I may meet you in the Heavens,
> Where I do hope to rest.[14]

Revere's representations in print of innocent Boston youth, martyred at the hands of British soldiers, were not difficult for Bostonians to interpret. The images were immediately, powerfully, and palpably compelling because for generations, English colonists in New England had catechized their young into the spiritual inheritance of English Protestant martyrdom, appropriated and adapted to their unique circumstances in North America.

"Heaven Is the Warrior's Shield"—Commemorating the Boston Massacre

In the years following the mass funeral marches of 1770, the Sons of Liberty worked diligently to keep the memory of their young martyrs alive, organizing annual commemorations on the anniversary of the March 5 Massacre on King Street. The climaxes of the commemorations were public orations delivered by notable Bostonians. Afterward, at the request of the Boston Town Meeting, these orations were circulated in print, a tradition that continued through the period of the American Revolution and beyond. James Lovell, a well-known local schoolmaster and orator, delivered the first commemorative address in 1771. Joseph Warren, who worked with Samuel Adams to convene the Massachusetts Committee of Correspondence, the first of what would become, in effect, shadow governments in each colony, spoke in 1772. Benjamin Church, a physician who had sealed his public reputations by championing the successful practice of smallpox inoculation, was the orator in 1773. John Hancock, the son of Samuel Hancock, one of Boston's wealthiest merchants, delivered the address in 1774. All were Harvard graduates.

Harvard College was founded in 1636 to provide the Massachusetts Bay Colony with a reliable supply of orthodox Calvinist clergy, a clear mission it maintained until the end of the seventeenth century. By the mid-eighteenth century, however, Harvard had expanded its mission to serve in large measure as a finishing school for Boston's elite. According to Conrad Edick Wright, the men of Harvard's "revolutionary generation" shared a common social profile, an early childhood training focused on "achiev[ing] a working level of literacy and numeracy" and a preparatory education, typically of four years, "where they would acquire the classical prerequisites of higher learning," specifically a full mastery of Latin and a working knowledge of Greek.[15] At Harvard, students were further schooled in ancient languages, opening to them the worlds of the Bible in the original Hebrew and Greek and to the world of the classics in the original Latin. Students at Harvard were immersed in the essential doctrines of the Christian faith, in the great truths they believed could be found in the annals of antiquity, and in the discoveries of what we now understand were but early expressions of modern science. As curious as it may seem today, even the most intellectual of the American revolutionaries did not perceive these traditions to contradict each other, nor did they seek to refute the findings of one with the findings of another. Rather, they expected that that great minds would find ways to reconcile and harmonize these many intellectual commitments.[16] The speeches offered at the annual commemorations of the Boston Massacre were entirely representative of this intellectual pedigree.

Understandably, the orators identified the quartering of British troops in the city as the proximate cause of what they called "the horrid massacre." This practice was deeply objectionable to Bostonians, and for many reasons. As expressed by James Lovell in his 1771 address, resident troops invited disaster by injecting uncertainty into the body politic and discouraged the orderly mustering of a local militia, a hallmark of colonial solidarity. In his 1772 address, Joseph Warren decried that the English ought to have been able to foresee "the ruinous consequences of standing armies to free communities," for these could be found "in the histories of SYRACUSE and ROME, and many other once flourishing STATES; some of which now have a scarce name!" In 1773, Benjamin Church declared that "words can poorly paint the horrid scene" but painted it nonetheless to make this same crucial point: "Defenceless, prostrate, bleeding countrymen—the piercing, agonizing groans—the mingled moan of weeping relatives and friends—These best can speak: to rouse the luke-warm into noble zeal, to fire the zealous into manly rage: against the *soul oppression, of quartering troops, in populous cities, in times of peace*."[17]

But this was not the only common theme evoked by the March 5 orators. Each also conjured the memory of the colony's ancestors, celebrated them for their demonstrations of fearlessness in the face of death, and challenged their listeners to carry this legacy forward. In this regard, the speeches commemorating the anniversary of the Boston Massacre are rightly understood as "panegyrics"—public speeches and commemorative writings by which surviving generations became custodians of the memories of Christian martyrs.[18] So the orators who commemorated the somber anniversary of March 5 took control of the public memory of the "bloody massacre," asserting divine approval for the entire enterprise of North American colonization. On March 5, 1771, Lovell declared, "Our fathers left their native land, risqued all the dangers of the sea, and came to this then-savage desart, with that true undaunted courage which is excited by a confidence in God." Warren picked up the same theme in 1772: "When they came to this new world, which they fairly purchased of the Indian natives, the only rightful proprietors, they cultivated the then barren soil by their incessant labor, and defended their dear-bought possessions with the fortitude of the Christian, and the bravery of the hero." Church concluded his 1773 address with instructions from the English poet Mark Akenside: "Go call thy Sons—instruct them what a debt / They owe their ancestors, and make them swear / To pay it, by transmitting down entire / Those sacred rights to which themselves were born."[19]

By the time of the massacre's fourth anniversary in March 1774, the relations between the colonists and the British had worsened further still. Protests on the shorefront of Boston Harbor in December 1773 had quickly come to be known as the Boston Tea Party, and in response, the British Parliament passed the Coercive Acts, a series of measures imposing further restrictions on colonial trade. Leading colonists in North America promptly dubbed the legislation the Intolerable Acts and, working together through a growing network of Committees of Correspondence, attempted a coordinated response. In this context—and clearly aware that his speech would reach an audience spanning the thirteen colonies—John Hancock delivered the 1774 commemorative address.[20] He opened by asserting as self-evident the Lockean creed: "Security to the persons and properties of the governed, is so obviously the design and end of civil government, that to attempt a logical proof of it would be like burning tapers at noon day, to assist the sun in enlightening the world." He then asked, "Is the present system which the British administration have adopted for the government of the colonies a righteous government? Or is it tyranny?" He did not leave the question in the rhetorical but answered it by asserting that "the troops of George the Third have cross'd the wide atlantick, not to engage an enemy, but to assist a band of TRAITORS in trampling on . . . those rights and liberties which as a father he ought ever to regard, and as a King he is bound in honour to defend." He then professed to "come reluctantly to the transactions of that dismal night, when in such quick succession we felt the extremes of grief, astonishment and rage; when Heaven in anger, for a dreadful moment, suffered hell to take the reins; when Satan with his chosen band opened the sluices of New-England's blood, and sacrilegiously polluted our land with the dead bodies of her guiltless sons." But rather than resign themselves to becoming passive victims, Hancock saw another possibility unfolding before what he called "the attentive gravity, the venerable appearance . . . which I behold in countenances of so many in this great Assembly." This alternative was "patriotism . . . this noble affection which impels us to sacrifice everything dear, even life itself, to our country."[21]

John Hancock's declaration illustrates how in the vernacular of the American Revolution, the word *patriot* could function as a precise substitute for the word *martyr*, such that calls to patriotism evoked a tradition steeped in generations, indeed centuries, of pathos. The hallmark of this true patriotism was now on display in the colonists, Hancock elaborated, by "patriots" demonstrating "a common sympathy and tenderness for every citizen" and "a *particular feeling* for one who suffers in a public cause." Hancock applauded the work of the Committees of Correspondence of the North American colonies, by whom "much has been done . . . for the Rights of Assembly in this and our Sister Colonies" and for "uniting the Inhabitants of the whole Continent for the security of their common interest." He then declared, "'Tis immortality to sacrifice ourselves for the salvation of our country. We fear not death." Conjuring the familiar motif of "playing the man," and asserting the ultimacy of divine judgment, Hancock concluded,

> I have the most animating confidence that the present noble struggle for liberty will terminate gloriously for America. And let us play the man for our God, and for the cities of our God while we are using the means in our power, let us humbly commit our righteous cause to the great Lord of the universe, who loveth righteousness and hateth iniquity. And having secured the approbation of our hearts, by

a faithful and unwearied discharge of our duty to our country, let us joyfully leave her important concerns in the hands of Him who raiseth up and putteth down the empires and kingdoms of the world as He pleases.[22]

By the time the organizing committee set their sights on the fifth anniversary of Boston's "bloody massacre," the outbreak of war with the British appeared inevitable. Samuel Adams had returned from the First Continental Congress prepared to go to war and convinced his fellow organizers that one of their own should speak again that year. And so Joseph Warren, who had been the principal orator at the 1772 commemorations, became the first to be honored by a repeat performance. As he had three years earlier, Warren began by rehearsing an idealized, and racist, version of the early colonial experience:

> Our fathers, having nobly resolved never to wear the yoke of despotism, and seeing the European world through indolence and cowardice, falling a prey to tyranny; bravely threw themselves upon the bosom of the ocean; determined to find a place in which they might enjoy their freedom, or perish in the glorious attempt. Approving Heaven beheld the favourite ark dancing upon the waves, and graciously preserved it until the chosen families were brought in safety to these western regions. They found the land swarming with savages, who threated death and every kind of torture. But savages, and death with torture were far less terrible than slavery: Nothing was so much the object of their abhorrence as a tyrant's power: They knew that it was more safe to dwell with man in his most unpolished state than in a country where arbitrary power prevails.[23]

Blaming "the hand of Britain" for the massacre of March 5, 1770, Warren lamented that "our streets are again filled with armed men" and "our harbour is again crowded with ships of war." Decrying British policies of taxation, he asserted that "some demon in an evil hour" must have "suggested to a short sighted financier the hateful prospect of transferring the whole property of the King's subjects in America to his subjects in Britain." He cautioned his listeners by saying that should they entertain even "the thought of giving up our liberty," they could no longer "reflect with generous pride on the heroic actions of our American fore-fathers" nor "boast our origin from that far famed island, whose warlike sons have so often drawn their well-tried swords to save her from the ravages of tyranny." Insisting that "where justice is the standard, Heaven is the warrior's shield," Warren doubled down on the tradition celebrating the virtue of fighting to the death:[24]

> Our country is in danger, but not to be despaired of. Our enemies are numerous and powerful, yet we have many friends; determine to be free, and Heaven and Earth will aid the Resolution. On you depends the fortunes of America. You are to decide the important question, on which rests the happiness and liberty of millions yet unborn. Act worthy of yourselves. The faultering tongue of hoary age calls on you to support your country. The lisping infant raises its suppliant hands, imploring defence against the monster slavery. Your fathers look from their celestial seats with smiling approbation on their sons, who boldly stand forth in the cause of virtue. . . . Having redeemed your country, and secured the blessing to future generations, who fired by your example, shall emulate your virtues, and learn from you the heavenly art of making millions happy;

with heartfelt joy, with transports all your won, you cry, the glorious work is done. Then drop the mantle to some young Elisha, and take your seats with kindred spirits in your native skies.[25]

Three months later, on June 17, 1775, Joseph Warren, newly elected as a major general, led troops from the Massachusetts provincial army into battle with British troops at Bunker Hill. According to reports from the field, Warren was one of the last defenders to retreat from the British attack, before being shot in the head.[26]

* * * * *

The notion that Boston functioned as the cradle of the American Revolution remains a staple of even elementary introductions to early American history—and rightly so. This depiction is apt in more than merely metaphorical terms. The laboring youth who marched against the Stamp Act in 1765—motivated in part by basic oppositional impulses that are foundational to the human experience of adolescence—were of precisely the age to become soldiers in the Continental Army a decade later.[27] Britain's postwar policies of taxation incited this oppositional spirit, and the decision to quarter troops in Boston inflamed it yet further. The stage had been set for a new generation of martyr-patriots to "play the man."

The public culture of New England had been shaped powerfully by an inheritance of Puritan resistance to authorities both ecclesial and political, and demonstrations of this kind of resistance represented to New Englanders the righteousness of their cause. As they constructed and propagated narrative traditions about the events surrounding "the bloody massacre," leading Bostonians readily appropriated the spiritual traditions of contending with death that they had inherited from their English forebears. As were their ancestors, New Englanders in the mid-eighteenth century were encouraged to consider their mortality throughout their lives. Likewise, they were exposed to the archetype of martyrdom at every turn—in their sacred texts, in sermons both spoken and published, when they shared in the memorial feast of the Lord's Supper, and as they accompanied their friends and loved ones to their graves. Indeed, they had been introduced to this tradition even as they learned to read, with John Rogers's martyrdom presented as a kind of capstone to their first book, *The New-England Primer*. This deep reservoir of cultural material championing the ideals of martyrdom made it possible for Bostonians to conjure and reinforce these ideals at any moment by marking and revisiting the deaths of revered pastors, notable citizens, and even kings. Even the deaths of ordinary people were perceived to be connected to the crucifixion of Jesus, the firstborn among the dead, such that everyone could perceive themselves as caught up in the majestic workings of God in human history. Just as Cotton Mather appended the printed narratives of his own children into *Janeway's Token*, English colonists in pre-Revolutionary Boston wrote themselves and their own children into this living tradition.

When Christopher Seider was killed on February 20, 1770, Edes and Gill hailed him as a martyr to the patriot cause in their *Boston-Gazette*, and thousands of Bostonians honored him by marching in his funeral procession, not yet knowing that this cause would lead eventually to revolution. When the events of March 5 took five more young lives, Paul Revere embraced them as martyrs in his famous engraving, and within a few years, the notion that Seider was the first to die was lost to all but local memory.[28] The wide circulation of Revere's engraving and woodcut illustrations in print brought the March 5 event to the attention of independence-minded Americans throughout the colonies, evoking powerful sentiments born from diverse local traditions of martyrdom and martyrology. As conflict with British troops and authorities continued to escalate, the anniversary commemorations of the massacre presented leading Boston elite, trained at Harvard College, the opportunity to remind their listeners that these occupying agents had allied themselves with spiritual forces of wickedness, even death itself.

Lurking not too far below the surface of these accusations was the enduring Protestant suspicion that a tyrannical ruler had final control of the apparatuses of power. Generations of English-speaking Protestants in North America had been trained to think of the pope as a beastly tyrant who must be opposed at all costs. But English kings were not immune from the wrath of English Protestants inclined to cast all their struggles in stark, all-or-nothing terms. It had happened before in the years of the English Civil Wars, and reminders of these battles still coursed through the popular culture, appearing routinely on the pages of colonial newspapers, almanacs, sermons, songs, and accounts. In this light, it was all but inevitable that colonists from elsewhere in North America—growing in their sense of a common identity and a shared destiny now soaked in the blood of American martyrs—would join with their brethren from Boston and turn their rebellious sights on their king.

6

Liberty or Death

American Martyrdom in the Continental Congresses

Across the months of September and October 1774, delegates from twelve colonies gathered in Philadelphia for what would come to be known as the First Continental Congress. The formal results of the Congress were a series of resolves expressing displeasure at British policy in North America and a decision to convene in Congress again the following year. But the unfolding crisis in Massachusetts dominated the proceedings, and perhaps the most significant achievement of this First Continental Congress was the forging of emotional bonds around the plight of the New England colony. Having concluded earlier in the year that "the Town of Boston, for ought I can see, must suffer Martyrdom," John Adams wrote to his wife, Abigail, from Philadelphia on September 14, 1774, "The Spirit, the Firmness, the Prudence of our Province are vastly applauded, and We are universally acknowledged the Saviours and Defenders of American Liberty."[1]

Adams attributed the birth of these bonds in part to Rev. Jacob Duchè, the assistant rector of Christ Church and St. Peter's, the leading Anglican parish of Philadelphia, describing the young clergyman as "one of the most ingenious Men, and best Characters, and greatest orators in the Episcopal order, upon this Continent—Yet a Zealous Friend of Liberty and his Country." When, on the first day of the Congress, Thomas Cushing of Massachusetts moved that the proceedings be opened with prayer, a number of delegates had objected, according to Adams, "because we were so divided in religious Sentiments, some Episcopalians, some Quakers, some Anabaptists, some Presbyterians and some Congregationalists, so that We could not join in the same Act of Worship." In response, Samuel Adams "arose and said he was no Bigot, and could hear a Prayer from a Gentleman of Piety and Virtue, who was at the same Time a Friend to his Country. He was a Stranger in Phyladelphia but had heard that Mr. Duchè (Dushay they pronounce it) deserved that Character, and therefore he moved that Mr. Duchè, an episcopal Clergyman, might be desired, to read Prayers to the Congress, tomorrow Morning. The Motion was seconded and passed in the Affirmative."[2] Adams's concession was strategic, a doff of the cap both to the delegates from Pennsylvania, as the hosts, and also to those delegates—including those from Virginia, the largest delegation—who were faithful, if sometimes dissenting, Anglicans.

The next day, John Adams continued, the Reverend Duchè "read several prayers, in the established form." He "then read the Collect for the seventh day of September, which was the Thirty fifth Psalm." The psalm begins with a plea—"Plead *my cause*, O Lord, with them that strive with me: fight against them that fight against me." But as it progresses it returns again and again to the faithfulness of the psalmist himself, who declares loudly that the Lord will deliver him: "And my soul shall be joyful in the Lord: it shall rejoice in his salvation." My opponents may rejoice in my adversity, the psalmist declares, and may "tear *me*" and gnash "upon me with their teeth." And yet "I will give thee thanks in the great congregation: I will praise thee among much people." Those "that rejoice at mine hurt," the psalmist says, shall "be ashamed and brought to confusion," while those "that favour my righteous cause" will be led to "shout for joy." Through it all, the psalmist will remain steadfast: "And my tongue shall speak of thy righteousness *and* of thy praise all the day long." The psalm was a favorite in tales of martyrdom down through the ages, celebrating the ultimate demonstration of faith—the vocal profession of one's faith in the face of persecution. In countless stories from Foxe's *Actes and Monuments*, for instance, the martyrs refused to cease from speaking the truth, often shouting until the cruel tyrants tore their tongues from their mouths before their ultimate execution. John Adams reported to Abigail, "I never saw a greater Effect upon an Audience. It seemed as if Heaven had ordained that Psalm to be read on that Morning."[3] Duchè continued in extemporaneous prayer, so impressing the delegates that he was forthwith invited by the Congress's president, the Virginian Peyton Randolph, to serve as the body's official chaplain.[4]

This precedent would prove an important one—across years of gatherings, the Continental Congresses came to rely on Duchè and other Protestant chaplains to open their sessions with prayer, to preach on special occasions, and to preside over traditional observances like fast days and Christian holidays. These acts served to reinforce among delegates the belief that the cause for which they were meeting in Congress was divinely ordained. Likewise, Congress depended on Protestant chaplains in the Continental Army to keep American troops devoted to what they routinely portrayed as a holy war.[5] These chaplains also took for granted that martyrdom was the proper frame for understanding the deaths of those who lost their lives in battle. As one chaplain summed things up while addressing troops under the command of General Arthur St. Clair in October 1776, any soldier who might fall in the Revolutionary cause "will be justly esteemed a *Martyr* to liberty."[6]

More broadly, Protestant clergy from across the colonies joined with chaplains to the Congress and to the Continental Army, providing constant, indispensable ideological support to the Revolutionary cause.[7] But clergy were not alone in appropriating and adapting the oppositional spirit of English Protestantism—including the practices of English Protestant martyrdom—to the new circumstances of the American Revolution. Orators, printers, songwriters, and pamphleteers joined with chaplains and soldiers in putting on the mantle of American martyrdom. Often, they would simply call it patriotism.

"Give Me Liberty or Give Me Death"—Patrick Henry at Virginia's Second Revolutionary Convention

On March 23, 1775—two weeks after Joseph Warren's speech commemorating the Boston Massacre—things were coming to a head in the fourth day of meetings at what would come to be known as Virginia's second Revolutionary Convention. Having met for the first time in August of the preceding year, delegates from across the English colony had returned to the city of Richmond for a second multiday gathering, and they had come well prepared. Edmund Pendleton, a respected judge from Caroline County, first urged the body to "petition" England's King George III. Modeled after a recent petition from the colony of Jamaica, Pendleton's proposal defended colonial rights but also renounced armed rebellion.

Countering this more compromising approach, a group of younger delegates introduced three resolutions. The first stated that "a well-regulated militia, composed of gentlemen and yeomen, is the natural strength and security of a free government," an entirely uncontroversial point of view. The second asserted that "the establishment of such a militia is, at this time, peculiarly necessary."[8] The third authorized that a Virginia militia be activated to put the colony in a state of defense. Taken together, these resolutions came close to a declaration of war, and having brought them to the floor of the convention, Patrick Henry stood to speak in their support.

Henry had attended the sessions of the First Continental Congress in the fall of 1774, and he was now in regular communications and correspondence with leaders from other colonies. Impressed by the sense of urgency communicated by his colleagues from Massachusetts, he was persuaded by their view that war was now inevitable. And so, after arguing his case before his fellow Virginians, Henry worked himself to a fever pitch. According to oral tradition, he closed with these words: "What is it that gentlemen wish? What would they have? Is life so dear, or peace so sweet, as to be purchased at the price of chains and slavery? Forbid it, Almighty God! I know not what course others may take, but as for me, give me liberty or give me death!"[9]

We cannot know with certainty that Henry spoke the words with which he would become forever associated. In 1817 William Wirt, Henry's first biographer, drew on the recollections of witnesses to reconstruct the speech, and it is Wirt's version that was passed down in American lore.[10] Whatever the specific words he spoke, Henry's famous speech resonated with much more than mere politics. The delegates to Virginia's Revolutionary Convention were seated in church pews in the chapel of St. John's Episcopal Church in Richmond, and all but a few in over one hundred in attendance that day were vestrymen (lay leaders) in their hometown Anglican churches.[11] As remembered uniformly by those who heard it, Henry's oration was replete with biblical imagery and allusions.[12] It was also delivered in a style shot through with personal emotion—just a few weeks earlier, Henry had buried his first wife, Sarah, who three years earlier had fallen into madness (probably what today we would call postpartum depression) after giving birth to the couple's sixth child. Henry, the grieving widower, served as an embodied reminder to his listeners that the threat of death was ever present.

The other delegates would have found none of this surprising. Neither the rallying cry with which Henry was destined to be forever associated nor the pathos with which he was remembered as having delivered it was in any way out of character. Henry's declaration in the spring of 1775 represented a closing argument in a case that he had been building for over a decade. In the 1763 case that came to be known as "the Parson's Cause," Henry gave voice to the resentment that Virginians—and Americans, more generally—felt toward distant authorities of the Church of England. In his defense of the Stamp Act Resolves at the 1765 Stamp Act Convention, he focused this same resentment on the English Parliament. And in his speech at Virginia's second Revolutionary Convention in 1775, he set his sights squarely on the king. Henry would remain a controversial figure in Virginia politics, hailed by some as a visionary leader and by others a political opportunist. In either case, during this buildup to the American Revolution, Henry was always one step ahead of his times.

While it cannot be proven that Henry conjured it on March 23, 1775, the slogan "liberty or death" was widely familiar in Revolutionary circles. In Joseph Addison's *Cato*, the popular eighteenth-century play, the title character declares, "It is not now a time to talk of aught / But chains, or conquest; liberty, or death." Beginning in May 1775, just six weeks after Henry's speech, the editors of the *Massachusetts Spy* added the slogan to the masthead of their Revolutionary newspaper. And in July, a pseudonymous American author, "Lucius," writing in the *London Evening Post* declared with a kind of hyperbole characteristic of the era that "the whole Continent, with one Voice, is crying Liberty or Death."[13]

This cry—and others like it that resonated with the same sentiment—challenged all who heard or read it to confront both the prospect of British domination and the prospect of their own mortality, just as Samuel Davies's muster sermons had challenged an earlier generation of militiamen during the period of the French and Indian War. In this frame of understanding, the threat of temporal domination was analogous to the threat of mortality, and the truly virtuous would rise to the challenge presented by both. The pathos born of this tradition explains why the clarion call with which Henry would forever be associated—"Give me liberty or give me death!"—resonated so powerfully across Revolutionary America. It did so because it was easily and intuitively recognizable as the utterance of a virtuous man declaring himself ready to go to battle—a man ready, if need be, to die for a sacred cause.

"Noble Martyrs to Liberty"—Joseph Warren as the First American Martyr

By the time delegates from Britain's thirteen North American colonies gathered in Philadelphia in May 1775 for the opening sessions of the Second Continental Congress, tensions were at a hot boil. Weeks earlier, on April 19, Massachusetts militia had resisted efforts by British troops to seize caches of arms at Lexington and Concord, marking the outbreak of formal hostilities. With Boston now under siege, delegates from Massachusetts came to Philadelphia ready to declare war, and radical delegates from Virginia, elected in the aftermath of Patrick Henry's rousing speech before Virginia's Revolutionary Convention in March, were prepared to join them. Delegates from the mid-Atlantic colonies of New York, Pennsylvania, New Jersey, and Delaware, however, continued to profess their hopes of reconciling with the British Crown.

The escalation of hostilities would soon force Congress's hand. On June 17, some 140 soldiers in the Massachusetts provincial army—and perhaps twice as many British troops—were killed at Bunker Hill. As tales from the battle spread through the colonies, the bravery and ferocity displayed by Joseph Warren and other Massachusetts militiamen quickly became the stuff of legend. The fallen were hailed as true patriots—which is to say, as martyrs—as in this report from the survivor Jonathan Williams Austin to John Adams on July 7, 1775: "They fight like Men who are conflicting . . . for all that is dear to them, and seem to die with the Enthusiasm of martyrs. I love my Countrymen, and when I go into Battle, I go with a Band of Brothers, who seem to be animated with one Soul."[14]

The tribute offered to Warren in Daniel George's *Cambridge Almanack for 1776*, published in late 1775, was representative of the response in print. The bottom of the pages in the almanac's first edition contained a running list of "those noble Martyrs to Liberty who fell in action" at Lexington and Concord. But in the second edition, Warren was paid special homage with an engraved portrait, occupying a full page and entitled "The late Magnanimous and Heroic Gen. Joseph Warren, Slain fighting in the cause of Liberty, at Bunker Hill."[15]

"For We Will Rather Die"—the *Pennsylvania March*

On July 6, 1775, the Congress approved *A Declaration Setting Forth the Causes and Necessity of Their Taking Up Arms*. Drafted by John Dickinson, the declaration asserted, "We are reduced to the alternative of choosing an unconditional submission to the tyranny of irritated Ministers, or resistance by force. The latter is our choice."[16] Before adjourning on August 1 for a monthlong recess, the delegates placed the army in Massachusetts Bay under the direction of the Virginian George Washington, and they allocated an unprecedented sum of $500,000 to the equipping and support of what would become the Continental Army.[17] The war was on, and the Congress that some delegates had hoped would simply further enhance communication and collaboration among the colonies was confronted, suddenly, with much more fundamental challenges—conducting a war, creating an intercolonial government, and consolidating an already-emergent sense of national identity.[18]

The lyrical labor of the Revolution continued even as the Continental Congress was in recess. On Monday, August 7, 1775, the week after Congress broke for the summer, Thomas Dunlap's weekly newspaper, the *Pennsylvania Packet*—which had distinguished itself as the Revolution's de facto journal of record through its consistent publication of congressional minutes and notes—published this song on its penultimate page:

We are the troop that ne'er will stoop,
To wretched slavery,
Nor shall our seed, by our base deed
Despised vassals be;
Freedom we will bequeath them,
Or we will bravely die;
Our greatest foe, ere long shall know,
How much did Sandwich lie.

CHORUS
And all the world shall know
Americans are free;
Nor slaves nor cowards we will prove,
Great Britain soon shall see.

We'll not give up our birthright,
Our foes shall find us men;
As good as they, in any shape,
The British troops shall ken.
Huzza! Brave boys, we'll beat them
On any hostile plain;
For freedom, wives, and children dear,
The battle we'll maintain.
   CHORUS

What! Can those British tyrants think,
Our fathers cross'd the main,
And savage foes, and dangers met,
To be enslav'd by them?
If so they are mistaken,
For we will rather die;
And since they have become our foes,
Their forces we defy.
   CHORUS[19]

While the *Packet's* readers were instructed to sing the *Pennsylvania March* to the tune of a Scottish folk song, "Sandy O'er the Lea," Pennsylvanians of almost any heritage would have been able to sing these lyrics to any of innumerable tunes. So, too, would residents of other British colonies when it was republished in their newspapers in the ensuing weeks.[20] The verses of the *Pennsylvania March* were written in the most familiar of all these meters, the "common meter" of 8.6.8.6 (eight syllables in the first line, six in the second, eight in the third, six in the fourth). The chorus was metered in an almost equally familiar 6.6.8.6.

The formal declarations approved by the delegates to the Continental Congresses were, in many ways, efforts to capture in prose an identity that had been birthed across several decades. But, like an infant being sung to in a cradle, the emerging nation was raised in a sonic environment that was dominated by metered verse—from the singing of psalms and sacred hymns to the practice of public rhyming and melody making. As this genre of metered verse spread through the colonies, in the form of both spoken rhyme and sung lyric, Americans of every persuasion embraced it as they contested ecclesial and political turf. So in the 1770s American colonists went writing and corresponding, rhyming and singing, preaching and proclaiming their way to independence from the British Crown. As they did, they bucked each other up, witnessing that the defining challenge of life was that of preparing to die a faithful death.

Death, the Last Enemy—the Memorializing of Samuel Ward

As the Second Continental Congress continued to meet through the fall of 1775 and into 1776, their sessions continued to be marked by significant deaths. On October 22, 1775, the Virginian Peyton Randolph died while still formally occupying the position of president of Congress. The funeral celebrations were reported to have been the largest ever seen in Philadelphia, and Randolph's presence seemed to linger, in part because his body remained in Philadelphia through the winter, awaiting the spring thaw to be returned for burial in Virginia. At year-end, General Richard Montgomery fell in battle during an attempted New Year's Eve surprise attack on the city of Quebec. After learning in mid-January of Montgomery's perishing, Congress resolved on January 25 that Dr. William Smith, provost of the College of Philadelphia, "prepare and deliver a Funeral Oration in honour of General MONTGOMERY, and of those Officers and Soldiers who magnanimously fought with him in maintaining the principles of American liberty." Smith's oration, delivered on February 19, 1776, generated some controversy. Smith lauded Montgomery's heroism, and that of "the officers and others who fell with him," but his characterization of the patriot cause was widely panned as unsuitably ambivalent.[21] Even the inscription that Smith chose for the title page of the sermon's printed version seemed to many insufficiently militant for the moment:

> *O thou, who bad's them fall with honour crown'd,*
> *Soon make the bloody pride of war to cease!*
> *May these the only sacrifice by found*
> *To public freedom and their country's peace.*[22]

In this light, when the Rhode Island delegate Samuel Ward succumbed to smallpox in Philadelphia on March 26, 1776, his death presented an opportunity for leading members of Congress to get things right. While he had not occupied a formal position of leadership in the Continental Congress, Ward was no minor character in the buildup to revolution. The great-great-grandson of Rhode Island's founder, Roger Williams, Ward was known for his religious devotion and was well connected across the vast networks of relationships that spanned the Continental Congress. More importantly, Ward had earned a colonies-wide notoriety in 1765, when, as governor of Rhode Island, he became the sole royally appointed governor in North America to enforce the Stamp Act. His subsequent conversion to an unqualified support of the Revolutionary cause was seen by many as an important marker that a corner had been turned. At year-end 1775, in a letter to his brother Henry, Ward had articulated his conviction that war with Britain was now inevitable: "When I first entered this contest with Great Britain . . . I saw clearly that the last act of this cruel tragedy would close in fields of blood. I have traced the progress of this unnatural war through burning towns, devastation of the country and every subsequent evil. I have realized with regard to myself, the bullet, the bayonet, and the halter; and, compared with the immense object I have in view, they are all less than nothing. . . . Heaven save my country, is my first, my last, and almost my only prayer."[23]

Congress chose Samuel Stillman to eulogize Ward, a logical choice because both men were Baptists but also because Stillman was by this time a celebrated practitioner of the long-standing New England craft of the funeral sermon. The pastor of Boston's First Baptist Church since 1765, Stillman's 1773 collection of two sermons "occasioned by the condemnation and execution of Levi Ames" had run through four editions and an unknown number of printings in the hands of two Boston printers, John Kneeland and Ezekiel Russell. To the two sermons, Stillman appended, "at the Request of many," an account of Ames's conduct and conversation in his final hours, by which "he may be thought in a Judgment of Charity, to have died A Penitent Thief." Kneeland's imprint included a striking cover in a "tombstone" format, topped by the "death's head" image of a skull, conjuring funereal customs that reached back to the very earliest days of colonial New England.[24]

On March 27, 1776, the day after Ward's death, Samuel Stillman addressed the Congress, delivering a sermon entitled *Death, the*

Last Enemy. Encouraging the delegates to consider the loss of Ward within a longer sweep of devastation, Stillman began by recalling the legendary plague that struck London beginning in 1665, resulting in the death of "sixty-eight thousand persons; and in a single week of that time, not less than seven thousand one hundred and sixty-five." Sometimes, he intoned, the "grand destroyer death . . . threatens totally to depopulate." Insisting, therefore, that even the deaths of "crowds on crowds unnumbered" should not deter them in the Revolutionary struggle, Stillman recited for the assembled Congress a litany of celebrated names from among those who had perished in the first year of armed confrontation with the British.[25] The litany included Joseph Warren and Richard Montgomery and others who had died in battle but also Peyton Randolph and Samuel Ward, who died while serving in Congress:

> Among the band of WORTHIES, whom death's rapacious hand hath snatched from the bosom of their friends and country, we place, with deepest sorrow, a WARREN, that Proto-Martyr to the Liberties of America—a MONTGOMERY—a MACPHERSON—a CHEESMAN—a HENDRICKS;— with all those worthy heroes, who have fought and bled, and died in freedom's glorious cause.—To the venerable catalogue, with deep felt anguish, I am forced to place the honorable name of RANDOLPH, that distinguished patriot, and friend to God and man. For the loss of whom, we have scarce had time to dry our weeping eyes, before all the avenues of grief again are opened, by the present mournful providence, the untimely death of the no less honorable WARD; over whose remains, with undissembled sorrow, we now perform the solemn obsequies!—Thus death destroys,—or WARD had still lived to bless his family, to serve his country, and

make the people happy.—But stop my soul!—It was heaven ordained the blow by which he finished life; and therefore it must be right!²⁶

Stillman concluded by assuring the members of their Congress of Ward's comportment in his final days, a sure sign of his eternal fate: "In his last illness he appeared composed, having placed his expectation of eternal merits of Jesus Christ . . . his immortal part hath joined the spirits of just men made perfect, who continually surround the throne of God." When the Philadelphia printer Joseph Crukshank brought Stillman's sermon to press the following week, it included a preface in which Stillman addressed Ward's surviving children as "my Dear Young Friends," counseling them that their "strongest Consolation, under this heavy Affliction, must arise from the Confidence You have, That He is now with God; in whose Presence is Fulness of Joy: And at whose Right Hand are Pleasures forever."²⁷

"Sacrifices upon the Altar of Liberty"—the Incitements of Thomas Paine

Across their meetings in Philadelphia in the spring of 1776, the delegates to the Second Continental Congress grew more and more emboldened, in part because facts on the ground seemed continually to outpace their formal deliberations. The Continental Army, created and placed under George Washington's command the preceding June, had engaged the British in battles from New York to Quebec across the first months of 1776, and in this same period a little booklet written by Thomas Paine, a recent immigrant from London to Philadelphia, had taken the colonies by storm. In *Common Sense*, Paine hammered the economic and political themes that were the immediate focus of the colonists' outrage, but he placed these themes within the frame of a larger spiritual struggle. Americans ought not to seek merely to replace King George III with a monarch who would respect their liberties, he argued. Instead, he proposed that Americans jettison the "base remains of two ancient tyrannies. . . . *First*—The remains of monarchical tyranny in the person of the king. [And] *secondly*—The remains of aristocratical tyranny in the persons of the peers." Rooting his claims in a distinctive reading of the Hebrew scriptures, Paine claimed that the very notion of monarchy had been created by the devil for the promotion of idolatry and that Americans would be wise to construct a new government based solely on "republican materials, in the persons of the commons, on whose virtue" freedom depends.[28] The distribution of *Common Sense* in pamphlet form, and excerpts from it in colonial newspapers, lit up the network of print production that had been generations in the making. "The period of debate is closed," Paine had declared.[29] Indeed, the eventual outcome of Congress's deliberations—a declaration of formal separation from England—seemed all but decided.

The cover of Paine's *Common Sense* included an excerpt from a poem by the Scottish poet James Thomson: "Man knows no master save creating Heaven / Or those whom choice and common good ordain."[30] The larger context of this quote makes clear that Paine was conjuring the notion that a fully realized manhood required resistance to tyrants and obedience to the demands of the divine, even to the point of martyrdom:

> *Erect from nature's hand, by tyrant force,*
> *And still more tyrant custom, unsubdued,*
> *Man knows no master save creating Heaven,*
> *Or such as choice and common good ordain.*[31]

The following year, Paine made this connection more explicit. In the fifth essay of his new series—American Crisis—Paine conjured Thomson's poem once more, including its assertion that Americans were bound to no earthly master. This time, though, he elaborated, just as "the blood of the martyrs has been the seed of the Christian church, so the political persecutions of England will and have already enriched America." Once, he explained, America had been "a mere chaos of uncemented colonies, individually exposed to the ravages of the Indians and the invasion of any power that Britain should be at war with." Now that period was past, he concluded, "and she is no longer the dependent, disunited colonies of Britain, but the independent and United States of America, knowing no master but heaven and herself."[32]

But Paine did not wait until 1777 to make transparent that he considered his *Common Sense* to be endorsed by the legacy of English Protestant martyrdom. After an anonymous author took the name "Cato" to issue a rebuke of Paine in a series of public letters, Paine responded in kind and published a pamphlet entitled *A Dialogue between the Ghost of General Montgomery Just Arrived from the Elysian Fields; and an American Delegate, in a Wood near Philadelphia*. Published in May 1776, as Congress was moving toward declaring independence, Paine's dialogue opened with Montgomery's ghost responding to a greeting from the unnamed delegate by declaring, "I still love liberty and America, and the contemplation of the future greatness of this Continent now forms a large share of my present happiness. I am here upon an important errand, to warn you against listening to terms of accommodation from the court of Britain." The ghost concluded by rehearsing the surnames of the first martyrs of the Revolutionary War ("Hampden—Sidney—Russell—Warren—Gardiner—Macpherson—Cheeseman") and describing them as "heroes who have offered themselves as sacrifices upon the altar of liberty."[33] Montgomery's ghost then conjured the memory of James Wolfe, a celebrated British general in the French and Indian War who died in battle at Quebec in 1759:

> It was no small mortification to me when I fell upon the Plains of Abraham, to reflect that I did not expire like the brave General Wolfe, in the arms of victory. But I now no longer envy him his glory. I would rather die in attempting to obtain permanent freedom for a handful of people, than survive a conquest which would serve only to extend the empire of despotism. A band of heroes now beckon to me. I can only add that America is the theater where human nature will soon receive its greatest military, civil, and literary honors.[34]

In Paine's summation, Richard Montgomery was among the first to be martyred to the cause of the American Revolution. And now he spoke from beyond the grave, beckoning those he left behind him to join him in "a band of heroes."

"Our Lives, Our Fortunes and Our Sacred Honor"— Thomas Jefferson and the Declaration of Independence

Thomas Jefferson was absent from the opening sessions of the Second Continental Congress, and for a specific reason: he had been slow to emerge from a prolonged period of grieving. The grief itself was nothing new—born in 1743 to Peter Jefferson and Jane Randolph Jefferson, Thomas Jefferson's coming-of-age had been marked profoundly by death. His father, Peter, had died at the age of fifty in 1757, leaving the fourteen-year-old Jefferson with—as he would recall years later—"the whole care and direction of myself . . . thrown on myself entirely, without a relative or friend qualified to advise or guide me."[35] His older sister, Jemimah—called "Jane," after her mother—died at the age of twenty-five in 1765. His best friend and brother-in-law, Dabney Carr, died at the age of twenty-nine in 1773. Another sister, Elizabeth, died at the age of nineteen in 1774. And in September of 1775, just before he traveled to Philadelphia for the opening sessions of the Second Continental Congress, Jefferson had been sent into a profound tailspin when his second child, named Jane Randolph Jefferson—formally after his mother but also in memory of his beloved deceased sister—died at the age of eighteen months. Jefferson had returned to Virginia in December and did not return when Congress resumed its sessions in January. Just as he prepared to depart from his home in Monticello to join his colleagues in the Congress, his mother, Jane Randolph Jefferson, died at the age of fifty-seven on March 31, 1776. It was in this season of mourning that Jefferson finally arrived in Philadelphia in mid-May of 1776, two months after the Congress had reconvened.[36]

On June 7, Richard Henry Lee, acting on behalf of the delegates from Virginia, presented this resolution to Congress: "*Resolved.* That these United Colonies are, and of right ought to be, free and independent states, that they are absolved from all allegiance to the British Crown, and that all political connection between them and the state of Great Britain is, and ought to be, totally dissolved." Anticipating that unanimous support of the resolution would soon be achieved, Congress appointed a committee of five to prepare a Declaration of Independence: Thomas Jefferson of Virginia, Benjamin Franklin of Pennsylvania, Roger Sherman of Connecticut, Robert Livingston of New York, and John Adams of Massachusetts.[37] By this time Adams was well established as a leader of the Congress, but he was convinced that Jefferson should make the first draft of a declaration. Jefferson was a Virginian and—as Adams would recall later in his autobiography—had been elected to Congress in larger part for having authored *A Summary View of the Rights of British America*, a 1774 essay that "had given him the Character of a fine Writer." Adams also considered Jefferson's relative lack of exposure an advantage. Just thirty-three at the time, Jefferson had not represented Virginia at the First Continental Congress, which convened in 1774. He had participated actively but unremarkably in the opening sessions of the Second Continental Congress in late 1775, and he had arrived late at its spring sessions in 1776. He had fought few battles in Congress, and a draft drawn by his hand was likely to be met with less preconceived opposition.[38] Jefferson did not disappoint Adams's expectations, and his draft, as amended and improved by his fellow committee members, was approved by the Congress on July 2, 1776. Generations of historians have parsed the Declaration of Independence, including its articulation of core human rights—"life, liberty, and the pursuit of happiness."[39]

The way Thomas Jefferson rendered it in the Declaration of Independence, the Americans' predicament was quite simple: a single tyrannical figure, England's King George III, was obstructing their pursuit of happiness. In his 1774 *Summary View of the Rights of British North America*, Jefferson had opined that "bodies of men, as well as individuals, are susceptible of the spirit of tyranny," but he had linked this threat to the British Parliament and to the injustice that "160,000 electors in the island of Great Britain should give law to four millions in the states of America"—"parliamentary tyranny," he called it.[40] But in the Declaration of Independence, Jefferson escalated and dramatized the confrontation, concentrating the threat of tyranny in a single person: "The history of the present King of Great Britain is a history of repeated injuries and usurpations, all having in direct object the establishment of an absolute

Tyranny over these States." Jefferson followed with a lengthy list of these "injuries and usurpations," written in the eighteenth-century equivalent of bullet point form. This listing was bookended by another even more direct accusation leveled at King George III: "A Prince whose character is thus marked by every act which may define a Tyrant, is unfit to be the ruler of a free people."[41]

Not all members of the drafting committee were comfortable with this strident approach. John Adams wrote later, "There were other expressions which I would not have inserted if I had drawn it up, particularly that which called the king tyrant. I thought this too personal; for I never believed George to be a tyrant in disposition and in nature. I always believed him to be deceived by his courtiers on both sides of the Atlantic, and in his official capacity only, cruel. I thought the expression too passionate, and too much like scolding, for so grave a solemn document."[42] But in casting the American predicament in this light, Jefferson tapped a stream of oppositional Protestantism that reached back centuries requiring that resistance to a monarch (or "prince") be predicated on his possessing the character of a tyrant.[43] The discourse was the same one that Benjamin Franklin would conjure the next month in his draft proposal for a "Great Seal" of the new nation labeled "Rebellion to Tyrants Is Obedience to God." Thomas Jefferson liked the motto so much that he chose it later for his own personal seal.[44]

Most proximately, Jefferson's portrayal of King George III as a tyrant connected the American Revolution directly to an idealized, and distinctly Protestant, rendering of English history.[45] In this rendering, the English Civil Wars of the sixteenth and seventeenth centuries amounted to an extended battle for natural liberty, the liberty of the individual. And this battle culminated finally in the Glorious Revolution, which inaugurated the reign of the Protestants William and Mary in 1688 and enshrined the English Bill of Rights the following year. The Bill of Rights had opened with an accusation leveled at King James II: "By the assistance of divers evil counsellors, judges and ministers employed by him," it asserted, James "did endeavour to subvert and extirpate the Protestant religion and the laws and liberties of this kingdom." This depiction of the Catholic monarch as a tyrant was followed by a litany of complaints. The Bill of Rights then resolved that the Protestants "William and Mary, prince and princess of Orange, be and be declared king and queen of England, France and Ireland and the dominions thereunto belonging."[46] Jefferson replicated the essential structure of the English Bill of Rights in the body of the Declaration of Independence, making clear the colonists' intent.[47]

Thomas Jefferson's Declaration of Independence shared something else in common with the English Bill of Rights—both documents concluded with what amounted to sacred oaths. The Bill of Rights concluded with two oaths, crafted to be taken by magistrates and other officials "of whom the oaths have allegiance." The first oath required the individual to state his name and then "sincerely promise and swear that I will be faithful and bear true allegiance to their Majesties King William and Queen Mary. So help me God." The second required the individual again to state his name, to renounce the authority of the pope, and then to declare that "no foreign prince, person, prelate, state or potentate hath or ought to have any jurisdiction, power, superiority, pre-eminence or authority, ecclesiastical or spiritual, within this realm. So help me God."[48] Likewise, Jefferson concluded his Declaration of Independence with an oath that was clearly intended to be read aloud. Specifically, he envisioned that the document would be read in public and ceremonial fashion, a vision that was fulfilled routinely in assemblies throughout the colonies and in proclamations to gatherings of Continental Army troops under the command of George

Washington.[49] Whether they read the declaration or heard it read aloud, those who composed its intended audience were invited to embrace it in the most personal of terms, joining (or imagining their voices joining) with the voices of countless others: "And for the support of this Declaration, with a firm reliance on the protection of divine Providence, we mutually pledge to each other our Lives, our Fortunes and our sacred Honor."[50] This closing oath was more than mere rhetorical flourish—it was an invitation to martyrdom.[51]

* * * * *

The men at the vanguard of the American Revolution were inspired not just by their growing thirst for greater economic and political self-determination but also by the conviction that God was acting providentially through them in human history.[52] This conviction was evident in the ritual life of the Continental Congresses, which hosted public prayers and fast days, funeral sermons, and memorial commemorations of many different kinds. Clergy played an indispensable role in promoting this conviction, working in close collaboration with members of Congress, leaders of the Continental Army, and provincial leaders throughout the colonies. This collaboration proved indispensable in fashioning a sense of national identity that scholars sometimes refer to as an "imagined community."[53]

This process of constructing a new American identity is easy to see in the work that leading clergy undertook to memorialize their fallen war heroes as martyrs—beginning in the period of the French and Indian War, continuing in the buildup to revolution and during the Revolution itself, and in the period of nation building that followed. But these first generations of self-identified Americans did not have to conjure the ideals of martyrdom from scratch; their predecessors had been leading purveyors of this tradition for generations. Across the long expanse of English colonization in North

America, Protestant clergy had inserted representations of martyrdom into the catechetical material they produced for children and the sermons they preached and printed for adults, into harrowing tales of Indian captivity, into poems and lyrics written in simple meters to be sung to popular tunes, and into their prolific production of written accounts of death. In times of war, these same preachers rallied colonial troops with muster sermons, war cries, and battlefield commemorations. All these were part of a larger process, the process by which the inherited tradition of English Protestant martyrdom was appropriated and adapted to the new context of North America.

The ideals of American martyrdom circulated freely through Revolutionary circles from 1774 through 1776, years that saw the establishment of the Continental Congresses and the formal onset of war with the British. John Adams, Joseph Duchè, Patrick Henry, the author of the *Pennsylvania March*, Samuel Stillman, Thomas Paine, Thomas Jefferson—these men shared with virtually every English-speaking person in eighteenth-century America a basic understanding that the central spiritual question of human existence was whether one was prepared to die. They also shared with a great many of their contemporaries the presumption that the struggle to live virtuous lives might someday require them to die virtuous deaths, as it had from time immemorial. As they committed themselves wholeheartedly to the cause of the American Revolution, these men drew on a spiritual heritage that they traced back from England's Glorious Revolution of 1688 to John Foxe and the martyrs of the English branch of the Protestant Reformation and from there to the martyrs of the early Christian church and to those of Greek and Roman antiquity. Each made explicit, unmistakable appeals to their audiences that the American cause was worth dying for, and each did so in a specific idiom steeped in pathos. Understanding this idiom of American martyrdom is essential to understanding American calls for revolution in full dimension. Understanding this idiom and how powerfully it resonated in the hearts and minds of young American men in the 1770s is also essential to answering the central question of this book:

What animated so many young men—young men like Nathan Hale—to risk sacrificing their lives for the Revolutionary cause?

7

Nathan Hale

An Exemplary American Martyr

By the time the American Revolution came into view, the tradition of English Protestant martyrdom had found varied expression across centuries among English-speaking peoples. The ideal of dying willfully and self-sacrificially for a sacred cause was embraced ferociously by all sides to the many conflicts in the mid-seventeenth century, the era of the English Civil Wars. Survivors of these wars bequeathed this ideal to their descendants, who deployed it across the seventeenth and eighteenth centuries in the prosecution of wars to maintain and expand England's far-flung empire. As part of this empire, English colonists in North America sustained their commitment to these ideals through many varied circumstances. Even those who did not become martyrs themselves believed that their deaths could be meaningful in the eyes of God, and so they looked to the martyrs who had gone before them—their forefathers, their loved ones, their heroes—as sources of inspiration, both in the essential work of preparing to die and in the unavoidable work of dying itself. Most powerfully, English Protestants in North America kept this tradition alive as they engaged in armed conflict with their erstwhile neighbors—the Native peoples of North America and their colonial competitors, the Spanish and the French. In these martial endeavors, martyrs remained for English-speaking Protestants exemplars of true Christian faith, paragons of virtue, and paradigms of fully realized masculinity. Through the conduct and aftermath of the great midcentury war that they called the French and Indian War, a new generation of English colonists identified a new cause—the "continental" or "American" cause—as worthy of the price of martyrdom.

The entire weight of this tradition was felt by young men who came of age in the years leading up to the American Revolution—young men like Nathan Hale. As were previous generations of English colonists in North America, these young men were trained from childhood to prepare themselves for that moment, which could be any moment, when they would be forced to confront the reality of death. Born into families and communities chock-full of men who fought in what they considered a holy war—the French and Indian War—they were groomed to take seriously the possibility that they too might be called by providential design to give their lives in self-sacrifice for a sacred cause. As the rebellion against British authorities in North America gained momentum through the 1770s, and as talk painting King George III a tyrant spread through the colonies, the American cause took on Revolutionary form. The War of Independence represented a perfect opportunity for young men like Nathan Hale to demonstrate their spiritual virtuosity by becoming true patriots, which is to say willing martyrs. They each had but one life to give.

Raising and Rallying an American Martyr

Born on June 6, 1755, in the farming village of Coventry, Connecticut, Nathan Hale was the son of Richard Hale and Elizabeth Strong, each descended from early New England families.[1] From an early age, the Hales encouraged Nathan and his older brother, Enoch, to consider the possibility that God was calling them to become pastors in the Congregational Church. This encouragement—unsurprising given that Richard's family tree was dotted with Congregationalist ministers and Elizabeth's densely populated with them—means that the young Hale boys were raised in a rigorous process of Puritan catechism.[2] Even as they learned to read, they began to be steeped in themes of mortality and ideals of martyrdom that composed their Puritan spiritual inheritance. A practice of not just reading the Bible but in fact seeking to embody it; habits of daily study that embedded an ethos of self-sacrifice in the very acts of reading and writing; a catechetical curriculum providing both guidance for preparing to die and inspiring models suitable for emulation in the work of dying itself; and a perpetual reaffirmation of the biblical narrative, with Jesus's own martyrdom presented as the very crux of human history—these practices shaped the early spiritual formation of Nathan and Enoch Hale. Their parents immersed the two brothers and their nine siblings in this way of orienting to the larger world precisely because they believed it was uniquely suited to meeting the kinds of challenges that had confronted the faithful from time immemorial.

Like so many of their peers, the Hale brothers' coming-of-age was cast in the long shadow of death. Nathan Hale was approaching his twelfth birthday and Enoch was just thirteen and a half when their mother, Elizabeth, died in early April 1767 from postpartum complications after giving birth to her twelfth child.[3] Their mother's death cast in dramatic relief a series of rites marking the passage of the Hale boys to adulthood. Within a year of their mother's burial, Nathan and Enoch made their own professions of faith before their father and the other men who served as deacons at the Coventry Congregational Church; they submitted to the ordinance of baptism, in which, standing before the entire congregation, they pledged to unite themselves spiritually with the suffering, death, and resurrection of Jesus Christ; and they announced an intention to explore a pastoral calling or vocation.[4] In the fall of 1769—just over two years after their mother's death—Nathan, then just fourteen, and Enoch, turning sixteen, enrolled at Yale College, an institution dedicated at its founding in 1701 to "educate and train up youth for the ministry, in the Churches of the Colony, according to the doctrine, discipline and mode of worship received and practice in them."[5] The brothers would graduate from Yale together four years later in the summer of 1773. As things turned out, Enoch would go on to become a Congregational pastor, as had always been the plan. Nathan's calling would take on a different shape, but one of which his elders would have been equally, perhaps even more, proud.

The most influential person in the Hale brothers' coming-of-age was the young clergyman Joseph Huntington, pastor of their family church, Coventry's Congregational Church. Their declaration of intent to seek admission to Yale College ushered the Hale brothers into the young clergyman's office, where he assisted them in exploring their calls to ordination and tutored them as they prepared to sit Yale's entrance exams. Barely thirty and a graduate of Yale College himself, Joseph Huntington was uniquely qualified to mentor Enoch and Nathan Hale—and his record of publication gives a clear picture of the intellectual pedigree he passed on to his young disciples. While at Yale, Huntington published *College*

Almanack, containing a compendium of useful information. As was customary for almanacs of the period, Huntington imparted formal catechetical information to faithful Christians—devotional prayers, hymns, poems, and the like—alongside basic astrological, meteorological, and historical information laid out in the form of monthly calendars. Huntington's mélange of Christian orthodoxy, reflections on the human condition, and astronomical investigation was entirely reflective of the intellectual trends at Yale College—and, more broadly, in educated circles of America—in the middle decades of the eighteenth century. In his almanac for the year 1761, the young seminarian expounded in an introductory note to the "Courteous Reader" on the organization of the solar system, offered an extended defense of "Copernican calculation" and "Newtonian philosophy," and protested the "incrudility [*sic*] of the vulgar, who pretty generally (with great confidence, and assurance) deride and explode it." But Huntington did not perceive astronomy and physics and mathematics to be at odds with faith. As he summed up after counting the staggering multitude of bodies known to exist in the solar system, "What then is earth, with regard to the whole? Like a miserable hospital, amidst unnumbered, stately palaces! But to conclude. What lessons of humility do these considerations teach us? Sure, man is by the Poet fitly stiled, 'An atom, of this atom world.' Shall he then fight against the whole universe? Shall he propose his own good to the good of the whole? Be still then my complaining spirit; remember that the common PARENT OF ALL has large provision to make for infinite numbers of far, far greater conference."[6] Students at Yale College in the 1760s and 1770s neither perceived nor sought to perceive any contradiction between theology and science, between faith and reason. Preachers in training like Joseph Huntington and Enoch Hale—and even students like Nathan Hale, who, it turns out, was uncertain of a clerical vocation—were taught to resist the notion that these great streams of thought ran at crosscurrents to each other. Rather, they were encouraged to identify how these diverse streams were being channeled in a common direction by providential design. As Huntington explained to the "Courteous Reader" of his 1761 *College Almanack*, "As the great design of all curious science, astronomical, philosophical, or of any other denomination whatsoever, is to subserve and promote the interest of religion, & good morals amongst mankind; so there is a wonderful and wise concerted aptitude and fitness in every kind of liberal science, to accomplish this grand, this important effect."[7]

As was also typical for the genre, Huntington squeezed aphorisms and miscellany into what little space might have otherwise remained in the monthly calendars of his almanac. True to form, Huntington presumed that human mortality would be a prevailing interest of his readers, as is suggested by aphorisms like this from his *College Almanack* for 1762:

- One eye on earth; and one full fix'd on Heaven, becomes a mortal and immortal man. (March)
- Death treads in pleasure's footsteps round the world! (April)
- To trifle, is to live (say the gay and fashionable) and is it likewise a trifle to die? (August)
- The funeral of all nature, which we see every winter, ought, methinks, to admonish of our own. (December)[8]

This preoccupation was also reflected in the holdings of the extracurricular reading society Linonia, to which Huntington and Nathan and Enoch Hale all belonged while students at Yale College.[9] The society's collection included works not just from across the vast expanse of the Christian tradition, and not just from the early generations of what we now think of as modern science, but also from the "classics" of Roman antiquity. Scattered throughout these classics were countless examples of noble deaths—accounts of the deaths of Socrates, Anaxarchus, Paetus Thrasea, Helvidius Priscus, Rubellius Plautus, and Seneca, to name just a few. When Helvidius Priscus, for example, was threatened with death by the emperor Vespasian, the Stoic philosopher responded, "When did I tell you I was immortal? You play your role and I will play mine. Your role is to cause my death, mine is to die without trembling."[10] Pervading this literature was the ancient Roman notion that the born male (*mas*) could become a true man (*vir*) by growth in the exercise of virtue (*virtus*). In this regard, the conduct of martyrs was celebrated as exemplary, none more so than Polycarp, who responded to a heavenly voice urging him to "play the man."[11]

Joseph Huntington retained these ideological commitments throughout his life, and he passed them on to his young students, including Enoch and Nathan Hale. We know that he did because on September 29, 1779, he preached at a service marking Enoch Hale's ordination and installation as the pastor of the Congregational Church of West Hampton, Connecticut. Affirming that God sought collaboration from human beings in the form of "moral virtue" or "holiness," Huntington used the terms interchangeably in the installation sermon: "Moral virtue, the love and practice of it, as we have opportunity in the world, is as necessary to salvation as the atonement of Christ, or faith in his blood, and is as much urged and insisted on in the word of God; the peace of moral virtue is distinct from the other, in the oeconomy of our salvation, but no less necessary. 'Without holiness no man shall see the Lord.'" For Huntington, this task of preparing to "see the Lord" was not metaphorical—to the contrary, this very real encounter was the logical and necessary conclusion of every human life. For precisely this reason, Huntington encouraged Enoch Hale—and the larger audience of listeners and readers to whom his sermon was ultimately addressed—to "take a more distinct view of the death of Christ" and to "consider the death of Christ in all its glorious connections and consequences." As he had throughout his career, he returned to the theme that dominated the preaching and teaching and writing of New England preachers straight through to the end of the eighteenth century: "It were indeed well for us, had we all the learned accomplishments of the most eminent legislators, philosophers and orators of Greece and Italy, of Athens, Corinth and Rome, in the most shining period of their days; these qualifications, sanctified, may be of great use to us, and the greatest degree of learning is to be sought by us: But in the sacred and important character of preachers of the gospel and guides of precious and immortal souls, we have nothing to do with any other theme, than JESUS CHRIST, and him crucified."[12] Just seven days earlier, Enoch Hale had marked the third anniversary of his brother Nathan's death as a martyr to the cause of the American Revolution.

No evidence survives to help us understand why Nathan Hale chose not to follow his older brother Enoch in seeking ordination as a minister of the gospel. The docents at the Nathan Hale schoolhouses in East Haddam and New London, Connecticut, have parsed fact from fiction to present to their visitors an honest accounting of Revolutionary America's most famous spy. But no written record details the decision-making that led him to take up work as a schoolteacher after graduating from Yale—nor that which led him to abandon this work after just eighteen months to enroll in Connecticut's colonial militia. The only impression left is of a young man in search of adventure or purpose, or perhaps both.

Nathan Hale's biographers, meanwhile, have reconstructed his largely uneventful military career by triangulating independent sources (news articles, battlefield accounts, and so on) with Hale's own diary. The diary begins on September 23, 1775, as Hale's company departs from New London, Connecticut. In its last entry, dated August 23, 1776, Hale remarks on the continuing buildup of British troops in occupied New York, the circumstance that would lead to his recruitment as a spy the following month. Nathan Hale's diary consists largely of routine notations of his company's comings and goings, but even in these notations can be found clues to Hale's experience as a member of George Washington's Continental Army.

We know, for instance, that Hale heard sermons while soldiering, including sermons encouraging him to prepare for his own self-sacrifice. Most but not all of the sermons noted in Hale's diary were delivered on Sunday, the Christian Sabbath, and most but not all of his entries about the sermons are brief and unadorned, the abbreviation *pr* standing in for the word *preached*. These two examples from October 1775 are typical:

8th. Sab. A.M. rainy—no meetg. Mr Bird pr. Watertown
P.M. Went to meetg on the hill. Mr. Smith pr.
Sab., 15th. Mr. Bird pr. P.M. After meeting walked to
Mystick.[13]

Every so often, however, a sermon merited Hale's special praise. On Sunday, November 5, 1775, a "Mr. Learned" preached from the Scripture John 13:19 and earned a notation of "excellentissime" in the diary. Two weeks later, Hale made the following entry: "Sabbath Day, 19th. Mr. Bird pr.—one service only, beginning after 12 o'cl. Text Esther 8th, 6: 'For how can I endure to see the evil that shall come unto my people, or how can I endure to see the destruction of my kindred?' The discourse very good, the same as preached to Genl Wooster, his officers and Soldiers, at Newhaven, and which was again preached at Cambridge a Sabbath or two ago. Now preached as a farewell discourse."[14] We do not know exactly what Rev. Samuel Bird, pastor of the Church of Christ in New Haven, preached to Nathan Hale's company of Continental Army soldiers on November 19, 1775. But we know from Hale's notation that Rev. Bird liked to recycle his sermons—Hale had apparently heard this sermon several times—and we also know the kind of farewell discourse Bird liked to preach to those preparing for battle. Some sixteen years earlier, on an unspecified date at the height of the French and Indian War, Bird had preached such a sermon to a company of Connecticut soldiers at the request of their colonel David Wooster. Entitled *The Importance of the Divine Presence with Our Host* and brought to press in 1759 by the New Haven publisher James Parker, Bird's sermon was based on Exodus 33:15, which he rendered, "And he said unto him, if thy Presence go not with me, carry us not up hence." The farewell sermon opens with a perfunctory caveat: "War is in itself very undesirable; but nevertheless, it is some Times an indispensable Duty, of absolute Necessity, and of great Importance to undertake it." After asserting "our absolute Dependence on the over-ruling Providence of God, for Success in all our Undertakings," Bird admonished his listeners (and readers) to "consider by what Means we should endeavor to secure the divine Presence with us." The heart of the sermon, though, is a clear vindication of the English cause and a clear and rousing call to arms.[15] Having noted that "a just War is rather to be chosen than an unjust peace," Bird exhorted, "May a noble Spirit of martial Courage and good Conduct, united with a divine Blessing, attend our Armies in the Field, and may sneaking Cowardice, and a dastardly Temper be banish'd from every Breast, and be abhorred by every New England Man. . . . Surely an honourable Death, in the Defence of our Country, is much rather to be chosen, than a Life of most wretched Slavery." Bird challenged the faithful to "draw the Sword in the Cause of King JESUS, the King of Kings" and "against the Emissaries and Incendiaries of Hell and Rome." He encouraged the soldiers to imagine the voices of their wives imploring them to "prevent my becoming a Sacrifice to the merciless Rage of tawny Savages" and the voices of their children likewise crying out, "O! dear and compassionate Father, Instrument of our Being, fight for us, and beat off the base Savages of the Wilderness, into whose Hands, if we should fall, we must expect to share the Fate of defenceless Lambs, among ravening Wolves." He exhorted them "to fight under the exalted Banner of the Lord Jesus, against your spiritual Enemies, the World, the Flesh and the Devil." He assures them that "however sharp and tedious the Conflict, the Victory will most assuredly turn in your Favour, and the Reward be very glorious; no less than an everlasting Kingdom; a Crown of unfading Glory." He concluded, "Put your trust in God, then may you stand intrepid amidst the hideous Terrors of Death: and if it should be your Log to fall among the Slain in Battle, holy Angels will be your kind and faithful Convoy to the Regions of undisturbed Tranquility, where the Noise of War shall be heard no more. Brave Soldiers, Farewell, be strong and of good Courage, and may the Presence of God be with you."[16]

Sermons were not the only form in which the heritage of English Protestant martyrdom was conjured for the young Americans who fought in the War of Independence. Dating to his time in the French and Indian War, George Washington favored his soldiers performing works of theater when not training for battle, and he carried this practice forward to his command of the Continental Army.[17] Among the preferred works was Addison's *Cato*, the theatrical performance of which was seen as a kind of dress rehearsal for battle. As one soldier, William Bradford Jr., wrote to his sister Rachel from Washington's encampment in Valley Forge, Pennsylvania, in May 1778, "The camp could now afford you some entertainment. The manoeuvering of the Army itself is a sight that would charm you.—Besides these, the Theatre is opened—Last Monday Cato was performed before a very numerous and splendid audience. . . . The scenery was in Taste—& the performance admirable—Col. George did his part to admiration—he made an excellent die (as they say)."[18] Nathan Hale would have seen countless such dramatizations—or performed in them himself—during his almost two years of soldiering, the participants actively (or vicariously) rehearsing their own deaths. In the play's climactic scene, Cato is presented with the body of his martyred son, and the proud, mournful father declares,

> *Welcome, my son! Here lay him down, my friends,*
> *Full in my sight, that I may view at leisure,*
> *The bloody corpse, and count those glorious wounds.*
> *How beautiful is death, when earn'd by virtue!*
> *Who would not be that youth? What pity is it,*
> *That we can die but once to serve our country!*[19]

Then pointing to the corpse, Cato concludes,

> *There the brave youth, with love of virtue fired,*
> *Who greatly in his country's cause expired,*
> *Shall know he conquer'd, the firm patriot there,*
> *Who made the welfare of mankind his care,*
> *Though still by faction, vice, and fortune crost,*
> *Shall find the gen'rous labour was not lost.*[20]

Soldiers under Washington's command near New York were also taught to revere the Declaration of Independence, with its rousing conclusion calling on fellow patriots to seal their commitment to the patriot cause. As Pauline Maier tells the story, on July 9, 1776, Washington "ordered officers of the several Continental Army brigades stationed in New York City to pick up copies of the Declaration at the Adjutant General's Office." Then, "with the British 'constantly in view, upon and at State-Island,' as one participant recalled, the brigades were 'formed in hollow squares on their respective parades,' where they heard the Declaration read, as the General had specified, 'with an audible voice.' The event, Washington hoped, would 'serve as a free incentive to every officer, and soldier, to act with Fidelity and Courage.'"[21] The hope expressed by Washington was not without foundation. Whether Captain Nathan Hale read the Declaration out loud to soldiers under his command or whether he heard it read out loud by one of his commanding officers, or both, the declaration's closing flourish would have packed a powerful punch—"And for the support of this Declaration, with a firm reliance on the protection of divine Providence, we mutually pledge to each other our Lives, our Fortunes and our sacred Honor."[22] It was the public declaration of a willingness to die for the sacred cause of American independence.

American Martyrs as Fruits of a Deeply Rooted Tree

Americans today are accustomed to thinking of the American Revolution as a singular and innovative event, a democratic revolution that set in motion a chain of events that would change the course of human history. But the young men who fought in the War of Independence were not soothsayers; their motivations were shaped not by subsequent events but rather by the traditions in which they had been raised. Even the most farsighted and visionary among them considered the American cause in the light of a centuries-long chain of Protestant wars, the virtues of which were proven by the willing self-sacrifices of generations of martyrs. As Thomas Jefferson himself wrote to his friend William Stephens Smith in 1787, "The tree of liberty must be refreshed from time to time with the blood of patriots and tyrants."[23]

The life and death of Nathan Hale were fruit of this ancient tradition, the tradition of English Protestant martyrdom appropriated to the context of colonial America and adapted to the cause of the American Revolution. Hale's conduct—including whatever words he spoke—in the moments preceding his execution on September 22, 1776, cannot be understood apart from a lengthy process that unfolded across generations.

Consider just one simple construction of this ancient cultural impulse—the construction calling on youthful Americans to "play the man."

This articulation of masculine virtue—its roots in the English language dating at least to John Foxe's sixteenth-century martyrology—circulated freely in eighteenth-century British North America, appearing routinely in a wide range of printed material. Nathan Hale could have read it in the King James Version of the Bible, and he could have read it in the famous account of the bishops Ridley and Latimer found in John Foxe's original *Book of Martyrs* and in every abridgment of it. He could have read it in the climactic scene of John Bunyan's *Pilgrim's Progress*, the most popular book for generations of young readers on both sides of the Atlantic. He could have read it in any of dozens of "muster sermons" printed in Boston in the decades leading up to the Revolutionary War—including Thomas Symmes's *Lovewell Lamented*, Peter Clark's *Christian Bravery*, William McClenachan's

The Christian Warrior, Thomas Prentice's *When the People, and the Rulers among Them, Willingly Offer Themselves to a Military Expedition against Their Unrighteous Enemies*, William Hobby's *The Soldier Caution'd*, Jonathan Todd's *The Soldier Waxing Strong and Valiant in Fight through Faith*, Samuel Checkley's *A Day of Darkness*, Isaac Morrill's *The Soldier Exhorted*, Gilbert Tennent's *The Happiness of Rewarding the Enemies of Our Religion and Liberty*, and Samuel Davies's *The Curse of Cowardice*.[24] He could have read it in Robert Eastburn's chronicle of his Canadian captivity, first published in Philadelphia in 1758 and reprinted the same year in Boston, or in any of a number of other narratives of Indian captivity.[25] He could have read it in John Hancock's 1774 speech to the crowd assembled at the annual commemoration of the Boston Massacre, which was published that same year in Boston, New Haven, and Newport (Rhode Island) and the following year in Philadelphia.[26]

Hale could have come across this evocative phrase in any number of print materials while soldiering in the Connecticut militia and the Continental Army. He could have read it—or heard it read aloud—in any of dozens of open letters published in New England newspapers like this one protesting the news that British authorities had issued orders that Samuel Adams, John Hancock, and others be "hanged in Boston." The letter's author signed off, "I shall only add, that my country may be free if she will and that she may have the virtue to play the man, is the aspiration of Sir, your most obedient servant."[27] The author of another such letter entitled "To the American Soldiery" printed in November 1775 in the *New England Chronicle* before appearing in newspapers in Pennsylvania, Maryland, and Virginia assured his colleagues, "We are engaged, my fellow soldiers, in the cause of virtue, of liberty, of God: For God's sake, then let us play the man for God's sake, let us neglect no requisite precautions to frustrate the cruel attempts of our remorseless foes."[28] He could have read it—or heard it read aloud—in this prayer composed by Abiel Leonard, chaplain to the Continental Army, and published in Cambridge in 1775 under the title *A Prayer, Composed for the Benefit of the Soldiery, in the American Army, to Assist Them in Their Private Devotions*:

> Teach, I pray thee, my hands to war, and my fingers to fight in the defence of America, and the rights and liberties of it! Impress upon my mind a true sense of my duty, and the obligation I am under to my country! And enable me to pay a due and respect to all my officers. Grant unto me a courage, zeal and resolution in the day of battle, that I may play the man for my people, and the cities of my God; chusing rather to lay down my life, than either through cowardice or desertion betray the glorious cause I am engaged in.[29]

In fact, Nathan Hale could have come across this exhortation in the very almanac that he likely carried in his pocket—*Watson's Register, and Connecticut Almanack, for the Year of Our Lord, 1776*. (See figures 5 and 6.) Published in Hartford in 1775, and the only almanac published in Connecticut that year, *Watson's Almanack* listed all of the colony's officers serving in the war, including Hale's position in the Nineteenth Regiment of George Washington's Continental Army. The almanac's calendar for April—just a few months before Hale would volunteer for service as a spy—was introduced with this poem:

> *With public Spirit let each Bosom glow,*
> *And love of Liberty direct the blow:*
> *Rouse, patriot Heroes, and pursue the Plan,*

Teach listless Souls what 'tis to play the Man.[30]

This formulation remained widespread in American print in the decades following the Revolution, appearing in sermons, orations, poems, concerts, almanacs, and encyclopedias.[31]

Young revolutionaries like Nathan Hale understood Jesus Christ to have been crucified as the very crux of divine intervention in human history. They understood the early Christian martyrs to have followed in the footsteps of Christ and to have suffered persecution to the point of death as witnesses to the truth. They understood their Protestant forebears to have stood up to the demonic power of Catholic popes, even at the cost of their lives. And they understood their immediate forefathers to have warred against the papist French and the savage Indians to preserve the providential experiment that was the English colonization of America. They understood the American cause not just in terms of political and economic aspirations but in terms of racial and religious supremacy, and they understood this cause to be divinely ordained. For them, the American Revolution was a holy war.

At every stop along the way, they understood that to confront the powers of death at work in the world was the very essence of the human task, that to die for a sacred cause was to fulfill a high calling, and that for many this calling would prove a necessary rite of passage to manhood. Nathan Hale was steeped in these ideals of English Protestant martyrdom from his early childhood, through the years of his coming-of-age, in his formal education at Yale College, and in his time of soldiering under George Washington's command. These ideals were bequeathed to him by his ancestors, cultivated in him by his parents, encouraged in him by his mentors, proclaimed to him by his preachers, and extolled by the leaders of the Continental Congress and by the chaplains of the Continental

Army. There is every reason to conclude that his decision to enlist in the Continental Army and his decision to volunteer as a spy were inspired by these high-minded ideals. And there is no reason to doubt that he took pains to express these ideals—in his comportment and in his last words—at the time of his execution.

For young men raised to esteem martyrs and rallied to the Revolutionary cause—young men like Nathan Hale—to die as American patriots at war with a tyrannical king was a supreme honor and a sign of fully realized masculine virtue. Such deaths held out the promise of being escorted by holy angels to eternal peace by Jesus's side. They also held out the possibility that some who died such deaths might find their lasting fame. Indeed, some did.

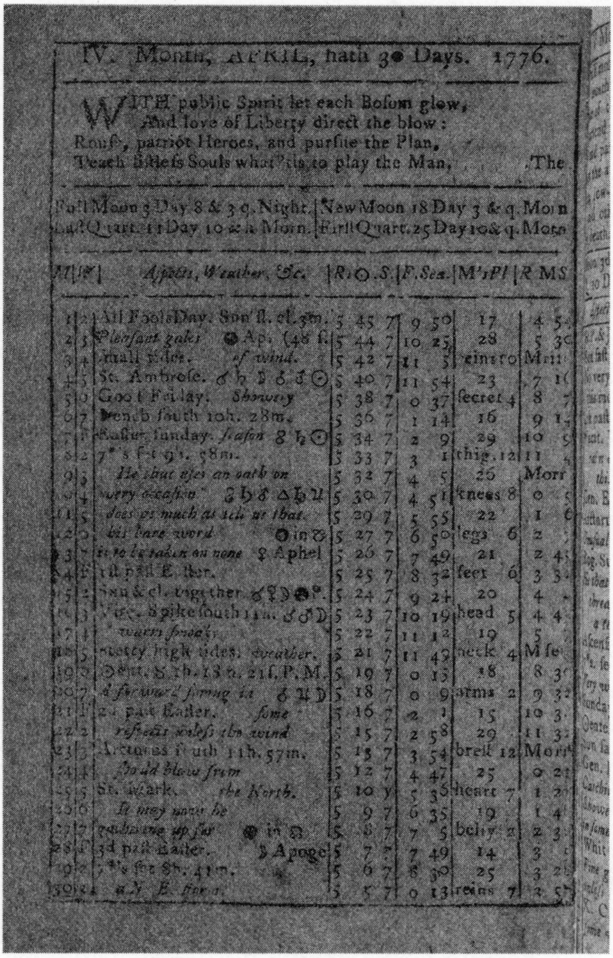
IV. Month, APRIL, hath 30 Days. 1776.

WITH public Spirit let each Bosom glow,
And love of Liberty direct the blow:
Rouse, patriot Heroes, and pursue the Plan,
Teach lifeless Souls what 'tis to play the Man. The

Full Moon 3 Day 8 & 3 q. Night. | New Moon 18 Day 3 & q. Morn
Last Quart. 11 Day 10 & a Morn. | First Quart. 25 Day 10 & q. Morn

M | W | Aspects, Weather, &c. | R. ☉ S. | F. Sea. | M's Pl. | R. MS

Figure 5. April calendar from Ebenezer Watson's *Connecticut Almanack* (1776)

The 1776 April calendar in *Watson's Register, and Connecticut Almanack* is introduced with a poem challenging young Connecticut soldiers to show others what it means to "play the man."

Ebenezer Watson, *Watson's Register, and Connecticut Almanack, for the Year of Our Lord, 1776* (Hartford, CT: Ebenezer Watson, 1775), 8. Reprinted with permission of the American Antiquarian Society.

NINETEENTH REGIMENT.

CHARLES WEBB, Colonel,
STREET HALL, Lieutenant Colonel,
------ BROOKS, Major.

Charles Webb, jun. *Adjutant*,   John Elderkin *Quarter Master*.

Captains.	*1st Lieutenants.*	*2d Lieutenants.*	*Ensigns.*
Joseph Hait	Joseph A. Wright	Reuben Scovil,	Stephen Betts
Nath. Tuttle	Eli Catlin	Jesse Grant	---- Johnson
Edw. Shipman	John Yates	---- Whitlesey	Selah Benson
Isaac Bostwick	---- Hurlburt	Elisha Bostwick	---- Vacant
Peter Perrit	Charles Pond	Samuel Sanford	---- Smith
Eli Levenworth	Robert Lewis	Cha. Webb, jun.	John Hall
William Hull	---- Shumway	William Clark	---- Whittlesey
Nathan Hale	---- Chapman	John Elderkin	---- Hurlbert

TWENTIETH REGIMENT.

BENEDICT ARNOLD, *Colonel*, JOHN DURKEE, *Lieut. Colonel*.
THOMAS KNOWLTON, *Major*, Daniel Tilden, *Adjutant*, Ebenezer Gray, *Quarter-Master*.

Captains.	*1st Lieutenants.*	*2d Lieutenants.*	*Ensigns.*
William Coit,	Leml. Bingham,	Beriah Bill,	Jon. Woodworth,
Eph. Manning,	Wills Cleft,	Nath. Bilhop,	Bryant Brown,
Jed. Waterman,	Wm. Lyon,	John Waterman,	Waters Clark,
Thomas Dyer,	Eben. Gray,	James Holt,	Benj. Durkee,
Tho. Grosvenor,	Dan. Tilden,	Ja. Sprague,	Tim. Cleveland,
Stephen Brown,	Ben. Durkee,	Josiah Fuller,	Silas Goodell,
John Keys,	Sam. Brown,	John Howard,	John Buall,
---- Ewing,	Wm. Adams,	Robt. Holland,	Jo. Durkee, jun.

TWENTY-SECOND REGIMENT.

SAMUEL WYLLYS, Colonel,
RUFUS PUTNAM, Lieutenant-Colonel,
RETURN J. MEIGS, Major.

Charles Whiting, Adjutant, Charles Knowles, Quarter Master.

Captains.	*1st Lieutenants.*	*2d Lieutenants.*	*Ensigns.*
Levi Walls,	Hen. Champion,	Warren Hunely,	Dudly Wright
Ab. Pettibone,	Nat. Humphry,	Jon. Pettibone,	Benj. Adams,
Ol. Hanckett,	Eb. Huntington,	Eliph. King,	Tho's Phelps,
Ezkiel Scoot,	Samuel Cooper,	Char. Knowles,	Jonath. Hart,
Eben. Sumner,	Abijah Savage,	Robert Warner,	Hez. Hulbard
Sam. Wright,	Steph. Goodrich,	Charles Butler,	Josiah Brown,
H. Holdridge,	Charles Whiting,	Eliza. Stillwell,	Tho's Hendar,
Amasa Mills,	Marcus Cole,	Bezakiel Ackley,	Sam. Richards

*** The shortness of the time since the formation and establishment of the army, we hope will apologize for any omission in the above list.

Figure 6. Listing of the Nineteenth Regiment from Ebenezer Watson's
Connecticut Almanack (1776)

The last pages of *Watson's Register, and Connecticut Almanack* list officers from Connecticut in George Washington's Continental Army, including Captain Nathan Hale.

Ebenezer Watson, *Watson's Register, and Connecticut Almanack, for the Year of Our Lord, 1776* (Hartford, CT: Ebenezer Watson, 1775), 24. Reprinted with permission of the American Antiquarian Society.

Conclusion

American Martyrdom,
the American Revolution, and Us

The story told in these pages sheds new light on the making of the American Revolution and on the American spirit.

Across the course of the eighteenth century, English-speaking colonists in British North America appropriated the tradition of English Protestant martyrdom, adapting it to their unique circumstances. In due course, they developed a distinctly American brand of martyrdom that helped fuel the American Revolution. The legend of Nathan Hale's death and final words did not spread widely until the early nineteenth century, but deaths like his were widely celebrated as acts of martyrdom straight through the Revolutionary period. As the Continental Army chaplain Hugh Henry Brackenridge put it in 1779, "It is the high reward of those who have risked their lives in a just and necessary war, that their names are sweet in the mouths of men, and every age shall know their actions."[1] Or as Israel Evans, one of George Washington's favorite chaplains, proclaimed that same year, fallen American patriots were "martyrs for the cause of freedom" whose deaths would surely animate their "countrymen to finish the glorious work of liberty!"[2] This tradition, this culture, this creed, is aptly called American martyrdom.

This tradition was not merely one of after-the-fact commemoration. Rather, the grooming of young American men like Nathan Hale for acts of martyrdom was an essential part of this tradition.[3] Print materials designed specifically for the instruction of the young in colonial America routinely celebrated martyrdom as an ideal type of death, and these materials still played an important role in the spiritual formation of America's Revolutionary generations. These materials were used for far more than mere reading—they were widely used in devotional practices like singing, praying, worshiping, teaching, preaching, writing, meditating, and so on. English-speaking colonists in eighteenth-century North America also developed a pan-Protestant vernacular that celebrated the ideals of martyrdom in both printed and oral forms. These printed texts and oral expressions may sound fanciful or delusional or hyperbolic in modern ears, and of course many of them were crudely crafted. But they were part of an ongoing and multidimensional cultural practice by which people told and retold, wrote and rewrote, imagined and reimagined narratives of martyrdom in ways that shaped their individual and collective identities. In this way of thinking, martyrs were worthy of emulation because they possessed a distinctively effective answer to the fundamental question of life, which was how to make meaning out of death.

The ideal type of the martyr inspired some in colonial America to adopt postures of pacifism that can be seen as precursors to modern strategies of nonviolent resistance.[4] But it inspired many more to assume postures of militant and martial opposition to what they perceived to be threats of tyranny. The idealized vision of dying a self-sacrificing death for a sacred cause inspired generations of Americans to "play the man"—what today we might call "manning up"—and to fight what they were taught to conceive of as fights to the death. Young Protestant men coming of age in colonial America understood their immediate forefathers and ancient heroes to have risked martyrdom by going to war to defend their honor and virtue. They understood that they should be prepared to do likewise as a rite of passage to manhood.

In prosecuting the mid-eighteenth-century war that they called the French and Indian War, leading English colonists fashioned a new collective self-understanding, embracing a shared vision of "continental" or "American" destiny. In the aftermath of the war, they adapted this language to their new circumstances as they began to rebel against the authority exercised by English institutions, first the Church and Parliament and eventually the Crown. As this rebellion gained momentum and took on Revolutionary form through the 1770s, the increasingly unhappy English colonists turned their ire on their king as their ancestors had before them.[5] By portraying King George III as a tyrant, they conjured the archetypal encounter in this tradition in which the martyr's essential test of virtue is his willingness to withstand the threats of a tyrant and confront bravely the prospect of death. The War of Independence represented a perfect opportunity for a new generation of young men to likewise demonstrate their masculine determination and devotion as martyrs to the patriot cause.

Of course, the origins of the American Revolution are many. These can be traced to a growing economic interdependence among the colonies, to a new ideological mix of ideas, to a growing democratic spirit across many dimensions of colonial life, and to new emerging cultural sensibilities. The story of Nathan Hale told in these pages shows that the roots of the Revolution can also be traced to a distinctively Anglo-American Protestant spirituality that celebrated the preparedness to die for a sacred cause as the paramount expression of human virtue.

This pan-Protestant tradition of American martyrdom helped make it possible for independence-minded people in eighteenth-century British North America to join forces across what otherwise might have been insurmountable divides of colony, culture, class, confession, color, and creed. Virginians like Thomas Jefferson, Patrick Henry, and George Washington; New Englanders like John Adams, Samuel Adams, Paul Revere, Joseph Warren, and John Hancock; and Pennsylvanians like Benjamin Franklin and John Dickinson—all appropriated the inherited tradition of English Protestant martyrdom and adapted it readily to the cause of the Revolution. Its potential for uniting an even wider range of peoples was undermined by the racism that was pervasive among English colonists and by the rank hypocrisy of slaveholding that was practiced by so many of them and sanctioned by so many others.

Inherently oppositional, this tradition of American martyrdom undergirded a shared Revolutionary identity that promoted open resistance to authorities, both ecclesiastical and political. Explicitly militant, it helped birth an ethos of martial valor and selfless patriotism that has been celebrated by Americans down through the ages. Entirely presumptive of divine sanction, it encouraged the demonization of enemies. Deeply racist, it sat comfortably with institutions and ideologies that dehumanized Native peoples and African slaves, among others. This tradition nurtured in those who embraced it both a kind of bravery and virtue and, simultaneously, a kind of arrogance and self-righteousness bred from certainty and zeal. Forged in the crucible of war, members of America's Revolutionary generations were, with rare exception, self-congratulatory about the former and entirely oblivious of the latter.

This tradition of American martyrdom is easy to overlook—in part because it is grounded in ancient history and in part because it lingers to the present day. This tradition provided the American revolutionaries a powerful reservoir of thought and sentiment to draw on as they encouraged each other and mobilized support for their cause. This reservoir had been filled by generations of Protestants who went to war against the "satanic" popes in the era of the English Civil Wars. Just as their forefathers in North America had demonstrated their masculine virtue in earlier wars against the "demonic" French and their "savage" Indian allies, the men reared in America's Revolutionary generations felt honor bound to demonstrate their own fearlessness in their war against the English monarch George III. They felt this way especially after they concluded—they could not help themselves—that George was a tyrant. As they prepared themselves to confront this earthly tyrant, it was only natural that they should, simultaneously, prepare themselves to face down the ultimate tyrant, death. In this way of thinking, death is a powerful spiritual force that is always seeking out earthly allies to conspire in the work of depriving the truly virtuous of life, liberty, and the pursuit of happiness. If the truly virtuous will remain faithful to their sacred cause, even as they die, they will triumph over this ultimate tyrant and enter heavenly realms.

Reframing the telling of the American Revolution in these terms invites us to reexamine the revolutionaries, but it also invites us to reexamine ourselves. This cultural inheritance has armed us, in moral and spiritual terms, with a double-edged sword. This inheritance can inspire a profound sense of purpose and destiny, imbued with the dimension of the divine. It can render us, as Americans, capable of extraordinary sacrifice for causes greater than ourselves.

It also predisposes us to absolutize our every cause and to demonize our every perceived enemy. Across the span of generations, English colonists in North America shifted the focus of their all-consuming animus quite readily from one adversary to the next: from French and Spanish Catholics, whom they characterized routinely as demonic "papists"; to Native peoples, in whom they often perceived little more than "bloodlust" and "savagery"; to Africans, whom they treated according to what they considered their "bestial" nature; and finally, to a king whom they portrayed as nothing more than a "tyrant." As inheritors of this tradition, we have been bequeathed this double-edged sword. We may be right to celebrate the distinctiveness of our identity as Americans, and we may find it inspiring to consider that God is acting providentially in our nation's history. But in doing so, we will always be tempted to draw distinctions between ourselves and others and to convert these distinctions into holy wars.

Afterword

Some ten years ago, I set out to pursue a conviction and a hunch. The conviction, born from my earlier work, was that how best to prepare for death remained the fundamental spiritual question confronting English-speaking peoples in British North America straight through to the end of the eighteenth century. Of this, I am now even more convinced. Across the eighteenth century—even as life expectancy increased dramatically in some parts—the visitations of death in colonial North America remained fundamentally unpredictable and beyond human control.[1] At the intimate levels of family, church, and town, the work of contending with death in colonial America remained woven into the very fabric of life and throughout the life cycle. Erik Seeman, a leading scholar of death in early America, cites the example of sea captain Aaron Bull, who wrote back to his family in Connecticut while sailing to Barbados in 1755 reminding his children to pray, read the Bible, and obey their mother. "You will one Day give an Account," Bull admonished, "and it a[i]nt improbable that that Time will be very soon, for you know you have lost two brothers and one sister and which God will call for next we cant tell."[2] Preoccupations like this are entirely representative of life in mid-eighteenth-century British North America.

The hunch I harbored, meanwhile, was that those who committed themselves to the cause of the American Revolution were not exempt from this fundamental concern but rather shaped powerfully by it. To start, this hunch was born from nothing more than my awareness that many celebrated slogans from the Revolutionary period conjured a kind of fearlessness in the face of death—"Give me liberty or give me death," "I regret that I have but one life to give for my country," "Live free or die," and so on. To explore this hunch, I immersed myself in streams of scholarship examining the ideological and cultural origins of the American Revolution,[3] perceptions of death and practices of dying in the early American experience,[4] how English speakers in early America were shaped by their engagements with printed text,[5] and the relationship between changes in early American religious landscapes and the rise of Revolutionary fervor.[6] At the intersection of these streams of scholarship, I found the ideal type of martyrdom. When I traced this ideal type through the historical record, it became clear to me that martyrdom was a driving force in the Revolutionary era, especially for young men coming of age. Hence this book, *One Life to Give*.

The first generations of English-speaking colonists in New England celebrated martyrdom as the paradigm of a faithful death—this much was well understood, and if any doubted it, Adrian Weimer's superb *The Martyr's Mirror*, published in 2011, dispelled any doubt. Anglicans, Separatists, Baptists, and Quakers in early New England all staked their claim to the heritage of the Protestant martyrs, Weimer explained, in order to "legitimize their status as the true church and their identity as a pure, persecuted community."[7] Likewise, Sarah Purcell's elegant *Sealed with Blood*, published in 2002, first demonstrated clearly that the motif of martyrdom was embraced roundly by Americans who memorialized their fallen heroes through a process of "memory making" both during and after the War of Independence. Along with other forms of public commemoration, Purcell explains, heroic narratives "created national identity by allowing early Americans to imagine a shared history of common sacrifice," so much so that in many ways, "the content of early American nationalism was reverence for sacrifice itself."[8] In other words, the ideal type of martyrdom was foundational to the identities of the first generations of English colonists in North America, and it was an indisputably important interpretive lens through which Americans in the early national period looked back on events of the Revolutionary era.

Between the time frames covered by these two books, however, I found a conspicuous gap. Several historians have rightly identified that the preaching of Protestant clergy—including much explicit talk of martyrdom—figured prominently in the martial culture of early America, including in the Revolutionary period. In *Sacred Scripture, Sacred War*, James Byrd has demonstrated that "wartime events were preaching events" in colonial America and that by grounding their appeals on the authority of the Bible and "by preaching sermons on the spiritual importance of martial service, ministers became authorities on war."[9] And in *Pulpit and Nation*, Spencer McBride has chronicled how "politicized clergymen" played an essential role in the Revolutionary War and the ensuing project of nation building and state formation.[10]

Most historians have concluded that apart from those spoken in the formal act of preaching, the persistent references to martyrdom in eighteenth-century America should not be taken too seriously—or at least not too literally. After all, overall life expectancy improved in many parts of colonial America across the course of the eighteenth century, and instances of religious persecution leading to archetypal acts of martyrdom grew evermore rare. If people were, on average, living longer and longer lives and fewer and fewer were being subjected to religious persecution, how could they really think of themselves as martyrs, and why should we? Talk of martyrdom in the eighteenth century was simply "rhetorical," this argument goes, or was an "exercise in special pleading" in which people used terms relating to martyrdom merely to conjure a "more capacious category of suffering."[11]

I am convinced that this way of thinking about martyrdom in British North America misses something fundamental about the American Revolution. Even as some lived longer lives, and even as overall instances of sectarian violence declined, English colonists in North America continued to produce, distribute, and devour texts extolling the virtues of martyrdom. Representations, allusions, and mentions of martyrdom—and related themes of masculinity, virtuosity, faithfulness, and truth witnessing—were widely scattered through print material that circulated widely in the trans-Atlantic book trade in the generations leading up to the American Revolution. The same was true of the pages that came rolling off English-language presses in North America with increasing efficiency through the middle decades of the eighteenth century. Childhood primers, captivity narratives, psalters, hymnals and songbooks, sermons, essays and accounts of death, poems, epitaphs, and other material printed routinely in almanacs and newspapers: all these remained drenched in these ancient themes.[12] The stories and images of clear-cut acts of martyrdom—like the deaths of the early English Protestant John Rogers or the early New England Quaker

Mary Dyer—served as archetypes that preachers, poets, printers, engravers, and artists could draw on in ways that were readily identifiable to English colonists of diverse ages and cultural backgrounds. Even noble deaths that were not acts of martyrdom in the strictest sense—like the deaths of the missionary David Brainerd or the Continental Congress delegate Samuel Ward—were understood to be deaths that were stretched along a spectrum of virtue or holiness, pointing in the direction of martyrdom as the ideal death. Undergirding this entire corpus of print material, and the entire range of spiritual practices associated with it, was the archetypal martyr's story, the story of Jesus's crucifixion as found in the Bible's New Testament.

Some English colonists in eighteenth-century North America may have read these materials in metaphorical and allegorical ways, but most did not. They were not merely "playing the martyr." Rather, they were participating actively in a formative cultural tradition by producing and consuming these print materials, as had their forebears, to prepare themselves and their children for their own confrontations with death.

Thomas Laqueur has characterized the dead as "social beings"— that is, "as creatures who need to be eased out of this world and settled safely into the next and into memory." Laqueur explains, "How this is done—through funeral rites, initial disposition of the body and often a redisposition or reburial, mourning, and other kinds of postmortem attention—is deeply, paradigmatically, and indeed foundationally part of culture. . . . Death in culture takes time because it takes time for the rent in the social fabric to be rewoven and for the dead to do their work in creating, recreating, representing, or disrupting the social order of which they had been a part." Laqueur names the "churchyard and later cemetery" as the "two quintessential physical places . . . in which the dead have done their work throughout the Western world over the past millennium."[13] In English Protestant variations of this ancient form, the dead have also done their work by way of the printed page, collaborating with the living through the manifold production, distribution, and use of print material drenched in the ideals of martyrdom and related themes.

It is my contention that many who came of age in the era of the American Revolution—especially young men—were steeped in these ideals and themes "from cradle to grave." As were their Protestant forebears, young men in early America were trained from infancy to understand that the most dramatic expression of fully realized virtue was to offer one's life self-sacrificially in the pursuit of a sacred cause. Whether they were conjuring the ideals of martyrdom in the 1750s and 1760s, during what came to be known as the French and Indian War; in the 1770s and 1780s, during the War of Independence; or in the 1790s and 1800s, during the period of the early American republic, American preachers were just one important piece in a vast and efficient martyr-making machinery—they were harvesting ripened fruit.

Many scholars today prefer a generic category—the Good Death—to describe a broad cultural fascination with the end of life and deathbed performance that emerged in the English-speaking world in the eighteenth and nineteenth centuries, tracing the origins of this fascination to a larger preoccupation with the "hour of death" that seemed to sweep the Western world in the wake of the Protestant Reformation.[14] In her celebrated work on death in the period of the US Civil War, for instance, Drew Gilpin Faust has chronicled the transformation of mid-nineteenth-century Americans' preoccupation with deathbed scenes and the "last words" of the dying. Faust traces this mid-nineteenth-century American fascination with "the Good Death" to the "arts of dying" (*Ars Moriendi*) traditions of the Middle Ages, to Anglican works like those of Jeremy Taylor that celebrated the work of "holy dying," and to the tradition of English Protestant martyrdom.[15] But there was little such general talk of the "Good Death" in British North America in the seventeenth and eighteenth centuries. English speakers in North America in this period were more likely to speak of noble deaths, holy deaths, heroic deaths, "excellent" or even "happy" deaths. The aspiration to die well—to die, that is, in an advantageous spiritual state—was so widely shared that it is hard to specify any single label that can encompass the entire domain of belief and practice. Across these many and varied expressions, though, one thing remained constant among English speakers in North America through to the end of the eighteenth century and beyond: martyrs remained the exemplars of true Christian faith, the paradigm of fully realized masculinity, and paragons of virtue, and it was taken for granted that almost anyone, no matter the specific circumstances of their living and their dying, could aspire to the spiritual virtuosity of the martyrs.[16]

Casting the American Revolution in this light helps us see it not as a singular event but instead as part of a long chain of events spanning generations. In retrospect, it may be rightly seen as the first in a wave of republican revolutions that would sweep through the Western world in the nineteenth century. But from the perspective of those English colonists who fought in it, the War of Independence surely felt much more like yet another in a centuries-long chain of English Protestant wars. The rank and file of the Continental Army had been prepared to interpret the War of Independence in these terms by earlier wars with the French and the Indians, just as earlier generations of English colonists in North America had been prepared to interpret those wars in this same way by the English Civil Wars. For those inclined to think in these terms, and there were many, the American Revolution fit nicely into the "beautiful historical summaries" and "chronologies of things remarkable" that printers like Benjamin Franklin and David Hall published periodically in their almanacs charting the "rapid and irresistible Progress of the Christian Religion." Leading revolutionaries often justified their cause by using multivalent words like *liberty*, *tyranny*, *virtue*, and *corruption*. Most commonly, historians associate this vocabulary with John Locke and the tradition of political liberalism that was ascendant among Revolutionary elite. But this vocabulary can just as easily be traced to John Foxe, who had embraced it in his *Book of Martyrs*, the landmark sixteenth-century martyrology that served as the taproot of the living tradition of English Protestant martyrdom, in which the revolutionaries were still steeped. Even the most enlightened of the revolutionaries routinely deployed words like these in close concert with other words that likewise conjured this tradition, language like *sacrifice* and *immortality* and *playing the man*.

This framing invites another conversation, one with an extremely long legacy in historical scholarship: the question of the relationship between religion and the Revolution. I have avoided telling the tale of *One Life to Give* in these terms—allow me to explain why. For much of the nineteenth and twentieth centuries, historians took for granted that sweeping revivals, or "awakenings," were the defining features of the religious landscape in mid-eighteenth-century British North America. When Jonathan Edwards published *A Faithful Narrative of the Surprising Work of God* in 1737, he contrasted the earlier "mirth and jollity" of the youth in Northampton, Massachusetts, with their later "sensible amendment to these evils," casting the transformation as a renewal of his forefathers' old-time Puritan religion. And when, four years later, Edwards published what would become his most famous sermon, *Sinners in the*

Hands of an Angry God, the title page described it as having been "preached at Enfield, July 8th 1741" and "at a Time of great Awakenings; and attended with remarkable Impressions on many of the Hearers." Edwards's framing and phrasing cast a long shadow.[17] A century later, in 1841, Joseph Tracy published a volume entitled *The Great Awakening* chronicling eighteenth-century religious upheavals elsewhere in the American colonies and aligning them always and everywhere with Edwards's ministry in Northampton.[18] Generations of narratives about early American religious history were written within this framework, and it is still employed widely today. This framework still has its more than capable defenders, but most scholars have concluded that this long-standing preoccupation with revivals has unduly narrowed our understanding of religious life in early America. Aware that the populations of British North America were far more diverse than has been commonly portrayed, scholars are busy constructing alternative frameworks within which to tell many different stories of the colonial experience in religiously inflected ways.[19]

This scholarly debate has played out against the backdrop of a simple fact, the importance of which is easily overlooked. Across their many differences, English-speaking peoples in eighteenth-century America shared a deep and abiding conviction that at the time of their deaths, all human beings would face a momentous transition from this life to the next.[20] This fundamental concern had been passed down through centuries, spreading across the expanse of branches in the Christian family tree. This concern continued to be shared across the entire cultural landscape of eighteenth-century British North America, and it led English colonists to engage in endless conversation and contestation with one another about the question of proper human conduct in the face of death. It also placed them on common ground—and ushered them into continual conflict—with their North American neighbors from other cultures and races, who also had their own ways of conducting themselves in the light of the prospect of death. Amid this conversation, contestation, and continual conflict, martyrdom remained for English-speaking peoples of all persuasions the paradigmatic answer to this fundamental question.

When the much-ballyhooed revivals of the eighteenth century are cast as specific and distinctive responses to the fundamental challenge of human mortality, preachers who engineered and trumpeted them are not banished from the stage of early America—their stories are not dismissed as inconsequential. But neither are they ensconced permanently in a place of privilege at center stage with all others cast into the shadows. Rather, all are rightly recognized for who they were, part of a bewilderingly diverse cast of characters struggling to make sense of life and death and life after death in a cultural context that was utterly unprecedented for all. The leading champions of the American Revolution were part of this drama, and they brought to it a unique mix of commitments. The new and rising philosophies of republicanism, the new and rising science made possible by the spread of Enlightenment thought, the new and rising sensibilities of passion and spirit—Americans living through the period of the American Revolution embraced these in varying combination as new means of protecting their liberty.

But for all this, the American Revolution did not result from a new blend of religion and politics, nor was the rhetoric of religion merely layered onto what was fundamentally a political cause.[21] As Robert Middlekauff has framed it, the American revolutionaries were "children of the twice-born"—they "valued liberty and representative government" but were also "marked by the moral dispositions of a passionate Protestantism. They could not escape this culture, nor did they try. They were imbued with an American moralism that colored all their perceptions of politics."[22] In Mark Noll's estimation, the mid-eighteenth century saw the beginning of an epochal transition—away from the assumption that "all spheres of life are intertwined" and toward "the distinguishing of the realms of religion and everything else."[23] But, with perhaps very few exceptions, this way of thinking had not taken hold of those who committed themselves in the mid-1770s to the cause of the War of Independence. For this reason, talk about "religion's role in the American Revolution" essentially obscures the motivations of those who committed themselves to the cause of Independence by implying that religion was an ancillary, or supplemental, source of motivation to what was essentially a political event. We do better to see the revolutionaries as animated in ways that were inherently, intrinsically, both religious and political at the same time, and we should not use our current standards to try to parse these components out.

Within this frame—a frame that considered the entirety of life to be defined by a single coherent search for purpose and meaning—the ideals of English Protestant martyrdom epitomized the revolutionaries' motivation. To oppose a perceived tyrant on grounds of principle, to conceive of this opposition as a sacred matter, and to conclude that virtue required making this opposition a fight to the death—these ideals had been passed down through the generations by English-speaking peoples for centuries. They were passed down for so long because they proved so easily appropriated and adapted to changing circumstances. It is not the case that these ideals were a compelling life force for English colonists in the seventeenth century, were then embraced in largely allegorical and rhetorical ways by colonists in the eighteenth century, and then were deployed strategically in the manufacture of national mythology in the decades following the American Revolution. This interpretation is too unilinear, too sequential, and too reductive—it flattens the experience of each generation. We do better to understand that English colonists in North America, and their descendants who came to understand themselves as "Americans," never disengaged from the tradition of English Protestant martyrdom. They never ceased from the work of appropriating this tradition and adapting it to their unique circumstances. The ideals of English Protestant martyrdom never fell out of favor. They remained central to the spiritual lives of English-speaking peoples in North America across this entire expanse of at least two centuries. This is true in significant measure because all were dedicated to catechetical practices that prepared their young, especially their young males, for acts of martyrdom.

Historians have long struggled with what to make of the American Revolution's Protestant hue, but none have traced it, as I have here, to this tradition of English Protestant martyrdom appropriated and adapted to the American context. This inheritance alone cannot account for the origins of the Revolution, but it facilitated the Revolution by providing a kind of spiritual foundation for countless young men who committed their lives to it. By surfacing and examining the roots of this tradition, this book has sought to complement rather than contest the central thrust of scholarship that has poured forth in recent generations about the dynamics that shaped the American Revolution. The surprising mix of ideas that birthed a new revolutionary ideology, the sermonizing that proved so influential in mobilizing American troops to serve in the Continental Army, the Revolutionary rhetoric that defies simple categorization as either religious or political, the ritual life of the Continental Congresses with their opening prayers and fast days and funeral sermons, the elaborate commemorations of the war dead during the period of the War of Independence and the construction of romantic narratives about them in the decades that followed—all these dynamics, surfaced in recent generations of scholarship, were indeed essential to the American Revolution. Running through them like a golden thread was the tradition of American martyrdom—a variation of English Protestant martyrdom appropriated and adapted to the cause of American independence.

Notes

Introduction

1 The details in this opening vignette are drawn from M. William Phelps, *Nathan Hale: The Life and Death of America's First Spy*, 1st ed. (New York: Thomas Dunne Books, 2008), 187–90. Phelps's is the most comprehensive and contemporary of many Hale biographies. See also Paul R. Misencik, *The Original American Spies: Seven Covert Agents of the Revolutionary War* (Jefferson, NC: McFarland, 2014), 11–13.

2 As one *New York Times* reporter concluded in 1997, "There are three places in New York where our hero was supposedly captured, four where he may have been detained, and no less than six where he is said to have been hanged." David Kirby, "Making It Work; Nathan Hale Was Here . . . and Here . . . and Here," *New York Times*, November 23, 1997, sec. 14, p. 3.

3 Joseph Addison, *Cato. A Tragedy, by Mr. Addison. [Seven Lines from Seneca]* (Boston: printed by John Mein and Fleeming, 1767), 60.

4 Jedidiah Morse, *Annals of the American Revolution*, cited in Kenneth A. Daigler, *Spies, Patriots, and Traitors: American Intelligence in the Revolutionary War* (Washington, DC: Georgetown University Press, 2014), 93. In 1799 an early chronicler of New England history could write, "So far . . . Hale has remained unnoticed, and it is scarcely known such a character ever existed." Hannah Adams, *The History of New England*, cited in George Dudley Seymour, *Documentary Life of Nathan Hale: Comprising All Available Official and Private Documents Bearing on the Life of the Patriot, Together with an Appendix, Showing the Background of His Life* (New Haven, CT: priv. printed for the author, 1941), 232. Biographies of Hale that proliferated in ensuing generations were hagiographic in the extreme, as exemplified by this excerpt from Charlotte Molyneux Holloway's 1899 portrayal: "Possessing genius, taste and ardor, he became

distinguished as a scholar, and endowed in an eminent degree with those graces and gifts of nature which add a charm to youthful excellence, he gained universal esteem and confidence. To high moral worth and irreproachable habits were joined gentleness of manner, an ingenious disposition, and vigor of understanding." Even Holloway acknowledged, "It was not until 1837 that patriotic sentiment in Connecticut demanded that there be fitting recognition of his great service, and the Hale Monument Association was formed." Charlotte Molyneux Holloway, *Nathan Hale: The Martyr-Hero of the Revolution with a Hale Genealogy and Hale's Diary* (New York: A. L. Burt, 1899), 165–66.

5 Quotations from Phelps, *Nathan Hale*, 187–88.

6 Elizabeth Castelli describes these ideas as "hardwired into the collective consciousness of Western culture" and "one of the central legacies of the Christian tradition." Elizabeth A. Castelli, *Martyrdom and Memory: Early Christian Culture Making* (New York: Columbia University Press, 2004), 33.

7 According to Daniel Boyarin and Moshe Lazar, within Judaism, there prevailed across centuries a "debate between tricksterism and martyrdom as the most honored and most valuable response to oppression." Daniel Boyarin and Moshe Lazar, *Dying for God: Martyrdom and the Making of Christianity and Judaism* (Stanford, CA: Stanford University Press, 1999), 55. Remarking on the description of Jesus as "the faithful witness" in Revelation 1:5, Jolyon Mitchell has written, "Even though this is rarely translated as 'faithful martyr,' many scholars interpret this to mean that Jesus is viewed here as the 'proto-' or even 'founding martyr,' who is then described as the 'first-born from the dead.' From this point of view, Jesus is portrayed [in early Christian writings] as both the pioneering martyr and the 'first' to overcome death." Jolyon P. Mitchell, *Martyrdom: A Very Short Introduction* (Oxford: Oxford University Press, 2012), 23.

8 Herbert Musurillo, *The Acts of the Christian Martyrs* (Oxford: Clarendon Press, 1972); Boyarin and Lazar, *Dying for God.*

9 Candida Moss, *Ancient Christian Martyrdom: Diverse Practices, Theologies, and Traditions* (New Haven, CT: Yale University Press, 2012), 28–29. Moss observes, "This association of courage, virtue, death, and masculinity meant that the notion of dying well was itself gendered. To die a good death, in or out of battle, entailed dying with self-control. In other words, it meant taking it like a man." In his pioneering early twentieth-century work, the French scholar Hippolyte Delehaye (1859–1941) listed as exemplary of this tradition the accounts of the noble deaths of "Socrates, Anaxarque, Paetus Thrasea, Helvidius Priscus, Rubellius Plautus and Seneca." When the emperor Vespasian threatened him with death, for instance, Helvidius Priscus is said to have responded, "When did I tell you I was immortal? You play your role and I will play mine. Your role is to cause my death, mine is to die without trembling." Hippolyte Delehaye, *Les passions des martyrs et les genres littéraires*, 2nd ed., reviewed and corrected (Bruxelles, Belgium: Societe des Bollandistes, 1966), 114. Still, most scholars today adhere to a long-standing consensus that it was during the first centuries of the Christian era that the Greek word *martyrios* (witness) came to be distinctly, indeed inextricably, linked to the ideal of proving willing to die for one's faith. Early Christian accounts of martyrdom built on these traditions, frequently conjuring one of two paradigms for conquering the final enemy, death: the triumphant athlete and the conquering warrior, each "crowned" with eternal glory. Of the warrior, Delehaye famously wrote, "His tent is his tomb, his armor is justice, his shield is the faith; he wears the helmet of salvation, the boots of the gospel and the sword of the spirit." (Sa tene est son tombeau, sa cuirasse le justice, son bouclier la foi; il porte le casque du salut, les cnemides de l'evangile, le glave de l'esprit.) Delehaye, *Les passions des martyrs*, 153–54. Cavan Concannon has shown that these two motifs of athlete and gladiator are often blended in early Christian literature. Cavan W. Concannon, "'Not for an Olive Wreath, but Our Lives': Gladiators, Athletes, and Early Christian Bodies," *Journal of Biblical Literature* 133, no. 1 (2014): 193–214. As suggested by these archetypes, the Christian martyrs were also understood to represent the fulfillment of idealized expectations of masculinity. This was true even when they

were undertaken by women—so the martyr Thecla cut her hair and dressed like a man; so Perpetua became a man in her dreams; so Blandina was transformed in the eyes of others into the male figure of Jesus. My thanks to Cavan Concannon for this helpful observation.

10 Performances of martyrdom are inherently public in nature—to be recognized as such, every martyr also requires an audience of people who live to tell the tale. As Daniel Boyarin has written, "Even more than tragedy," acts of martyrdom are "deaths that are seen . . . a practice that takes place within the public and, therefore, shared space." Boyarin and Lazar, *Dying for God*, 21. Or, as George Heyman puts it, martyrs are identified only by a process of "assessment" that, necessarily, can be made only after the fact: "Thus martyrs existed primarily as creations of those who wrote and assessed the nobility of a person's death." George Heyman, *Martyrdom and Sacrifice: Roman and Christian Representations of Power* (Minneapolis: Augsburg Fortress, 2007), xxii. Candida Moss considers martyrdom "a set of discursive practices that shaped early Christian identities, mediated ecclesiastical and dogmatic claims, and provided meaning to the experience described by early Christians as persecution, and in doing so produced a new economy of action." For Moss, the essential question is not "what really happened" but rather "how particular ways of construing the past enable later communities to constitute and sustain themselves" and how communities "make sense of their own present through recourse to constructed narratives of their past." Moss, *Ancient Christian Martyrdom*, 17, 5, 10.

11 Vasiliki Limberis has chronicled how the Cappadocian fathers of the fourth-century church deployed "panegyrics"—public speeches and writings commemorating the deaths of the early Christian martyrs—to mobilize the faithful and to fight their enemies, the Arians: "As they took control of the cult of the martyrs through conducting the panegyreis, retelling the narratives, preaching their mores in homilies, and making public their personal devotion to them, the Cappadocians engaged in a constant process of revising history. . . . The story of the martyrs became fluid under

their pens, as the Cappadocians conscripted them to bolster the reputation of Cappadocia, to help fight Arians, to encourage the faithful to imitate martyrs, and to ensconce them as the source of Christian doctrine." Vasiliki M. Limberis, *Architects of Piety: The Cappadocian Fathers and the Cult of the Martyrs* (Oxford: Oxford University Press, 2011), 31. Scholar of martyrdom Elizabeth Castelli describes this as the "construction of collective memory," arguing that this way of thinking allows us "to move past often unresolvable questions of 'what really happened'" to ask instead how "communities constitute and sustain themselves" across long expanses of time. Castelli, *Martyrdom and Memory*, 5, 29, 39. I am reminded of musicologist Bruno Nettl's struggle to identify what constitutes a musical piece for the purpose of analysis: "Let's agree that in European folk music, the piece is something that is created once, plus all the different ways in which it is performed." Bruno Nettl, *The Study of Ethnomusicology: Thirty-One Issues and Concepts*, new ed. (Urbana: University of Illinois Press, 2005), 114.

12 Brad S. Gregory, *Salvation at Stake: Christian Martyrdom in Early Modern Europe* (Cambridge, MA: Harvard University Press, 1999), 134:8. Gregory continues, "Were this not the case . . . attitudes linked to martyrdom, such as the importance of setting aside temporal concerns in the hope of eternal reward, would not have found such widespread expression; and fellow believers would not have championed so enthusiastically their martyrs as examples for others to follow." Christians throughout the ages considered their favorite martyrs to be "divinely revealed realities, and as such *more real* than the fleeting, temporal aspects of their lives." To call the lives and deaths of martyrs "symbolic," and then to contrast them with the "real" or the "material" dimensions of human life, Gregory explains, not only distorts the views of premodern peoples "but essentially inverts their whole way of seeing things." Gregory, 10.

13 Isaac Watts, *Horae Lyricae. Poems Chiefly of the Lyric Kind* (New York: James Parker, 1750), 79–80.

14 Adrian Chastain Weimer, *Martyrs' Mirror: Persecution and Holiness in Early New England* (Oxford: Oxford University Press,

2011), 49. For more on Weimer's work, see the afterword and note 7 in particular.

15 Henry Grove, *A Discourse concerning the Nature and Design of the Lord's-Supper* (Boston, 1766), 17–18, 25–26.

16 Carla Pestana has offered the most comprehensive accounting to date of the diverse international Protestant networks that gave shape to the "British Atlantic World." Carla Gardina Pestana, *Protestant Empire: Religion and the Making of the British Atlantic World* (Philadelphia: University of Pennsylvania Press, 2009). As to the spread of Grove's *Discourse* across this network, the date of its first publication is not known, but its second edition was published in 1738, the year of Grove's death, and in this edition, its London publishers (R. Ford and R. Hett) appended to Grove's *Discourse* his own *Devotional Exercises relating to the Lord's Supper*. In the same year, a third edition was published in Dublin (for Jonathan Smith and Abraham Bradley), an early indicator of its appeal across the extended communications network that some scholars of the early modern era today call "international Protestantism." In this third edition—also printed in London but by John Wilson in the year 1741—the contents of Grove's original began to be entitled as consisting of two parts: the original *Discourse concerning the Nature and Design* of the sacrament and now also a *Discourse on the Obligations to Communicate*. The resultant three-part structure—discourse concerning nature and design, discourse concerning obligations to communicate, devotional exercises—would be replicated in future editions. Grove's *Discourse* proved so popular through distribution on both sides of the Atlantic that in 1766, an unnamed Boston printer determined there was money to be made in supplementing its importation from England by reprinting the eighth edition on-site. This printer's hunch was correct—in the ensuing fifty years, Grove's *Discourse* would be printed at least seven times in the Massachusetts towns of Salem, Andover, and Dedham, as well as in New York and Dover, New Hampshire. Grove's *Discourse* exemplifies the multivalence of many eighteenth-century prints, as the author wrote routinely across the boundaries of literary convention that modern authors would be expected to

observe. For Grove, this notion of "shewing forth the death of Christ" was the very essence of the matter—he deployed the phrase over a dozen times.

17 Thomas Mall, preface to *The History of the Martyrs Epitomised. A Cloud of Witnesses* [. . .] (Boston: Rogers & Fowle, 1747). What Peter Brown has said of the early Christians was true for English Protestants in the early modern era: they attributed a unique power to their martyrs, who, "precisely because they had died as human beings, enjoyed close intimacy with God. Their intimacy with God was the *sine qua non* of their ability to intercede for and, so, to protect their fellow mortals. The martyr was the 'friend of God.' He was an intercessor in a way which the hero could never have been." Peter Brown, *The Cult of the Saints: Its Rise and Function in Latin Christianity*, enl. ed. (Chicago: University of Chicago Press, 2015), 5–6.

18 These definitions do not depart significantly from the scholars cited here, nor from those found in the dictionary of religious terms at the Association of Religion Data Archives (ARDA), according to which a martyr is "someone who dies, typically prematurely and violently, for a sacred cause." ARDA, s.v. "martyr," accessed February 13, 2021, https://tinyurl.com/yy8v2fcv. I am simply elaborating a constellation of interrelated definitions. Other related terms can be defined in these ways:

- A *martyrology* is a cultural representation of martyrs and martyrdom (such as a collection of written or printed narratives).
- *Martyrologists* are those who narrate or invoke stories of martyrdom to inspire and instruct.
- *Martyrological* is an adjective that can be used to describe material having the quality of martyrology.

I am, however, emphasizing the "catechetical" component of this tradition more than is typical of most scholars of martyrdom.

19 "Abigail Adams to Mercy Otis Warren, 5 December 1773," Founders Online, National Archives, accessed September 29, 2019, https://tinyurl.com/yaajau9w (original source: Lyman H. Butterfield, ed., *The Adams Papers*, Adams Family Correspondence,

vol. 1, *December 1761–May 1776* [Cambridge, MA: Harvard University Press, 1963], 88–90).

20 "John Adams to Abigail Adams, 12 May 1774," Founders Online, National Archives, last modified June 29, 2017, https://tinyurl .com/ycmumtzj (original source: Butterfield, *Adams Papers*, 1:107–8).

21 "General Orders, 2 July 1776," Founders Online, National Archives, last modified June 29, 2017, https://tinyurl.com/

yardjqpx (original source: Philander D. Chase, ed., *The Papers of George Washington*, Revolutionary War Series, vol. 5, *16 June 1776–12 August 1776* [Charlottesville: University Press of Virginia, 1993], 179–82).

22 With this litany I am conjuring just a few of the most famous scholarly arguments about the origins of the American Revolution. See the afterword for an extended historiographic comment, including on this question.

Chapter 1

1 David Hall sees this early New England way of life shaped by four great rites of passage: the conversion process, the "imperative for self-scrutiny when coming to the Lord's Table to receive communion," the suffering of "remarkable afflictions," and finally, the "art of dying well, of turning the terror of death into the joy of eternal life with Christ." Taken together, Hall concludes, these rites of passage represented a coherent and continuous path through the life cycle, "a mode of living and a mode of dying." He notes, "I am indebted to Charles Hambrick-Stowe's splendid study of Puritan devotional practice, *The Practice of Piety* (Chapel Hill, N.C., 1982) for this argument." David D. Hall, *Cultures of Print: Essays in the History of the Book* (Amherst: University of Massachusetts Press, 1996), 34–35.

2 Michael Wigglesworth, *Day of Doom: Or, a Poetical Description of the Great and Last Judgment* (Boston: Bartholomew Green and John Allen, 1701), 6. A few of many such works published on both sides of the Atlantic include Ellis Hookes's 1661 *The Spirit of the Martyrs Revived*; Michael Wigglesworth's 1662 *The Day of Doom*; James Worthy's 1667 *The Child's Plain Path-Way to Eternal Life*; Thomas Vincent's 1667 *Christ's Certain and Sudden Appearance to Judgment*; William Dyer's 1668 *A Cabinet of Jewels*; Benjamin Keach's 1684 *War with the Devil, Or, the Young Man's Conflict with the Powers of Darkness*; and Richard Sault's 1693 *The Second Spira, Being a Fearful Example of an Atheist* [. . .]. That titles like these were held in high esteem by English readers well into the eighteenth century is confirmed by their consistent republication and by the

frequency with which they appeared in catalogs of books for sale in both England and North America.

3 Some have seen the morbid preoccupations of early New England clergy as suggestive of their psychological withdrawal from the very suffering they so assiduously chronicled. See, for instance, E. Jennifer Monaghan, "Family Literacy in Early 18th-Century Boston: Cotton Mather and His Children," *Reading Research Quarterly* 26, no. 4 (Autumn 1991): 351. In this view, the early Puritans came to occupy an obsessive-compulsive, even delusional, world of phobia and paranoia. More commonly, modern interpreters see orthodox puritan theology as having produced a perfect, self-perpetuating feedback loop of emotional angst, first generating unrealistic expectations, both personal and collective, and then declaring the suffering resultant from inevitable failure to be the natural consequence of divine judgment, or Providence. But little psychoanalysis is required if, instead, these men are understood simply to be struggling, in the only way they knew how, with the incessant threat of death and with what they considered the fundamental spiritual challenge of preparing for it. Consider Cotton Mather's personal experience. Preceded in death by three wives, Mather fathered fourteen children, but seven died in infancy, one at the age of two, and of the six who reached adulthood, five died in their twenties—Samuel Mather was the only one of Cotton's fourteen offspring to live past his father's death in 1728. Stannard, *The Puritan Way of Death: A Study in Religion, Culture and Social Change* (New

York: Oxford University Press, 1977), 56. In the particularly cruel fall of 1713, measles swept through the city of Boston, and within a few short weeks, Mather lost his second wife, Elizabeth; her recently delivered twins; a maidservant from the household; and his two-year-old daughter, Jerusha. Mather described it in his diary as the "month which devoured my family" and penned for his "pretty little Daughter" both a tombstone epitaph—"Gone, but not lost"—and a poem with this first stanza:

The dearest Lord of heaven gave
Himself an offering once for me:
The dearest thing on earth I have,
Now, Lord, I'll offer unto Thee.

Monaghan, "Family Literacy," 357.

4 James Raven, *The Business of Books: Booksellers and the English Book Trade, 1450–1850* (New Haven, CT: Yale University Press, 2007), 34.

5 As Erik Seeman has described the piety of early eighteenth-century Boston carpenter John Barnard, "By candlelight late into the night and by the light of the rising sun, John Barnard read . . . the Bible, the Psalter, and books of piety and theology. He read books by his ministers and tracts composed thousands of miles away in England." And this despite that, according to Seeman, Barnard "was not formally educated," and "reading did not come easily" to him. Erik Seeman, *Pious Persuasions: Laity and Clergy in Eighteenth-Century New England* (Baltimore: Johns Hopkins University Press, 1999), 32.

6 David D. Hall, "The Uses of Literacy in New England, 1600–1850," in *Printing in Early America*, ed. William Joyce, David D. Hall, Richard D. Brown, and John B. Hench (Worcester, MA: American Antiquarian Society, 1983), 26.

7 Gary Ebersole, *Captured by Texts: Puritan to Postmodern Images of Indian Captivity* (Charlottesville: University Press of Virginia, 1995), 322.

8 The first printing press in North America was established in 1639, when the Reverend Jose Smith contracted the locksmith Stephen Daye to operate his Cambridge press, near the conclusion of a decade that saw the permanent settlement of some twenty thousand Puritan colonists in the Massachusetts Bay Colony. For the text of the New England Charter, see "History of the New England Company," New England Company, accessed February 13, 2021, https://tinyurl.com/y9fuc6gw. As Lawrence Wroth has summarized, the New England Company was an extensive enterprise in missionary propaganda:

> London was the natural center of its publishing operations, but the desire to print the Bible in the Indian tongue at the place where, from the translator's standpoint, that object could be most fittingly accomplished, led in the year 1659 to the sending of additional typographical equipment to Cambridge in the form of a second press and other fonts of letters. The *Whole Book of Psalmes*. . . , various catechisms, secular laws, college publications, almanacs, sermons and controversial tracts had been coming year by year, from the press. Now, in 1660, after twenty years of activity, the printing of the Bible, translated into the Indian tongue by John Eliot, was begun by Samuel Green and carried to completion by him and Marmaduke Johnson.

Lawrence C. Wroth, *The Colonial Printer* (New York: Dover, 1994), 17.

9 As David D. Hall has summarized, by the turn of the eighteenth century, Boston was "home to 19 booksellers, who trafficked in both imported and locally printed books, and seven publishing houses." Throughout this period, according to Hall, most people in colonial New England encountered "a limited number of books. Most had the use of, or owned, a Bible, psalmbook, primer, and catechism. Almanacs were widely available. Otherwise, the factors of cost and distribution were barriers to extensive reading." Hall, *Cultures of Print*, 62. Because the colonial book trade included not only the importation of books from England and other parts but also the widespread binding and selling of books at locations remote from the places where the pages went to press, tracking the stream of publication in colonial America cannot be taken as an accurate reflection of actual print distribution or the relative popularity of specific

works. According to Hugh Amory, "Since the technology of print changed little for three centuries, and since so many colonial books in any case were printed in Europe, the advent and spread of the craft in the colonies is of relatively little historical and cultural importance. More significant were the ways in which books were distributed and bound, the supply of paper and type, and the organization and recruitment of personnel." Hugh Amory, "Reinventing the Colonial Book," in *A History of the Book in America*, ed. Hugh Amory and David Hall (Chapel Hill: University of North Carolina Press in association with the American Antiquarian Society, 2007), 1:54. Patterns of publication do shed light, however, on what specific authors and printers perceived to be of value at specific times and places and where they perceived there to be niches in the colonial market that were not being presently filled by importation.

10 This martyrological tradition of early New England was exemplified by the Puritan clergyman Cotton Mather, who inherited his pastoral calling from not only his father, Increase Mather, but also his paternal grandfather, Richard Mather, and his namesake maternal grandfather, John Cotton. Born in 1663, Cotton Mather entered Harvard College at the age of twelve and graduated six years later with a degree presented by his father, the college's president at the time. Upon his death in 1728, he was succeeded in the pulpit of Boston's Second Church (the "Old North Church") by his son Samuel—together, Increase, Cotton, and Samuel Mather presided over the church from 1664 to 1741. As did his peers, Cotton Mather saw clearly that death could come calling at any time, and so he sought to prepare the faithful throughout the life cycle for this final, inevitable confrontation. Long one of the most treasured resources in the study of colonial America, Cotton Mather's lifetime literary production included over six hundred books; one of the most voluminous diaries surviving from the colonial era; sermons delivered across over forty years of pastoral ministry; countless poems, accounts, and essays; incessant correspondence; and a monumental, never-published commentary on the Bible, which Mather called the

"Biblia Americana." Monaghan, "Family Literacy," 350. The vast preponderance of Cotton Mather's corpus was published by Bartholomew Green, Timothy Green, and Samuel Kneeland—the son, grandson, and apprentice, respectively, of Samuel Green, one of the Bay Colony's first printers. According to Hugh Amory, the Greens represented the first true dynasty of American printing, eventually securing contracts not just in Massachusetts but in Connecticut, New Plymouth, and New Hampshire. He also observes, "The Greens and the Mathers are good examples of what the historian Edmund S. Morgan called Puritan 'tribalism,' associations that fitted smoothly into their intellectual and contractual commitments; they may even have been related by marriage." Hugh Amory, "Printing and Bookselling in New England, 1638–1713," in *History of the Book*, 86, 96. What Karen Halttunen has said of Mather's *Magnalia Christi Americana*—the sprawling and byzantine seven-volume project in which Mather attempted to summarize "The Ecclesiastical History of New England"—is an apt summation of the entire corpus: the works were "bound together by one dominant theme: the personal suffering of New England's greatest saints, the communal suffering of the New England people, and the martyrdom of Cotton Mather himself." Karen Halttunen, "Cotton Mather and the Meaning of Suffering in the *Magnalia Christi Americana*," *Journal of American Studies* 12 (1978): 314.

11 As Brad S. Gregory has observed, "Adriane van Haemsted's *History of the Death of the Devout Martyrs* was published in Dutch twenty-three times from 1590 through 1671. . . . Catholic Europe, too, was awash in martyrological literature." Gregory, *Salvation at Stake*, 3. Jolyon Mitchell has identified at least fifty works chronicling the persecution of Catholics published in English between 1550 and 1650. According to Mitchell, English Catholic literature heralded "the likes of Bishop John Fisher (1469–1535), Sir Thomas More (1478–1535) and the Jesuit Edmund Campion (1540–1581) . . . as genuine martyrs of the 'true' church." Mitchell, *Martyrdom*, 77–78.

12 For more detail, see the forthcoming section on *The New-England Primer*.

13 Elsewhere I have called this practice a "print practice of martyrology," which I define this way: "The production, distribution and use of printed material imbued with martyrological themes was a catechetical practice aimed at instructing and informing right conduct in individuals, and maintaining right order in communities, in the face of the prospect of death." John Fanestil, "The Print Practice of Martyrology in British North America, 1688–1787" (PhD diss., University of Southern California, 2017), 18.

14 John Foxe, *Actes and Monuments* (London: John Day, 1563). As Brad S. Gregory summarizes, "John Foxe's *Acts and Monuments*, first printed in 1563 (following his two Latin contributions to the genre), went through nine folio editions by 1684, including six by 1610. Jean Crespin's martyrology [*L'histoire des vrays tesmoins*] was published in some form at least thirty-seven times, beginning with thirteen installments and editions in French between 1554 and 1563." Gregory, *Salvation at Stake*, 10. Of fifty-four catalogs of books for sale surviving in the digital archive from the years 1688–1787, twenty-eight included John Foxe's martyrology—listed variously as *Actes and Monuments* or *Ecclesiastical History* or simply *Book of Martyrs*, often omitting the final *e* from Foxe's name—or one of the works that abridged or excerpted Foxe's martyrology, like Mall's *History of the Martyrs*, Hookes's *The Spirit of the Martyrs*, and Samuel Clarke's *General Martyrology*. These catalogs of books were frequently organized by subject matter or alphabetically, but when they were not so organized, Foxe's martyrology was often granted a place of privilege in the listings—for example, it received top billing in the 1718 catalog printed by Samuel Gerrish of Boston. Samuel Gerrish, *A Catalogue of Rare and Valuable Books* (Boston, 1717). Other martyrological titles were also referenced frequently in these American catalogs of books for sale. Of these same fifty-four catalogs, ten included works by Jeremy Taylor, and nineteen included works by John Bunyan (almost always *Pilgrim's Progress*).

15 Dominic Janes and Alex Houen put the number of burnings under Mary at 284. Dominic Janes and Alex Houen, *Martyrdom and Terrorism: Pre-modern to Contemporary Perspectives* (New York: Oxford University Press, 2014), 63.

16 In fact, there was much more going on than Foxe's summation would suggest. The lasting influence of his martyrology was due also to the illustrations accompanying his narrative accounts. In the earliest editions, these illustrations were simple representations made from woodcuts, but in later versions, these were replaced by copper engravings of great artistry, making for compelling viewing. As Catholics had for centuries venerated the shrines and relics of their saints and martyrs as places where the presence of God was mysteriously palpable, so Protestants turned to representations of martyrdom in print—including representations of Jesus's crucifixion—as sources of affective inspiration and divine revelation. For an excellent and more far-reaching discussion of Catholic-Protestant continuities in the early modern era, see Euan Cameron, *Enchanted Europe: Superstition, Reason, and Religion 1250–1750* (New York: Oxford University Press, 2010), 12–17. Cameron's central conclusion is this: "The evidence of continuing Protestant belief in a meaningful cosmos is copious and indisputable." Cameron, 12.

17 John N. King, *Foxe's "Book of Martyrs" and Early Modern Print Culture* (Cambridge: Cambridge University Press, 2006), xi. For an example of the scriptural references conjured by this story, see, to cite just one example, Isaiah 42:2–12.

18 John Foxe, *The Actes and Monuments* (1570), 110, available at The Acts and Monuments Online (TAMO; Sheffield: Digital Humanities Institute, 2011), http://www.johnfoxe.org.

19 Foxe, 228.

20 Foxe, 4.

21 Foxe marked the transition from ancient examples of martyrdom to present-day histories of ordinary people like "Wylliam Taylor an Englishman," who was burned at the pyre for his faith, with this note "to the gentle Reader":

When as it hath of long time been received and thought of the common people (gentle reader) that this religion now generally used hathe sprong up and risen but of late . . . we have thought good at this present to advertise thee how that not only the actes and monuments heretofore passed, but also histories hereafter following, that manifest and declare that this profession of Christes religion hathe bene spread abrode in England across the space of almost of CC [two hundred] yeres, yea and before that time, hath oftentimes sparkled although the flames thereof have never so perfectly burnt out.

Foxe, *Actes and Monuments*, 154–57.

22 Foxe, 1794.

23 Foxe, 65. The source of Foxe's account was Eusebius's *Ecclesiastical History*: "When the hour for departure had come, they set him on a donkey and led him into the city on a great Sabbath. Herod, the chief of police, and his father Nicetes met him and transferred him to their carriage. Sitting beside him, they tried to persuade him: 'What harm is there in saying "Lord Caesar" and sacrificing—and so be saved?' At first he did not answer them, but when they persisted, he said, 'I will not do what you advise.' . . . When Polycarp entered the stadium, a voice from heaven said, 'Be strong and play the man, Polycarp!' No one saw the speaker, but many of our people who were there heard the voice." Paul L. Maier, *Eusebius: The Church History* (Grand Rapids, MI: Kregel, 1999), 156.

24 Similar phrasing in the King James Version of the Bible is found in the deuterocanonical book of 1 Maccabees, where the elder Mattathias exhorts young Jewish rebels with these words: "Wherefore you my sonnes be valiant, and shew your selues men in the behalfe of the law, for by it shall you obtaine glory" (1 Macc 2:64). Later in the same book, the dying Eleazar's testimony offered a paradigmatic expression of the kind of witness that would be picked up in early Christian accounts of martyrdom: "For though for the present time I should be deliuered from the punishment of men: yet should I not escape the hand of the Almightie, neither aliue nor dead. Wherefore now manfully changing this life, I will shew my selfe such an one, as mine age requireth, and leaue a notable example to such as bee yong, to die willingly, and couragiously, for the honourable and holy lawes" (2 Macc 6:26–28).

25 Anne Spencer Lombard has written, "Seventeenth and eighteenth century New England ministers, evidently unaware of the irony in their choice of a theatrical metaphor, often exhorted their listeners to 'play the man.'" Anne Spencer Lombard, "Playing the Man: Conceptions of Masculinity in Anglo-American New England, 1675 to 1765" (PhD diss., University of California, Los Angeles, 1998), 6, https://tinyurl.com/y9t2v8tc. While I am building off Lombard's very helpful analysis of the construction of masculinity in eighteenth-century New England, the phrase is more accurately understood in a martyrological context.

26 The *Book of Martyrs* went through four folio editions before Foxe's death in 1587 (1563, 1570, 1576, and 1583), each more expansive and elaborate than the one before, but its reach grew exponentially in the ensuing century as it passed into the hands of other printers. Two more unabridged editions were published by 1610, at which time publication rights for the work were retained by the London Company of Stationers, affording wide access to both Foxe's text and its famous woodcuts. Three more complete editions were printed by 1684, but more affordable abridgments by Clement Cotton, Thomas Mason, and John Taylor made its contents available to the widest possible audience of English readers. Cotton's 240-page *The Mirror of Martyrs* alone went through at least nine editions—and an unknown number of print runs—between 1613 and 1685. For the most detailed account of this extraordinary literary legacy, see King, Foxe's "Book of Martyrs," 133–45.

27 Paul Leicester Ford, *The New England Primer: A History of Its Origin and Development* (New York: Dodd, Mead, 1897), cited in "A Famous Book—the 'New England Primer,'" *New York Times*, November 14, 1897.

28 *The New-England Primer* (Boston: Samuel Kneeland and Timothy Green, [1750?]), 13.

29 *New-England Primer*, 20.

30 *New-England Primer*, 20.

31 John Cotton, *Spiritual Milk for Babes* (London: Peter Parker, 1668), 15.

32 For example, Thomas Ken, *An Exposition on the Church-Catechism* (Boston: Richard Pierce, 1688); Benjamin Keach, *Instructions*

for *Children* (New York: William Bradford, 1695); Thomas Vincent, *An Explicatory Catechism* (Boston: Daniel Henchman, 1729); Samuel Phillips, *The History of Our Lord and Saviour Jesus Christ Epitomiz'd in a Catechetical Way* (Boston: Samuel Kneeland, 1738); Richard Allestree, *The Whole Duty of Man: Laid Down in a Plain and Familiar Way* (Williamsburg, VA: William Parks, 1746); and Cotton Mather, *The Way of the Truth Laid Out* (Boston: Samuel Kneeland, 1721).

33 *New-England Primer*, 24.

34 John Foxe, *Actes and Monuments* (London: London Company of Stationers, 1694), 249. The importance of Rogers's martyrdom is suggested also by Samuel Kneeland's 1736 publication *Martyrology: A Brief Account of the Lives* [. . .]. Kneeland encapsulated his account of Rogers's death: "Thus he took his Death with great Meekness and wonderful Patience, in the defence and quarrel of Christ's Gospel. When Fire was put to him, as it were, washing and rubbing his Hands in the midst of the Flame, he cryed out Lord receive my Spirit, till he was consumed to Ashes. He was the first Proto-martyr in Queen Mary's Days of all that blessed Company of Sufferers, and gave the first Adventure upon the Fire.".Samuel Kneeland, *Martyrology: A Brief Account of the Lives, Sufferings and Deaths of Those Two Holy Martyrs, viz. Mr. John Rogers and Mr. John Bradford* (Boston: Samuel Kneeland and Timothy Green, 1736), 9.

35 Jerome Griswold has estimated the total number of prints at six million between 1680 and 1830. See Kathleen Connery Fitzgibbons, "A History of the Evolution of the Didactic Literature for Puritan Children in America, 1656–1856" (EdD diss., University of Massachusetts, 1987).

36 James Janeway, *A Token for Children: Being an Exact Account of the Conversion, Holy and Exemplary Lives, and Joyful Deaths, of Several Young Children* (London: printed for Doman Newman, 1673), 17–18.

37 Janeway, preface.

38 As Janeway concluded his introductory remarks, "That you may be your Parents joy, your Countrey's honour, and live in Gods fear, and dye in his love, is the prayer of your dear Friend. J. Janeway." Janeway, 3.

39 James Janeway, *A Token for Children the Second Part: Being a Farther Account of the Conversion, Holy and Exemplary Lives, and Joyful Deaths* [. . .] (London: printed for Doman Newman, 1676); see also James Janeway, *A Token for Mariners Containing Many Famous and Wonderful Instances of God's Providence in Sea Dangers and Deliverances* [. . .] (London: printed by Hugh Newman and sold at his shop at the Grasshopper in the Poultry, 1698). For an excellent summary of *Janeway's Token*, see Stannard, *Puritan Way of Death*, 44–47.

40 Janeway, *Token for Children: Being*, 4.

41 Mather entitled his contribution to Janeway's martyrology *A Token for the Children of New England*, which he introduced by expressing concern that the children of New England know that "they will be condemned, not only by the Examples of Pious Children in other parts of the World, the Published and Printed Accounts whereof have been brought over hither," but also by "exemplary Children in the midst of New England itself, that will Rise up against them for their Condemnation." James Janeway and Cotton Mather, *A Token for Children. Being an Exact Account of the Conversion, Holy and Exemplary Lives and Joyful Deaths of Several Young Children* [. . .] (Boston: printed for Daniel Henchman over against the Brick Meeting House in Cornhill, 1728), 85–86.

42 As Glenda Goodman has thoroughly chronicled, Puritans found no biblical warrant for choral music in worship and so translated the psalms into English metered verse, singing them by "lining out the Psalms," a method that created the effect of a kind of communal chant. "Puritans believed psalmody created a channel between the singer and God: by singing, the devout glorified and praised God, but, through singing, the worshiper was also brought closer to the divine. The soul was lifted." According to Goodman, Puritans on both sides of the Atlantic relied on the Sternhold and Hopkins (1562) and Bay Psalm (1640) psalters until Nahum Tate and Nicholas Brady produced the popular *A New Version of the Psalms of David* in 1696. Glenda Goodman, "'The Tears I Shed at the Songs of Thy Church': Seventeenth-Century Musical Piety in the English Atlantic World," *Journal of the American Musicological Society* 65, no. 3 (2012): 700.

43 Watts's first collection of metered verse was published in London in 1706—a collection of poetry entitled *Horae Lyricae*: Isaac Watts, *Horae Lyricae: Poems, Chiefly of the Lyric Kind. In Two Books* [. . .] *By I. Watts* (London: printed by S. and D. Bridge for John Lawrence, 1706). The following year, Watts published *Hymns and Spiritual Songs*, in 1715 *Divine Songs Attempted in Easy Language for the Use of Children*, and in 1719 his own metrical psalter, *The Psalms of David*. Central to all these collections was Watts's view that the moment of death was of paramount importance to every individual.

44 My thanks to Andrew Cashner for this helpful articulation. That the question of proper Christian conduct in the face of death stood at the center of Isaac Watts's concern is evidenced by the way he put together his collections of verse. His original collection, *Horae Lyricae*, included countless poems touching on these themes—"Sickness Gives a Sight of Heaven," "The Day of Judgment," "Death a Welcome Savior," "The Happy Saint and Cursed Savior," "Longing for Heaven," to name just a few. The second and largest part of *Hymns and Spiritual Songs* opened with this series of songs:

 I. A Song of Praise to God from Great Britain
 II. The Death of a Sinner
 III. The Death and Burial of a Saint
 IV. Salvation in the Cross
 V. Longing to Praise Christ Better
 VI. A Morning Song
 VII. An Evening Song
 VIII. A Hymn for Morning or Evening
 IX. Godly Sorrow Arising from the Sufferings of Christ
 X. Parting with Carnal Joys
 XI. The Same

Death is mentioned explicitly in all but the first of these opening songs and then reappears continually throughout the remainder of the second part of the collection, as it does, inevitably, in the third part, containing songs for the celebration of what is, for Christians, the memorial feast of the Lord's Supper. Isaac Watts, *Hymns and Spiritual Songs in Three Books* (Boston: Zechariah Fowle and Samuel Draper, 1762). These themes are central, too, to Watts's *Divine Songs Attempted in*

Easy Language for the Use of Children, which was first published in 1715 in London and excerpted that same year for publication in Boston by Thomas Fleet under the title *Honey Out of the Rock Flowing to Little Children That They May Know to Refuse the Evil and Chuse the Good*. Ten of its twenty-eight songs included explicit mention of death and the promises of the afterlife.

45 Isaac Watts, *Sermons on Various Subjects, Divine and Moral: With a Sacred Hymn Suited to Each Subject* (London: printed for E. Matthews at the *Bible* in Paternoster Row, R. Ford at the *Angel*, and R. Hett at the *Bible* and *Crown*, both in the *Poultry*, 1734), 152–73, 492–93.

46 Watts, *Horae Lyricae. Poems Chiefly*, 79–80.

47 Cotton Mather, *Seasonable Thoughts upon Mortality: A Sermon Occasioned by the Raging of a Mortal Sickness in the Colony of Connecticut* [. . .] (Boston: sold by Timothy Green, 1712).

48 Isaac Watts, *Hymns and Spiritual Songs* (Boston, [1720?]). The only known copy of this first American print, held by the Massachusetts Historical Society, lacks the title page and is otherwise imperfect. By 1812 the volume had been reprinted in one form or another in America at least eighty-four times, and the work was such standard fare that new printers routinely included their own print runs of the songbook almost immediately upon attempting to break into established markets. A dramatic increase in its American publication during the early national era suggests disrupted importation from London.

49 Christopher Phillips, "Cotton Mather Brings Isaac Watts's Hymns to America; or, How to Perform a Hymn without Singing It," *New England Quarterly* 85, no. 2 (2012): 203. Watts's genius lay in his ability to encapsulate the Protestant gospel without resorting to complicated language or controversial doctrine. Watts himself recognized as much. As he put it in the preface to the edition of *Hymns and Spiritual Songs*,

> The whole Book is written in four Sorts of Metre, and fitted to the most Common Tunes. . . . The Metaphors are generally sunk to the Level of vulgar Capacities. . . . Some of the Beauties of Poesy are neglected, and some wilfully defaced . . . lest a more exalted

Turn or Though or Language should darken or disturb the Devotion of the weakest Souls. . . . I have avoided the more obscure and controverted Points of Christianity, that we might all obey the Direction of the Word of God, and sing his Praises with Understanding, Psalm xlvii, 7. The Contentions and distinguishing Words of Sects and Parties are secluded, that whole Assemblies might assist at the Harmony, and different Churches join in the same Worship, without Offence.

Watts, *Hymns and Spiritual Songs in Three Books*, vii–viii.

50 Isaac Watts was more than a hymn writer. His works included catechetical manuals for children and sweeping philosophical treatises with titles like *Discourses on the Love of God, and Its Influence on All the Passions* (Philadelphia: Woodward, 1799). Nonetheless, Watts's most lasting influence was as a lyricist. As William Dargan has compellingly chronicled, by the mid-eighteenth century, Isaac Watts "had become renowned in England and abroad, and his paraphrase of Psalm 90, 'Our God, Our Help in Ages Past,' had become a signal moment in the English Puritan epoch." Watts's unique blend of words and sounds also revolutionized the worship practices of the colonies' African American population, both slave and free. In Dargan's assessment, "Performances of Watts's lyrics became an artistic watershed for language contact between slave dialects and English verse" to such an extent that an entirely unique and distinctively American style of singing was born, which would come to be known across the African American landscape as, simply, "Dr. Watts." William T. Dargan, *Lining Out the Word: Dr. Watts Hymn Singing in the Music of Black Americans* (Berkeley: University of California Press, 2006), 94. For a sampling of recent works about Watts from a diversity of disciplinary approaches, see Richard Arnold, *Trinity of Discord: The Hymnal and Poetic Innovations of Isaac Watts, Charles Wesley, and William Cowper* (New York: Peter Lang, 2012), 162; John Knapp, "Isaac Watts's Unfixed Hymn Genre," *Modern Philology: Critical and Historical Studies in Literature, Medieval through Contemporary* 109, no. 4 (2012):

463–82; and J. F. Maclear, "Isaac Watts and the Idea of Public Religion," *Journal of the History of Ideas* 53, no. 1 (1992): 25–45. Only recently have scholars begun to treat Watts's oeuvre as a whole rather than parsing his works into categories conforming to the conventions of the modern academic disciplines. Watts conceived of his life's work not as fragmented but rather as all-encompassing in scope and all-embracing in reach. In Dargan's view, the common thread that bound these works together was Watts's "way of speaking on behalf of God's embattled people . . . fashioned in the crucible of Nonconformist persecutions." Dargan, *Lining Out the Word*, 95.

51 From the inception of their colonial enterprise, devout Puritans in New England understood themselves to have been sent on a divine "errand" to spread the truth contained in their Holy Scriptures. And so they attached preposterous expectations for Indian evangelization to early publications like *The Whole Book of Psalms*, known commonly as the *Bay Psalm Book*, and the Eliot Bible, a printed Bible translated into the Narragansett tongue by the Puritan John Eliot. Even as these expectations failed to be realized, with few exceptions, later generations of English in North America continued to embrace these same beliefs and assumptions, and they proliferated in print self-congratulatory assertions that theirs was an inherently benevolent mission, destined to transform Native peoples into good Englishmen. Perry Miller, *Errand into the Wilderness* (Cambridge, MA: Harvard University Press, 1956). This mission was institutionalized in 1649 with the creation in London of the Corporation for the Propagating the Gospel in New England, referred to most frequently as the New England Company. Following the tumultuous English Civil Wars of the 1640s and the restoration of the monarchy under Charles II in 1660, the New England Company was provided a royal charter to spread "the Gospel of Christ unto and amongst the heathen natives in or near New England and parts adjacent in America." "The Charter of New England: 1620," Lillian Goldman Law Library, accessed February 17, 2021, https://tinyurl.com/y5ee4p72.

52 As their preposterous evangelistic expectations met with repeated frustration, the English in North America attempted to justify in print the stubborn facts on the ground. As early as 1645, John Winthrop, writing "in the name of all the Commissioners" of the Massachusetts Bay Colony, published *A Declaration of Former Passages and Proceedings betwixt the English and the Narrowgansets, with Their Confederates*, commonly considered the first historical account published in North America. Intended as much for English as for American readers, Winthrop asserted that the English colonists "came into these parts of the world with desire to advance the kingdom of the Lord Jesus Christ, and to injoye his precious Ordinances with peace. Both in their treaties & converse, they have had an awfull respect to divine rules, endeavouring to walk uprightly and inoffensively, & in the midst of many injuries and instances to exercise much patience and long suffering." However, Winthrop continued, New England's Native "Pequots grew to an excesse of violence and outrage, and proudly turned aside from all wayes of justice and peace, before the sword was drawn or any hostile attempts made against them." John Winthrop, *A Declaration of Former Passages and Proceedings betwixt the English and the Narrowgansets, with Their Confederates* [. . .] (1645; Early English Books Online Text Creation Partnership, 2011), https://tinyurl.com/yadafrhs.

53 Rooted in conceptions of private property alien to North America, the conduct of the colonists was widely perceived by Native peoples as nonsensical and intrinsically predatory. As early as 1675, the Wampanoag sachem Metacom complained to the Rhode Island governor John Eaton that English presence in what they called New England boiled down to an unending campaign of "cheating, discrimination, and pressures to sell land, submit to the Plymouth Colony's authority, convert to Christianity and consume alcohol." Neal Salisbury, ed., *The Sovereignty and Goodness of God, by Mary Rowlandson, with Related Documents* (Boston: Bedford / St. Martin's, 1997), 19.

54 Other early works of this sort include Increase Mather's *A Brief History of the Warr with the Indians in New-England* (Boston:

printed and sold by John Foster over against the Sign of the Dove, 1676); see also William Hubbard's *A Narrative of the Troubles with the Indians in New-England, from the First Planting Thereof in the Year 1607* [. . .] (Boston, 1677). According to Wroth, this latter work included a map marking the beginning of "a native school of book illustration." Wroth, *Colonial Printer*, 18.

55 Archibald Loudon, *A Selection of Some of the Most Interesting Narratives of Outrages, Committed by the Indians, in Their Wars, with the White People* [. . .] (Carlisle, PA: from the press of Archibald Loudon, 1808), vi.

56 Some of these Native practices had—or came to have—their approximate parallels in English traditions. Many Native tribes practiced ritual washing as a rite of initiation, for instance, and this observance bore striking resemblance to baptism by immersion, which—perhaps not coincidentally—became increasingly popular among English colonists in the eighteenth century. Smith, for instance, described his initiation this way in his *Account of the Remarkable Occurrences in the Life and Travels of Captain James Smith*: "At length one of the squaws made out to speak a little English (for I believe they began to be a little afraid of me) and said, no hurt you, on this I gave myself up to their ladyships, who were as good as their word; for though they plunged me under water, and washed and rubbed me severely; yet, I could not say they hurt me much." James Smith, *Account of the Remarkable Occurrences in the Life and Travels of Captain James Smith (Now a Citizen of Bourbon County, Kentucky) during His Captivity* [. . .], in Loudon, *Most Interesting Narratives*, 155. After being dressed, painted, and seated with the men of the tribe, Smith was invited to share in the smoking of a pipe, after which "at length one of the chiefs made a speech which was delivered to me by an interpreter and was as followeth":

> My son, you are now flesh of our flesh and bone of our bone. By the ceremony which we have performed this day, every drop of white blood was washed out of your veins; you are taken into the Caughnewago nation, and initiated into the warlike tribe; you are adopted into a great family, and now received with

great seriousness and solemnity in the room and place of a great man after what has passed this day, you are now one of us by an old strong law and custom—My son, you have now nothing to fear, we are now under the same obligations to love and defend one another, therefore you are to consider yourself as one of our people.

Recalling his experience years later, Smith recounted that "from that day I never knew them to make any distinction between me and themselves in any respect whatever until I left them." Loudon, *Most Interesting Narratives*, 155–56.

57 See, for instance, Harold E. Selesky, *War and Society in Colonial Connecticut* (New Haven, CT: Yale University Press, 1990). The English were not averse to taking captives themselves—the story of Pocahontas, for instance, which enthralled generations of young English readers on both sides of the Atlantic, was the tale of a Native American princess kidnapped as a young woman. For the most part, however, the English took captives without the intent, or the acquired skill, of incorporating them into English culture, preferring instead to treat them as prisoners of war or as slaves. And because they conceived of war fundamentally as a contest over land, English colonists commonly characterized Native practices of captive taking as morally abhorrent. Anna Mae Duane, *Suffering Childhood in Early America: Violence, Race, and the Making of the Child Victim* (Athens: University of Georgia Press, 2010), 25, 31. For more on the history of Indian slavery in New England, see Margaret Ellen Newell, *New England Indians, Colonists, and the Origins of American Slavery* (Ithaca, NY: Cornell University Press, 2015).

58 John Bunyan, *Grace Abounding to the Chief of Sinners: Or, a Brief and Faithful Relation of the Exceeding Mercy of God in Christ to His Poor Servant, John Bunyan* [. . .] (Boston: printed by John Allen for Nicholas Boone at the Sign of the Bible in Cornhill, 1717); John Bunyan, *The Pilgrim's Progress from This World to That Which Is to Come* (London: printed for Robert Ponder, 1693).

59 Bunyan, *Pilgrim's Progress*, 123.

60 According to Phillips, "While most books, especially those of ten sheets or more,

were imported rather than printed in New England in the seventeenth and eighteenth centuries, Boston editions of *Pilgrim's Progress* had appeared as early as 1681, just three years after the London original." Phillips, "Cotton Mather Brings," 12.

61 Well aware of this, Bunyan penned a self-congratulatory introduction to the diaspora of readers anxiously awaiting the second part of his allegory, which was first published in 1682:

> My Pilgrim's Book has
>   travell'd sea and land,
> Yet could I never come to understand
> By any Kingdom, were
>   they rich or poor.
> In France and Flanders, where
>   men kill each other,
> My Pilgrim is esteem'd a
>   Friend, a Brother.
> In Holland, too, 'tis said, I am told,
> My Pilgrim is with some
>   worth more than Gold.
> Highlanders and Wild Irish can agree
> My Pilgrim should familiar
>   with them be.
> 'Tis in New England under
>   such advance,
> Receives there so much
>   loving countenance,
> As to be trimm'd, new cloth'd,
>   and deck't with Gems,
> That it may shew its features
>   and its limbs,
> Yet more, so comely doth
>   my Pilgrim walk
> That of him thousands
>   daily sing and talk.

John Bunyan, "The Author's Way of Sending Forth His Second Part of 'The Pilgrim,'" cited in David E. Smith, *John Bunyan in America* (Bloomington: Indiana University Press, 1966), xiii.

62 Because the trials and tribulations of the young Pilgrim became touchstones for children's literature produced in the era of the early American Republic, some scholars have argued that its greatest influence in North America was felt in the decades leading up to the US Civil War. But throughout the eighteenth century, generations of American preachers referenced Bunyan's allegory almost as casually as they referenced

the most familiar stories from the Bible. For one discussion of this lasting influence, see Ruth K. MacDonald, *Christian's Children: The Influence of John Bunyan's the Pilgrim's Progress on American Children's Literature* (New York: Peter Lang, 1989).

63 While earlier generations of historians commonly characterized the Indian captivity narrative as the first distinctly American genre of literature, today's scholars are less inclined to emphasize the novelty of the form. The experience of captivity was central to some of the most important biographies in the Hebrew Bible—including those of Joseph, Samson, David, and Daniel, to name just a few—and constituted the very heart of the founding narrative of the people of Israel, whose liberation from bondage in Egypt was chronicled in the book of Exodus. More proximately, the narratives shared much in common with English tales of shipwreck and piracy and with tales of English captivity in other regions of the world. Billy Stratton, *Buried in the Shades of Night: Contested Voices, Indian Captivity, and the Legacy of King Philip's War* (Tucson: University of Arizona Press, 2013), 17.

64 Mary Rowlandson, *A True History of the Captivity and Restoration of Mrs. Mary Rowlandson, a Minister's Wife in New-England* (London: Joseph Poole, 1682).

65 As Teresa Toulouse has aptly summarized, these early captivity narratives pointed "to the representative quality of the woman captive's experience"—the Puritan woman, who "manifested culturally valorized qualities of religious acceptance, humility, and obedience," did not stand for women's experience alone but, viewed in scriptural terms, for the experience of the entire colony. Teresa Toulouse, *The Captive's Position: Female Narrative, Male Identity, and Royal Authority in Colonial New England* (Philadelphia: University of Pennsylvania Press, 2007), 7. Young soon-to-be men, meanwhile, were instructed that their coming-of-age would demand of them demonstrations of valor and endurance in the face of physical pain and psychological torment. Ruth Bloch has argued that even some of the narratives featuring female captives were intended primarily to communicate expectations of the male gender. She sees Hannah Dustin and Mary Rowlandson, for example, as having

been celebrated as exceptional women who "went so far beyond expectations: they proved themselves neither weaker nor less capable of absorbing and retaining the standards of civilization than men." Ruth H. Bloch, "The Gendered Meanings of Virtue in Revolutionary America," *Signs* 13, no. 1 (1987): 42.

66 Across the turn of the eighteenth century, the downward spiral of their relationships with their Indian neighbors seemed even more threatening to the English because their principal colonial competitors, the French, had proven consistently more adept at forging alliances with the continent's Native peoples. The first generations of French explorers in North America had forged these alliances on the simple basis of trade, a basis far less threatening than the English quest for the proprietary acquisition of land. Over time, English colonists came to think of themselves as surrounded by a "wilderness" that was occupied by the "savage" Indians and the "popish" French, whose cordial relations enjoyed by "the French and the Indians" came to represent a diabolical conspiracy. Toulouse, *Captive's Position*, 11. According to Toulouse, the American wilderness aligned in the English imagination with "the moral and psychological Babylon of Catholic Europe." In this way, English colonists came to think of armed conflict with their neighbors not just as a physical threat. Rather, wars with the French and the Indians—and the fears of such wars, reinforced continually by frontier skirmishes at the periphery of perpetually expanding colonial populations—came to be seen as an existential threat to the entire enterprise of the English in North America. The account of John Gyles, published in 1736 in Boston, illustrates the depth of this belief and how this belief shaped the expectations cultivated in young men coming of age in colonial New England across several generations. Taken captive by Maliseet Indians at the age of ten from his hometown of Pemaquid, Maine, in 1699, the last words Gyles recalled hearing from his mother were these: "If it is God's will, I had rather follow to your grave, or to never see more in this world than you should be sold to a Jesuit. For a Jesuit will ruin you body and soul." Gyles survived his six years in captivity without

converting to Catholicism, but as Peter Mancall has observed, Gyles's mother "ironically, got her wish: she died while he was in captivity." Conversation with Peter Mancall, University of Southern California, spring 2016.

67 Beginning with Williams's autobiographical account, men became more and more the featured protagonists in the most widely distributed captivity narratives, and by this time the basic template of the form was well established. Later narratives included the first-person narratives of John Gyles, John Norton, Nehemiah How, and David Brainerd, the latter famously distributed by the revivalist preacher Jonathan Edwards, who appended an elaborate preface and concluding remarks to his 1749 account of Brainerd's life and death. John Norton, *The Redeemed Captive. Being a Narrative of the Taking and Carrying into Captivity the Reverend Mr. John Norton* [. . .] (Boston: printed and sold opposite to the prison, 1748); Nehemia How, *A Narrative of the Captivity of Nehemiah How* [. . .] (Boston: printed and sold opposite to the prison, 1748); Jonathan Edwards, *An Account of the Life of the Late Reverend Mr. David Brainerd, Minister of the Gospel, Missionary to the Indians* [. . .] (Boston: printed for and sold by Daniel Henchman in Cornhill, 1749).

68 Hugh Amory has summarized this consensus neatly:

> Advocates of an alternative church order, the 'Congregational Way,' the immigrants quickly realized that both the preservation of 'Learning' and the success of their new system of church government depended on producing more clergy. Plans were therefore laid in 1636 for a college, soon to be named Harvard, in honor of a wealthy young minister who, dying in 1638, left half of his estate and the entirety of his books for the benefit of the institution. The first class graduated in 1642. . . . One central purpose of a Harvard education was to acquire a mastery of Latin, Greek and Hebrew; to be learned meant being 'literate' in the root sense of knowing Latin. . . . When a second college eventually named Yale, was founded in Connecticut in 1701, its organizers, all

of them Harvard graduates, re-created this curriculum.

Amory, "Printing and Bookselling," 131. Students at Harvard and Yale in the eighteenth century were introduced to the latest discoveries of the Copernican and Newtonian revolutions, but they were simultaneously immersed in the practices of devotion that would prepare them, should they choose, for careers as preachers and teachers of the Christian gospel. Having mastered the ancient languages Latin and Greek in their preparatory studies, Harvard men and "Yalensies" read what they called the Old Testament in the original Hebrew and the New Testament in the original Greek, and they immersed themselves in the works of Greek and Roman antiquity. According to Conrad Edick Wright, this curriculum and educational format "had a specific social function. It prepared boys and young men for genteel leadership in a community in which most adult males had a rudimentary education but little more. Harvard and other colleges of colonial New England were gateways to the region's upper reaches, places of status, respect, power, wealth, and refinement. Ambition ordinarily began at home. And its path often led through Harvard College." Conrad Edick Wright, *Revolutionary Generation: Harvard Men and the Consequences of Independence* (Boston: University of Massachusetts Press, 2005), 120. Tied together through relationships of both competition and collaboration, Harvard and Yale continued to prepare the vast preponderance of clergy serving established churches in New England through this period. Even less rigorous dissenting "academies" that trained preachers for service in Presbyterian and Baptist networks were founded by men who themselves were graduates of Harvard or Yale.

69 Of the eighty or so surviving Cotton Mather poems, for instance, at least two dozen were elegies, occasioned by the deaths of family members—"On the Death of a Son," "Go, Then, My Dove, No Longer Mine"—or friends, parishioners, and colleagues: "Some Offers to Embalm the Memory of the Truly Reverend and Renowned John Wilson"; "Lamentations for the Death, and Loss of the Every Way Admirable Mr. Urian Oakes"; "An Elegy upon the Death of

Mrs. Mary Brown; Who Dyed in Travail (with Her Unborn Child)"; and so on. Cotton Mather, *Maternal Consolations. An Essay on, the Consolations of God; Whereof, a Man Whom His Mother Comforteth, Receives a Shadow* [. . .] (Boston: printed by Thomas Fleet for Samuel Gerrish, 1714); Cotton Mather, *Memoria Wilsoniana. Or, Some Dues Unto the Memory of the Truly Reverend & Renowned Mr. John Wilson, the First Pastor of Boston* [. . .] (Boston: Michael Perry, 1695); Cotton Mather, *A Poem Dedicated to the Memory of the Reverend and Excellent Mr. Urian Oakes, the Late Pastor to Christ's Flock, and Praesident of Harvard-Colledge* [. . .] (Boston: John Ratcliff, 1682); Cotton Mather, *Eureka. The Vertuous Woman Found. A Short Essay on the Memory of Mrs. Mary Brown, Late Consort of Benjamin Brown Esq. In Salem* [. . .] (Boston: printed by Bartholomew Green, 1704). And of the eighty sermons published by Mather that survive, at least twenty can be formally categorized as "funeral sermons," while countless others conjured the memories of the recently departed. Of Mather's formal funeral sermons, half were printed together with a separately titled account of the death of the departed. For examples of these, see the following works of Cotton Mather: *A Devout and Humble Enquiry into the Reasons of the Divine Council in the Death of Good Men* (Boston: Thomas Fleet, 1715); *A Brief Enquiry into the Reasons Why the People of God Have Been Wont to Bring into Their Penitential Confessions* (Boston: Thomas Fleet, 1716); *The Death of God's Saints Precious in His Sight* (Boston: Bartholomew Green, 1723); *The Prophet's Death Lamented and Improved* (Boston: Thomas Fleet, 1723); *The Faithful Ministers of Christ Mindful of Their Own Death* (Boston: Daniel Henchman, 1729); and *Dying in Peace in a Good Old Age* (Boston: Samuel Kneeland, 1730).

70 Published by John Allen in 1717, Mather's *Instructions to the Living, from the Condition of the Dead* is representative of this practice of combining sermons and accounts of deaths under a single cover. The bulk of the sixty-four pages were dedicated to "a Brief Relation of REMARKABLES in the Shipwreck of above One Hundred PIRATES, who were Cast away in the Ship *Whido*, on the Coast of *New-England, April 26,*

1717. And in the Death of Six, who after a Fair Trial at *Boston*, were Convicted & Condemned, *Octob. 22.* And Executed, *Novemb. 15, 1717.* With some Account of the Discourse had with the on the way to their Execution." In this extended account, Mather recounted the harrowing details of the shipwreck itself but also shared the substance of his extended conversations with the six condemned men—"Simon Vanvoorst, who was Born in New-York. John Brown, Born in Jamaica. Thomas Baker, Born at Flushing in Holland. Henrick Quinter, Born in Amsterdam. Peter Cornelius Hooss, Born in Sweden. And T. S. Born at Boston in New-England." Cotton Mather, *Instructions to the Living, from the Condition of the Dead* (Boston: John Allen, 1717), 8. To each, Mather offered the opportunity of a last-chance repentance, with mixed results, the outcome of which apparently inspired the sermon that Mather requested Allen append to the published account. Mather based this sermon on Jeremiah 17:2, which he rendered, "He that getteth Riches and not by Right, shall leave them in the midst of his Days, and at his End shall be a Fool"—and he titled it *Warnings to Them That Make Haste to Be Rich.* In it, he expounded at length on the eternal peril risked by covetous individuals like the pirates. He also saw their demise unambiguously as the handiwork of God: "Our Gracious GOD has Wondrous Tenderness for *Humane Society*; And when men grow so Outrageous in the Ways of *Dishonesty,* that *Humane Society* suffers Insupportable Damages from them; Now there goes up that Cry to Heaven, *'Tis Time, Lord, for thee to Work!* And, GOD comes down, GOD steps in, GOD in compassion to *Humane Society,* fulfills that word upon the man who *trusted in the abundance of his Riches, and Strengthened himself in his Wickedness.*" Mather.

71 Cotton Mather, *Just Commemorations: The Death of Good Men, Considered* (Boston: Bartholomew Green, 1715), 48.

72 Mather, 52.

73 Mather, 7.

74 Mather, 7.

75 See Fanestil, "Print Practice."

Chapter 2

1   For an excellent early summary of this spread of print in the colonies of British North America, see Wroth, *Colonial Printer*.

2   Perry Miller long ago described print production and distribution in early colonial North America as reflective of a Puritan "errand into the wilderness." Miller, *Errand into the Wilderness*. In his 2007 *The Puritan Origins of American Patriotism*, George McKenna embraced Cotton Mather's summation of this narrative as emblematic— "to seek a place for the exercise of the Protestant Religion, according to the light of their consciences in the deserts of America." McKenna summarizes the narrative as composed of the following: (1) a vision of America as ancient Israel, (2) an "activist" brand of Christianity, (3) covenant theology, (4) a cosmic war against the antichrist, and (5) a predisposition to anxious introspection. I would add the "ideals and practices of martyrdom" to this list. And what McKenna says of the other components of this narrative is equally true of what I am calling English Protestant martyrdom: "It was an attractive story and a very adaptable one because it would be creatively reinterpreted in a variety of ways. Its geographical source was New England, but the movement of New England's large and ethnically homogeneous population, the compactness of its culture, and the enormous volume of New England writings—books, sermons, periodicals and newspapers—insured the Puritan narrative reached a colonywide audience years before the American Revolution." George McKenna, *The Puritan Origins of American Patriotism* (New Haven, CT: Yale University Press, 2007), 50.

3   Stoddard presided over the Northampton church for almost sixty years beginning in the 1670s, and his influence spread through a vast network of relationships that included five daughters who married Congregational clergy. Stoddard held to the orthodox puritan view that the true church was a community of "saints" whose faith could be made "visible" to others in the form of a professed experience of personal conversion. At the same time, however, Stoddard embraced an expansive vision of who could participate in the life of his congregation, admitting a form of provisional, or "halfway," membership to those who led godly lives, even if they had not yet experienced such a conversion. This unique blend of orthodox puritan theology and generous church practice proved so distinctive that it earned its own shorthand, "Stoddardean." It also earned Stoddard a nickname—the "Congregational Pope"—that was taken by his supporters as a source of pride and his opponents as an epithet.

4   John Williams, *The Redeemed Captive, Returning to Zion* (Boston: Bartholomew Green for Samuel Phillips, 1707). Williams glossed over the fact that his oldest daughter, Eunice, aged seven at the time of her capture, remained with her captors willingly. Later, as John Demos so engagingly chronicled in his landmark book *The Unredeemed Captive*, Eunice would convert to Catholicism, marry into the tribe, and remain a member of the Mohawk Nation through to her death. John Demos, *The Unredeemed Captive* (New York: Random House, 1995).

5   In his magisterial biography, George Marsden summarizes,

> Since before Jonathan could remember, family prayers included petitions for Uncle Williams . . . and cousins, captive in Canada. After Williams and two of his three remaining captive children returned in the fall of 1706, petitions continued for the one remaining child, Eunice (aged seven at the time of her capture), still with the Indians and, far worse, reportedly under Romish delusions. By the time the precocious Jonathan was old enough to read, he would have discovered . . . his uncle's *The Redeemed Captive, Returning to Zion*. John Williams' best-selling narrative vividly recounted the horrors of the Indian attack, the agony of seeing two children killed and losing his wife, and the pain of his long captivity among the Indians and French in Canada.

George M. Marsden, *Jonathan Edwards: A Life* (New Haven, CT: Yale University Press, 2003), loc. 332, 441 of 8774, Kindle.

6   As Marsden has summarized, Jonathan Edwards emerged from his Yale education "intensely committed to demonstrating how his heritage was not only viable but *the* answer to all the questions posed by the new world of his day." Marsden, *Jonathan Edwards*, loc. 187 of 8774.

7   John B. Blake, "The Inoculation Controversy in Boston: 1721–1722," *New England Quarterly* 25, no. 4 (1952): 489–506.

8   Jonathan Edwards, *A Faithful Narrative of the Surprising Work of God in the Conversion of Many Hundred Souls in Northampton* [. . .] (Elizabethtown, NJ: Shepard Kollock, 1740).

9   Edwards, 34–35.

10 Jonathan Edwards, *The Great Concern of a Watchman for Souls, Appearing in the Duty He Has to Do, and the Account He Has to Give, Represented & Improved* [. . .] (Boston: printed by Green, Bushell, and Allen for Nathaniel Proctor at the Bible and Dove in Ann Street, near the drawbridge, 1743), 6–7.

11 Delivered from pulpits above—sometimes remarkably high above—the level of meetinghouse floors, sermons were widely understood by New Englanders to represent a unique form of speech that bridged the gap between the heavens and the earth. Congregationalists commonly characterized the words of their preachers' mouths as supernaturally inspired, and even the sounds of their voices as supernaturally charged, though differences of opinion within congregations at times produced suspicions of demonic, as much as divine, influence. When they were brought to print, the sermons of celebrated preachers were commonly characterized—sometimes by the publisher, sometimes by the preacher himself, oftentimes by the two working in collaboration—in ways that suggested their inherent transcendence. Notable sermons were *verba vivifica* (living words) or "calls from the dead to the living" or "outpourings of the Holy Ghost." Cotton Mather, *Verba Vivifica* (Boston: Bartholomew Green, 1714); Samuel Dexter, *A Call from the Dead to the Living* (Boston: Bartholomew Green, 1727); Charles Chauncy, *The Out-Pouring of the Holy Ghost* (Boston: Thomas Fleet, 1742).

12 The first generations of Puritans in New England had consistently argued that the correct answer to this question was an experience of personal conversion or new birth. This understanding had found an early and powerful expression in Richard Baxter's *A Call to the Unconverted, to Turn and Live*, a combined treatise and prayer book that ran through dozens of editions from the time of its first publication in London in 1651 and was widely imported to North America before being first printed in Boston in 1731. Baxter, a Puritan of "non-Separatist" and yet "nonconforming" views, composed his *Call* "to be read in families where any are unconverted" and explained to his readers that their ministers were "set over you to advise you, for the saving of your Souls, as Physicians advise you for the curing of your Bodies." Richard Baxter, *A Call to the Unconverted, to Turn and Live and Accept of Mercy While Mercy May Be Had* [. . .] (Boston: printed for Samuel Kneeland and Timothy Green, 1731), 33. Across sixty years in the Northampton pulpit, Solomon Stoddard had embraced Baxter's counsel, mastering a form of sermonizing that came to be known as the jeremiad. Jonathan Edwards continued in this vein after taking over the Northampton pulpit in the early 1730s but over time delivered sermons of an astonishing diversity of kinds. As his many biographers routinely and rightly emphasize, popular portrayals of Edwards's sermonizing are often unbalanced, in part for the title of his most famous sermon, *Sinners in the Hands of an Angry God*. For Edwards's God was a God of both righteous anger and providential mercy. In fact, the point of departure for the sermon was that the life of man was "always exposed to *sudden* unexpected Destruction," a simple observation that Edwards clearly assumed his audience of listeners and readers would accept as a matter of fact, and its central message was that their mere survival evidenced the abundant mercy of God. Jonathan Edwards, *Sinners in the Hands of an Angry God. A Sermon Preached at Enfield, July 8, 1741. At a Time of Great Awakenings* [. . .] (Boston: Samuel Kneeland and Timothy Green, 1741), 4. As Patricia Tracy has summarized, the critical point of the sermon was that "although man earns his own damnation, the angry God nevertheless sustains him—for the moment—out of pure mercy." Patricia J.

Tracy, "Edwards, Jonathan (1703–1758), Congregational Minister and Philosopher," *American National Biography*, June 7, 2018, https://tinyurl.com/y7l65re8.

13 Marsden, *Jonathan Edwards*, loc. 3386, 3457 of 8774.

14 Jonathan Edwards, *True Saints, When Absent from the Body, Are Present with the Lord* (Boston: printed by Rogers & Fowle for Daniel Henchman in Cornhill, 1747), 7.

15 Edwards, 8.

16 Edwards, 25.

17 That same year, in 1747, Edwards reached a firm and final conclusion that the Stoddardean practices of more expansive church membership could not produce what he had famously described in a 1741 treatise as "the distinguishing marks of a work of the spirit of God." Jonathan Edwards, *The Distinguishing Marks of a Work of the Spirit of God. Applied to That Uncommon Operation That Has Lately Appeared* [. . .] (Boston: printed and sold by Samuel Kneeland and Timothy Green in Queen Street over against the prison, 1741). Having aligned himself with other "New Light" pastors, Edwards had long advocated a return to a more restrictive practice of membership, judging that only those who had experienced a personal conversion—and could evidence the experience through demonstrations of personal piety or "awakening"—merited full participation in the church. When he restricted access to the communion altar at the Northampton church, Edwards met with fierce opposition from so-called Old Lights, who remained committed to the more moderate practice of the "halfway" covenant and who remained suspicious of overly "enthusiastic" demonstrations of supposed conversion. Jonathan Edwards spent his last years in the Northampton pulpit struggling to make sense of the collapse of his pastorate, delivering sermons with titles like *An Humble Attempt to Promote Explicit Agreement and Visible Union of God's People* [. . .] and *An Humble Inquiry into the Rules of the Word of God, concerning the Qualifications Requisite to a Compleat Standing* [. . .]. Jonathan Edwards, *An Humble Attempt to Promote Explicit Agreement and Visible Union of God's People* [. . .] (Boston: printed for Daniel Henchman in Cornhill, 1747); Jonathan Edwards, *An Humble Inquiry into the Rules of the Word of God, concerning the Qualifications Requisite to a Compleat Standing* [. . .] (Boston: printed and sold by Samuel Kneeland in Queen Street, 1749). Finally, on June 22, 1750, Edwards preached his final sermon as the called pastor of the Northampton church. Published the next year, it was poignantly titled *A Farewel-Sermon Preached at the First Precinct in Northampton, after the People's Publick Rejection of Their Minister* [. . .]. Edwards was dismissed from the Northampton pulpit by Congregational vote. Edwards's final years in Northampton were also marked by profound intimate loss. In February of 1748, he was traumatized by the death of his beloved daughter Jerusha at the age of seventeen. In her funeral sermon, which he titled *Youth Is like a Flower*, Edwards forged his way through "very heavy and sorrowful" affection to find solace in the promise of his daughter's salvation. As she lay dying, he reported, Jerusha told her parents that "she had not seen one minute in several years that, for matter of any other good she saw in the world besides an opportunity to serve and glorify God in it." A year before dying herself, Jerusha had nursed David Brainerd on his deathbed and had attracted the interest of Samuel Hopkins, another of Edwards's Yale students who had followed him to Northampton. Edwards concluded that his daughter, once apparently destined to extend the family tradition of marrying into the clergy, was nonetheless being used by God for divine purpose: "O that this instance of death . . . might be a means of awakening the young people! If it might be so . . . and so be the beginning of a general awakening and reformation among you, the young people of my flock—it would abundantly add to the comforts I have in the circumstances of this providence, in itself so bitter and afflictive to me." "'A Heart Uncommonly Devoted to God': The Life of Jerusha Edwards," *Eusebeia* 10 (Fall 2008): 43, https://tinyurl.com/y732fcop. Three months later, Edwards delivered the funeral sermon for another family member, this one for his uncle John Stoddard, Esq. The older brother of his mother, Esther, John Stoddard was "a strong rod broken and withered," in Edwards's portrayal: "But now this strong Rod is broken and withered, and

surely the Judgment of GOD therein is very awful, and that Dispensation that which may well be for a Lamentation. Probably we shall be more sensible of the Worth and Importance of such a strong Rod by the Want of it. The awful Voice of GOD in this Providence is worthy to be attended. . . . We have now this Testimony of the divine Displeasure, added to all the other dark Clouds GOD has lately brought over us." Jonathan Edwards, *A Strong Rod Broken and Withered. A Sermon Preach'd at Northampton, on the Lord's Day, June 26. 1748* [. . .] (Boston: printed by Rogers & Fowle for Jonathan Edwards in Cornhill, 1748), 28. Chastened at being rejected by his congregants in Northampton, Edwards took a pastorate in Stockbridge, a newer settlement in western Massachusetts, beginning in 1750. From this post he attempted, unsuccessfully, to replicate his hero Brainerd's ministry with surrounding Native populations. He continued, however, his prolific production of theological and philosophical treatises, an undertaking that earned him, in 1757, an invitation to become president of the College of New Jersey, the institution that would later become Princeton University. The invitation was a bittersweet one, however, for it was brought about by the death of Aaron Burr Sr., the then president who died in September of 1757 at the age of forty-one. Five years earlier, Burr had married the eldest of Jonathan and Sarah Edwards's eleven children, Esther. The following year, as Jonathan assumed his first year of duties in the office he took over from his son-in-law, smallpox once again spread through New England. The Edwards clan joined with thousands in seeking to inoculate themselves from the disease, with mixed results. Rev. Timothy Edwards, Jonathan's father, succumbed at the ripe age of eighty-eight in January, but Jonathan followed him in March at the age of fifty-four, and sixteen days later, Esther succumbed as well at the age of twenty-six. Sarah Edwards died in October, reportedly of dysentery. Marsden, *Jonathan Edwards*, loc. 6832 of 8774.

18 Edwards, *Account of the Life*.

19 Edwards, 309–10.

20 Raised in a dissenting Leicestershire family, George Fox had launched the Religious Society of Friends—the movement that would come to be known as the Quakers—in 1647. Fox was convinced, as summed up by Frederick Tolles, that "to seek and follow the leadings of the Inward Light," Quakers must be "free from all outward coercion by church or state." Only by opening themselves fully to the "inshinings" of the Light could the faithful inherit the essential promise of the gospel—"Ye shall know the Truth, and the Truth shall make you free"—and only then would they be able to live freely in obedience to the teachings of Christ, as distilled in Christ's Sermon on the Mount. Quakers considered this conviction a logical, if radical, extension of the quintessentially Puritan principle that the individual's relationship to God was paramount in the life of faith. It provoked rabid opposition, however, from more traditional Puritans, as well as from the broader community of dissent in England. Within a few years of its establishment, Fox's society began to explore colonization as an escape from this persecution, sending missionaries to both northern Europe and North America in the mid-1650s. The early Quaker experience in New England was not markedly different from what Fox's society had experienced in England, however, and in short order, the self-understanding of Quakers on both sides of the Atlantic became rooted in their identity as a society forged in the crucible of suffering. F. B. Tolles, *Quakers and the Atlantic Culture* (New York: Octagon Books, 1960), 11.

21 Edward Burrough, *A Standard Lifted Up* (London, 1658), 10, cited in Weimer, *Martyrs' Mirror*, 103.

22 From the time he brokered the colony's founding in 1681 to the time of his death in 1718, Penn was convinced that his "holy experiment" in religious liberty should lead naturally to social harmony among Quakers and non-Quakers alike. In fact, Pennsylvania's commitment to freedom of religious expression produced a proliferation of divisions among Pennsylvania Quakers—what the New York governor Thomas Dongan in 1687 called "an abundance of Quakers . . . singing Quakers, ranting Quakers, Sabbatarians, anti-Sabbatarians, some Anabaptists, some Independants," and what Penn himself decried as "scurvy quarrels that break out to the disgrace of the Province." Tolles, *Quakers*, 13.

23 Weimer, *Martyrs' Mirror*, 99.

24 According to Shy, "To the relatively homogeneous English population of the seventeenth century were added about 200,000 Scotch-Irish and almost 100,000 Germans in the four decades after 1715, while as many as 250,000 blacks were forced to migrate to the continental colonies between 1700 and 1775." John W. Shy, *A People Numerous and Armed: Reflections on the Military Struggle for American Independence* (Ann Arbor: University of Michigan Press, 1990), 123.

25 Simon Finger, *The Contagious City: The Politics of Public Health in Early Philadelphia* (Ithaca, NY: Cornell University Press, 2012). Nonetheless, Philadelphia remained the preferred destination for immigrants, even after the Quakers abdicated their political control of Pennsylvania in 1756, in large part because the city had developed what Bernard Bailyn calls "a human warehousing capacity." In Bailyn's estimation, this "second circuit" of "the peopling of North America," which revolved around Philadelphia as its hub, extending "from the Hudson River South to the Delaware," was characterized by "ethnic diversity of the most extreme kind, and not a single expanding network of communities impelled outward by the distinctive dynamics of a distinctive demographic process, but half a dozen different demographic processes moving in different phases at different speeds." Bernard Bailyn, *The Peopling of British North America: An Introduction* (New York: Knopf, 1986), 95–97.

26 In 1685, William Bradford asserted in a publication called *Kalendarium Pennsilvaniense* that "after great charge and trouble, I have brought the great Art and Mystery of Printing into this part of America." After running afoul of Pennsylvania's governors for publishing the controversial tracts of the schismatic Quaker George Keith, Bradford moved to New York in 1692, where he became that colony's official printer. His son, Andrew, however, returned to Philadelphia in 1712 and resumed the family's business as the unofficial provincial printer. The Bradfords also launched the first newspapers in each colony: Andrew the Philadelphia-based *American Weekly Mercury* in 1719 and William the *New York Gazette* in 1725. By this time, the Bradfords

had established themselves, in effect, as the hub of a larger network of printers in Philadelphia and New York, whose collective production lagged only slightly behind that of the Boston-based network linked to the descendants of Samuel Green. A founding generation of Philadelphia printers included, among others, the Bradfords, Benjamin Franklin, Robert Bell, Christopher Sower, William Dunlap, and David Hall. See Rosalind Remers, *Printers and Men of Capital: Philadelphia Book Publishers in the New Republic* (Philadelphia: University of Pennsylvania Press, 2000).

27 As Nick Bunker has summarized, by the middle of the 1740s, "Franklin had become clearly the dominant, the most successful, the most entrepreneurial, the most accomplished printer on the eastern seaboard." Nick Bunker, "Episode 207: Nick Bunker, Young Benjamin Franklin," interview by Emily Sneff, *Ben Franklin's World*, October 9, 2018, https://tinyurl.com/yb8tntvl.

28 Franklin described the consequences this way in his autobiography:

> Mr. Denham took a store in Water-street, where we open'd our goods; I attended the business diligently, studied accounts, and grew, in a little time, expert at selling. We lodg'd and boarded together; he counsell'd me as a father, having a sincere regard for me. I respected and loved him, and we might have gone on together very happy; but, in the beginning of February, 1726/7, when I had just pass'd my twenty-first year, we both were taken ill. My distemper was a pleurisy, which very nearly carried me off. I suffered a good deal, gave up the point in my own mind, and was rather disappointed when I found myself recovering, regretting, in some degree, that I must now, some time or other, have all that disagreeable work to do over again. I forget what his distemper was; it held him a long time, and at length carried him off.

Walter Issacson, *A Benjamin Franklin Reader* (New York: Simon & Schuster, 2005), 445.

29 Issacson, 97.

30 The worldview embodied in this early raft of publications is encapsulated nicely by Ralph

Sandiford's 1729 antislavery tract *A Brief Examination of the Practice of the Times*. In a preface addressed to "my Friendly Reader," the Quaker Sandiford explained the inspiration for his abolitionist views: "UNDER the consideration of the shortness of the life of Man, and the end for which he was created, [I] engaged my mind to the Lord that he would make known his truth unto me, beyond custom or tradition in which most content themselves." Addressing himself directly to "whomsoever thou art that deals in slaves," Sandiford counseled his readers to remember that upon their death, they would be judged as belonging to God or to Lucifer. Ralph Sandiford, *A Brief Examination of the Practice of the Times, by the Foregoing and the Present Dispensation* [. . .] (Philadelphia: Benjamin Franklin and Hugh Meredith, 1729), ix, 1.

31 From his experience growing up in Boston, and from his time as an apprentice to his older brother James, Franklin knew that the publication of newspapers in colonial America was inherently controversial. The first newspaper ever published in North America, beginning in September 1690, was the Boston printer Benjamin Harris's "genuine periodical journal": "Publick Occurrences both Foreign and Domestick, a small folio of two leaves with a colophon on page three, reading: 'Boston, printed by R. Pierce, for Benjamin Harris, at the London-Coffee-House. 1690.'" Harris had promised his Boston readership "Publick Occurrences both Foreign and Domestick," but his paper had been suppressed almost immediately by the council of the Massachusetts Bay Colony. Fifteen years later, when Bartholomew Green launched a new weekly, the *Boston Newsletter*, its first issue, dated April 24, 1704, made clear that it was published "by authority" of then Massachusetts governor Joseph Dudley: "*The Boston News-Letter*, April 24, 1704, published by authority and 'Printed by B. Green.'" Wroth, *Colonial Printer*, 19. When James Franklin launched his own newspaper, the *New England Courant*, in 1721, it quickly earned a reputation as a vehicle for expression of protest and dissent. Patrick G. Williams, "Franklin, James (1697–1735), Printer," *American National Biography*, June 7, 2018, https://tinyurl.com/bhraa3ez. For this reason,

newspapers printed in North America were viewed with continued suspicion by English authorities on both sides of the Atlantic throughout the colonial period, their practice of airing public controversy deemed inherently oppositional. For more on this, see J. C. Roney, *Governed by a Spirit of Opposition: The Origins of American Political Practice in Colonial Philadelphia* (Baltimore: Johns Hopkins University Press, 2014).

32 See "The Pennsylvania Gazette," Accessible Archives, accessed February 19, 2021, https://tinyurl.com/ya3tv8hm.

33 For entirely representative examples, see "Attempt towards an Epitaph," *Philadelphia Gazette*, June 1, 1738, 2 (published after the 1737 death of Queen Caroline, the wife of England's King George II); and "On the Death of the Late Celebrated Mrs. Rowe," *Philadelphia Gazette*, July 26, 1739, 2.

34 *Philadelphia Gazette*, March 20, 1740, 3.

35 Richard Saunders [Benjamin Franklin], *Poor Richard, 1733: An Almanack for the Year of Christ 1733* (Philadelphia: Benjamin Franklin, 1733). T. J. Tomlin cites just one instructive data point: "Franklin's business partner, David Hall, reported that between 1752 and 1765 he printed 141,257 copies of *Poor Richard's Almanack* (averaging around 10,000 per year); this alone equaled one almanac per one hundred colonists." T. J. Tomlin, "Astrology's from Heaven Not from Hell," *Early American Studies* 8, no. 2 (Spring 2010): 294. Franklin's launch of an almanac for the Philadelphia market was based on precedents established in his native Boston. By the turn of the eighteenth century, students and tutors at Harvard College had been producing almanacs for decades. While neither was schooled at Harvard, James and Benjamin Franklin were raised in this literary environment, and they sought early on in their publishing careers to capitalize on it. From his publishing house on Queen Street in Boston, James first printed Nathan Bowen's *New England Diary and Almanack* in 1725, and then, after opening a press in Newport, Rhode Island, he produced under the pseudonym "Poor Robin" his own *The Rhode-Island Almanack*, the first issue printed in 1727 (for the year 1728).

36 Richard Saunders [Benjamin Franklin], *Poor Richard, 1734* (Philadelphia: Benjamin

Franklin, 1734). Richard Saunders [Benjamin Franklin], *Poor Richard, 1736* (Philadelphia: Benjamin Franklin, 1736).

37 Saunders, *Poor Richard, 1733.*

38 In these materials, too, Franklin routinely conjured the subject of death, as well as other themes reflecting the predilections of his readership, which he presumed to be male—the dangers of food and medicine, the burdens of wives, and so forth.

39 As Tomlin explains, "Astrology had always been a flexible and diverse system. As it entered the eighteenth century, it had already been made fully compatible with an array of religious opinions. . . . The starting point for understanding . . . almanac astrology is the belief that God disclosed himself and his ways through the workings of the natural world. Reading the skies for signs assumed the presence of an omnipotent sign-sender." According to Tomlin,

> The natural astrology found in almanacs offered a clear and comprehensive explanation of how the universe functioned. Almanacs detailed the influence of the planets on a variety of earthly affairs. Each of the seven planets—the sun, the moon, Saturn, Jupiter, Mars, Venus, and Mercury—were believed to be a combination of hot, cold, dry, and moist qualities. The four elements that constituted the physical composition of terrestrial matter were also made up of these qualities: fire was hot and dry; air was hot and moist, water was cold and moist; earth was cold and dry. Likewise, the four humors that filled the human body exhibited these traits: choler, or yellow bile, was hot and dry; blood was hot and moist; melancholy, or black bile, was cold and dry; phlegm was cold and moist.

Tomlin, "Astrology's from Heaven," 296.

40 Saunders, *Poor Richard, 1733.*

41 His religious views squarely within the fold of an ascendant deism that imagined a supremely rational God. Franklin formed the Society for Useful Knowledge in 1743, calling for "virtuosi or ingenious men residing in the several colonies" to share the fruits of the intellectual and technological labors. Inspired in part by, and partly in contradistinction to, the Anglican Church's historic Society for the Propagation of Christian Knowledge (SPCK), Franklin's society had helped establish Philadelphia as the central node in an intercolonial network of science, arts, and letters. J. Lyons, *The Society for Useful Knowledge: How Benjamin Franklin and Friends Brought the Enlightenment to America* (New York: Bloomsbury, 2013). After the 1751 publication of his *Experiments and Observations on Electricity*, Franklin was awarded honorary degrees by both Yale and Harvard and the Copley Medal, the Royal Society of London's highest honor. Franklin had become a bona fide and uniquely multidimensioned celebrity on both sides of the Atlantic, a kind of combined Steve Jobs and Oprah Winfrey for the eighteenth century.

42 In this, Franklin was following a well-traveled path—new publishers in North America routinely opened their houses by selling "steady sellers," like Bibles, psalmbooks, and primers, while simultaneously printing locally authored works that they hoped would be found attractive by the readers in their local markets. Working closely with printers, booksellers, bookbinders, newspaper editors, and authors—and often working in more than one of these capacities themselves—homegrown American publishers expanded dramatically their share of the growing North American market, even as the bulk of print material consumed in the colonies continued to be imported from London. A representation of what Franklin offered for sale can be found in the summary listing of items "sold by the Printer hereof," with which he concluded his *Poor Richard's Almanack*, as in this edition for the year 1734: "Large Quarto Bibles of good print, small Bibles, Testaments, Psalters, Primers, Hornbooks, Account-books, Demi-royal and small Paper, Ink, Ink-powder, Dutch Quills, Wafers, New Version of Psalms, Watts's Psalms, Practice of Piety, Whole Duty of Man, Barclay's Apology, Beavan's Primitive Christianity, Vade mecum, New Help to Discourse, Pope's Miscellany Poems, Life Actions and End of Dr. Faustus, Aristotle's Works, Argalus and Parthenia, History of Fortunatus, with several other diverting and entertaining Histories." Saunders, *Poor Richard, 1734.*

43 Isaac Watts, *A Preservative from the Sins and Follies of Childhood and Youth, Written by Way of Question and Answer* [. . .] (Philadelphia: printed and sold by Benjamin Franklin in Market Street, 1744). Isaac Watts, *Divine Songs Attempted in Easy Language for the Use of Children*, 16th ed. (Philadelphia: printed and sold by Benjamin Franklin and David Hall at the New-Printing Office, 1760). By this time, Watts's works—which were both widely imported and prolifically printed in Boston—were also being published by Franklin's colleagues Hugh Gaine in New York; James Parker in Woodbridge, New Jersey; and Daniel Fowle in Portsmouth, New Hampshire. Phillips, "Cotton Mather Brings," 203.

44 According to Shy, "Blacks, who had done so much to solve the chronic labor shortage, caused a growing fear of bloody insurrection, especially after about 1740, when New York City and South Carolina had each felt the terror of slave uprisings. The Scotch-Irish, hardly indistinguishable from other English-speaking people today, were widely regarded in the eighteenth century as dirty, lazy, disorderly, and generally undesirable. And Germans, more orderly and diligent, were disliked for being non-English-speaking, remaining clannish, and practicing some of the more bizarre forms of Protestantism." Shy, *People Numerous and Armed*, 123. According to P. R. Silver, this rhetoric and identity would prove indispensable to the colonists as they fought wars not just against the Delaware and other Native peoples—the Conestogas, Tuscaroras, Tutelos, Nanticokes, Shawnees, and Senecas—but also, ironically, against the French and, finally, the British. The "crisis of Indian war," Silver concludes, "had tilted public life toward the celebration of a suffering people, creating a new politics that was harsh and ruthless, if recognizably democratic." See P. R. Silver, *Our Savage Neighbors: How Indian War Transformed Early America* (New York: W. W. Norton, 2008).

45 See "The Holy Club," in *John Wesley: A Plain Account of His Life and Work, by a Methodist Preacher* (New York: Eaton and Mains for the Methodist Book Concern, 1903), 68–82.

46 According to Ann Taves, "By 1700 there were more than forty of these 'little devotional cells' in London and the surrounding towns." See Ann Taves, *Fits, Trances, and Visions: Experiencing Religion and Explaining Experience from Wesley to James* (Princeton, NJ: Princeton University Press, 1999), 64. Among the most successful of these societies were the Society for the Propagation of Christian Knowledge and the Society for the Propagation of the Gospel (SPG). Founded by Thomas Bray, who had served in the 1690s as the Church of England's commissary in Maryland, these organizations were dedicated to strengthening the Anglican mission in North America—the SPCK by sending books and printed matter to the colonies and the SPG by sending Anglican ministers. See Jon Butler, *Awash in a Sea of Faith: Christianizing the American People* (Cambridge, MA: Harvard University Press, 1990), 104.

47 Peter Charles Hoffer, *When Benjamin Franklin Met the Reverend Whitefield: Enlightenment, Revival, and the Power of the Printed Word* (Baltimore: Johns Hopkins University Press, 2013), 10.

48 According to Richard Cullen Rath, preachers in North America began to "claim their own voices as God's thunder," taking to the emerging public squares of the colonies with animated speeches, orations, sermons, and pronouncements. As Rath has documented, these practices combined with practices of Native peoples and African slaves and their descendants—drumming, shouting, stomping, groaning, war crying, for instance—to create an entirely new American "soundscape." Richard Cullen Rath, *How Early America Sounded* (Ithaca, NY: Cornell University Press, 2003). This new sonic environment was one of profound mutual influence, even as the English were, characteristically, unaware of how their own behaviors were being changed and even as they routinely portrayed their own soundings as "civilized" while deeming those of others as "savage" or "backward." See David Cressy, *Bonfires and Bells: National Memory and the Protestant Calendar in Elizabethan and Stuart England* (Berkeley: University of California Press, 1989), 50.

49 See, for example, George Whitefield, *A Further Account of God's Dealings with the Reverend Mr. George Whitefield, from the Time of His Ordination to His Embarking for Georgia*

[. . .] (Boston: printed by Rogers & Fowle in Queen Street, next to the prison, 1746), 37–38.

50 Harry S. Stout, *The Divine Dramatist: George Whitefield and the Rise of Modern Evangelicalism* (Grand Rapids, MI: William B. Eerdmans, 1991), 85–95, 104.

51 "To the Rev. Mr. Whitefield," *Philadelphia Gazette*, December 27, 1739. Franklin returned to laud Whitefield at year-end 1740 with the publication of a poem, presumably of his own composition, "On Hearing George Whitefield at the New Building in Philadelphia," *Philadelphia Gazette*, December 18, 1740. Throughout his life, George Whitefield's legendary manner of performance was recognized for its dramatic and musical quality. As Stout has chronicled, Whitefield frequently acted out the many parts of biblical narratives in what amounted to one-man theater, a practice especially popular in America, where theatrical institutions had not yet been established. Stout calls it "biblical history in a theatrical key." Specifically, according to Stout, Whitefield inserted his body into his discourse: "Even though his sermons were written out in classic Anglican fashion, his body did not—could not—remain still in the prescribed fashion. From the start of his preaching, apparently without premeditation or guile, he evidenced a dramatic manner that remained a hallmark of his preaching style throughout his career." Franklin's admiration for Whitefield would only grow across the middle decades of the eighteenth century—despite that the two men were, as Stout has summed up, "on public record as opposing much of the philosophy the other stood for." Stout, *Divine Dramatist*, 222. Whitefield was also a masterful innovator of his sonic and visual environment, routinely incorporating elements from his surroundings into the drama of his sermonizing. According to Mark Noll, a Boston listener recounted one occasion on which Whitefield used "a passing thunderstorm to compare human life to a transitory cloud, the wrath of God to a lightning bolt, and his divine mercy to the sun emerging after rain." When asked afterward if he would make a text of his sermon available for printing, "Whitefield replied, 'I have no objection, if you will print the lightning, thunder and rainbow with it.'" Mark A. Noll, *America's God: From Jonathan Edwards to Abraham Lincoln* (New York: Oxford University Press, 2001), 105. Through his collaboration with Franklin and Franklin's associate David Hall, Whitefield's evangelistic operation in North America remained effectively headquartered in Philadelphia until his death in 1770. As Peter Charles Hoffer has chronicled, this partnership was based on much more than entrepreneurial opportunity—rather, it was rooted in a shared understanding that their "world could be knit together more closely by words." In Whitefield's view, the tightest weave was composed of words that could be both printed and spoken aloud or, perhaps even better, both printed and sung. And most powerful of all, in this regard, were words that could be printed and spoken and sung about the individual's spiritual journey and its ultimate destination, death. Hoffer, *Benjamin Franklin Met*, 11.

52 For generations, this fact inspired puzzlement—or avoidance—among historians who preferred to cast Franklin's life journey as a one-dimensional and unilinear unfolding of reasoned speculation. More recent research has shed light on the bond shared by Franklin and Whitefield. At its most elemental level, this bond was rooted in a simple shared conviction, as aptly summarized by Peter Charles Hoffer, that the "Atlantic world could be knit together more closely with words." Hoffer, *Benjamin Franklin Met*, 5. More specifically, this bond was rooted in a common Protestant vernacular that writers and publishers, preachers and hymnodists, used to construct bridges of common sentiment across cultural gaps in the colonial landscape.

53 As George McKenna has summarized, Franklin printed works by Whitefield—and some by those who opposed the controversial revivalist—in unprecedented numbers. These works proved popular throughout the North American colonies and "reached a mass readership through quantity discounts, prepayment incentives, serial publication, convenience packaging, and home delivery." McKenna, *Puritan Origins*, 59. For an excellent discussion, see James N. Green, "English Books and Printing in the Age of Franklin," in *History of the Book*, 259–65.

54 John Wesley, "On the Death of the Rev. Mr. George Whitefield," in *The Sermons*

of John Wesley (1872), available at the Wesley Center Online (Nampa, ID: Wesley Center at Northwest Nazarene University, 1999), https://tinyurl.com/neeueb7. Whitefield shared this concern and preoccupation with his intimate friend from Oxford, Charles Wesley, the prolific lyricist who published two complete collections titled *Funeral Hymns* (1746, 1759) and *Hymns on the Preparation for Death* (1772).

55 Stout, *Divine Dramatist*, 199.

56 See my *Mrs. Hunter's Happy Death* (New York: Doubleday, 2006).

57 Methodists and Quakers also shared with these other Pietists the view that true Christian faith required an openness to what they called "the religion of the heart." Also called "experimental religion" (the word *experimental* had much the same meaning in the eighteenth century as the word *experiential* does today), the hallmark of this way of thinking was that the *experience* of the faithful was decisive in giving shape to the Christian life. For this reason, they resisted rigid adherence to complex articulations of Christian doctrine.

58 Tolles, *Quakers*, 99.

59 Jonathan Warne, *The Spirit of the Martyrs Revived in the Doctrines of the Reverend Mr. George Whitefield, and the Judicious, and Faithful Methodists* [. . .] (London: printed and sold by Thomas Cooper, 1740).

60 First published in London in 1682, Hookes's martyrology was published in 1750 in North America (publisher unknown, presumed to be in New London, CT).

61 Warne, *Spirit of the Martyrs*, ii.

62 George Whitefield, *Some Remarks on a Pamphlet Entituled, the Enthusiasm of Methodists and Papists Compare'd* (Philadelphia: printed and sold by William Bradford in Second Street, 1749), 25, 34, 41, 42.

63 George Whitefield, "Ah! Lovely Appearance of Death," in *A Collection of Hymns for Social Worship* (Philadelphia: David Hall, 1768), 156. The hymn was often published under Charles Wesley's name, but Wesley attributed it to Whitefield himself in a handbill that went through several print runs on both sides of the Atlantic.

64 Cynthia Z. Stiverson and Gregory A. Stiverson, "The Colonial Retail Book Trade: Availability and Affordability of Reading Material in Mid-eighteenth-century Virginia,"

in *Printing and Society in Early America*, ed. William Leonard Joyce and American Antiquarian Society (Worcester, MA: American Antiquarian Society, 1983), 140. For a history of the *Virginia Gazette*, see "A History of the Virginia Gazette," *Daily Press*, August 19, 2002, https://tinyurl.com/yhcezr65.

65 Rhys Isaac, *The Transformation of Virginia, 1740–1790* (Chapel Hill: published for the Institute of Early American History and Culture, Williamsburg, VA, by University of North Carolina Press, 1982), 17.

66 Church of England, *The Book of Common Prayer and Administration of the Sacraments, and Other Rites and Ceremonies of the Church* [. . .] (Cambridge, 1701). These and all other quotes are from different editions of the 1662 version of the Book of Common Prayer, which succeeded revisions of 1549 and 1559 and was used for well over a century. The 1789 version, which finally succeeded it, was so similar that revisions can only be identified painstakingly. The Common Prayer also prescribed death-centered liturgies as rites of passage for individuals, walking the faithful through the life cycle in ways that encouraged them to prepare for their deaths by conforming themselves to the image of the crucified Christ. As infants, Anglicans were baptized "into the death and resurrection of Jesus Christ"; they married by taking vows to be faithful "'til death do us part," and they celebrated the sacrament of Holy Communion as a commemoration of Jesus's Last Supper, pledging, "And here we offer and present unto thee, O Lord, our selves, our souls, and bodies, to be a reasonable, holy, and lively sacrifice unto thee." When they gathered at the gravesides of their loved ones, they heard their priests utter these austere words, prescribed by the Common Prayer for the moment of burial: "Man that is born of a woman hath but a short time to live, and is full of misery. He cometh up, and is cut down, like a flower; he fleeth as it were a shadow, and never continueth in one stay. In the midst of life we are in death." When they read aloud—or, more probably, recited from memory—the twenty-third Psalm and came to the line that says, "Yea, though I walk through the valley of the shadow of death, I will fear no evil," they would not have understood themselves,

as modern people might be inclined to do, to be referring to a set-apart season of dying in this life. Rather, they would have understood that the entirety of human life on this earth was characterized by walking through this valley.

67 Jeremy Taylor, *The Rule and Exercises of Holy Living. In Which Are Described the Means and Instruments of Obtaining Every Vertue, and the Remedies against Every Vice* [. . .] (London: printed by Roger Norton for Richard Royston, 1650). Taylor had served as a chaplain in the Royal Army and as a personal chaplain to Charles. His devotion to the ideals of martyrdom found its first expression in the 1649 publication of his biography of Jesus, *The Great Exemplar of Sanctity and Holy Life according to the Christian Institution Described in the History of the Life and Death* [. . .], and would continue throughout his life, resulting in the posthumous publication of *Antiquitates Christianae, or, the History of the Life and Death of the Holy Jesus as Also the Lives Acts and Martyrdoms of His Apostles: In Two Parts.*

68 Taylor, *Rule and Exercises of Holy Living.* Jeremy Taylor, *The Rule and Exercises of Holy Dying. In Which Are Described the Means and Instruments of Preparing Ourselves and Others Respectively for a Blessed Death* (London: printed by Roger Norton for Richard Royston, 1651).

69 Taylor, *Rule and Exercises of Holy Living,* 59, 1, 87.

70 Evidence of their availability in North America is found in their regular listing in catalogs of books for sale.

71 In his 1975 classic *American Slavery, American Freedom,* Edmund Morgan chronicled the cataclysmic founding of the Virginia colony—how the first expedition, led by John White up the Roanoke River in the winter of 1585–86, "simply disappeared," never to be heard from again; how the March 1622 massacre of 347 men, women, and children by neighboring Algonquin Indians "released all restraints that the company had hitherto imposed on those who thirsted for the destruction and enslavement of Indians"; how the first generations of English to successfully settle in the Chesapeake suffered rates of mortality "comparable only to that of severe epidemic years in England." Even as average longevity began

to climb, overall rates of mortality remained extreme—as a common saying had it, "The swamps and Tuckahoe marshes breed into the air a something that makes both widows and widowers." Edmund S. Morgan, *American Slavery, American Freedom: The Ordeal of Colonial Virginia,* Norton pbk. ed. (1975; repr., New York: Norton, 2003), 17. Citations refer to the 2003 edition.

72 As John Shy has summarized, in practice, "Virginia relied on a buffer of friendly Indians, on several forts along the frontier, and . . . on a few dozen paid, mounted soldiers who 'ranged' between the forts—the first rangers of American history." Shy, *People Numerous and Armed,* 33.

73 As some historians have told the story, this cultural upheaval swept through Virginia in neat ecclesial waves—Presbyterians beginning in the 1730s, Baptists beginning in the 1760s, Methodists beginning in the decades following the American Revolution. But the turmoil roiling Virginia's Anglican parishes was not nearly so orderly. People who were resistant to, or distant from, the authority of the Church of England had been present from the colony's inception. Over time, Virginians dissatisfied with the established church began to organize themselves as local elders, or "presbyters," who considered themselves the rightful leaders of their local congregations. Some advocated formal "separation" from the Church of England, while others championed reform of it through practices described, variously, as "dissenting" or "nonconforming."

74 Both perceptions appear to have been grounded in fact. As James Blair, the commissary of Virginia's colonial church, reported to the bishop of London with alarm in 1727, "Nothing was such a great disservice to Religion as the leaving of so many Parishes destitute of ministers, and the Supplying of so many with indifferent ones, either as to their ministerial talents or the good life." The locals, Blair concluded, were "taking advantage of the want of Ministers" and "are very busy, fitting up meetings in many places where they had none heretofore." Robert Douthat Meade, *Patrick Henry: Patriot in the Making* (Philadelphia: Lippincott, 1957), 115.

75 Until 1744, the law of the Commonwealth allowed county courts to fine residents who absented themselves from Anglican services

of worship, but by the early decades of the eighteenth century, members of dissenting sects were almost uniformly exempted from the imposition of these fines. Instead, the fines were reserved for noncompliant members of the Anglican Church—people whose absence was perceived to be a direct affront to the properly established authorities of vestry and parish priest. Lieutenant Governor Sir William Gooch acknowledged this reality in his 1728 inaugural address, declaring, "If there are among you any dissenters from this Church with consciences truly scrupulous, I shall think an indulgence to them to be so consistent with the genius of the Christian Religion that it can never be inconsistent with the interest of the Church of England." Arthur Pierce Middleton, "Anglican Virginia: The Established Church of the Old Dominion 1607–1786," *Colonial Williamsburg Library Research Report Series* 0006 (1954): 150.

76 "Letters of Patrick Henry, Sr., Samuel Davies, James Maury, Edwin Conway and George Trask," *William and Mary Quarterly* 1, no. 4 (October 1921): 261–81, 265.

77 "Letters of Patrick Henry, Sr.," 264.

78 The colony's royal governors had outlawed printing of any kind up through the year 1690, and even after that date they retained the right to license—and, conversely, forbid—all manner of publication. Sir William Berkeley, the longest tenured of the colony's seventeenth-century governors, had expressed succinctly the prevailing suspicions: "I thank God, there are no free schools nor printing, and I hope we shall not have these hundred years; for learning has brought disobedience, and heresy, and sects into the world, and printing has divulged them, and libels against the best government. God keep us from both." Efforts to establish other newspapers in the years leading up to the Revolution were only sporadically successful. Years later Thomas Jefferson would recall, "We had but one press, and that having the whole business of the government, and no competitor for public favor, nothing disagreeable to the governor could be got into it. We procured Rind to come from Maryland to publish a free paper." George F. Willison, *Patrick Henry and His World*, 1st ed. (Garden City, NY: Doubleday, 1969), 26.

79 Edmund Gibson, *The Sacrament of the Lord's Supper Explain'd: Or the Things to Be Known and Done, to Make a Worthy Communicant* [. . .] (Williamsburg, VA: William Parks, 1740), 2–3.

80 William Sherlock, *A Practical Discourse concerning Death. By William Sherlock, D. D. Late Dean of St. Paul's* (Williamsburg, VA: William Parks, 1744), 58–59, 107, 109.

81 New England Historic Genealogical Society, *The New England Historical and Genealogical Register*, vols. 16–17 (Boston: Joel Munsell, 1862–63), 360, https://tinyurl .com/ycdjpjn9. Blair's son, of the same name, would later assist Davies at the College of New Jersey, now Princeton University, and become the second chaplain to the Continental Congress.

82 Henry Mayer, *A Son of Thunder: Patrick Henry and the American Republic* (New York: Franklin Watts, 1986); Harlow G. Unger, *Lion of Liberty: Patrick Henry and the Call to a New Nation* (Cambridge, MA: Da Capo, 2010), 37.

83 Samuel Davies, *A Sermon Preached before the Reverend Presbytery of New-Castle, October 11. 1752. By S. Davies, V. D. M. in Hanover, Virginia* [. . .] (Philadelphia: printed by Benjamin Franklin and David Hall, 1753), 27.

84 Thomas Gibbons, "Divine Conduct Vindicated, or the Operations of God Shown to Be the Operations of Wisdom," in *Sermons on Important Subjects, by the Late Reverend and Pious Samuel Davies, Sometime President of the College in New-Jersey* [. . .] (New York: Thomas Allen, 1792), xiv.

85 The quotations are from *Encyclopedia Virginia*, s.v. "Samuel Davies (1723–1761)," by W. B. Whitley and the *Dictionary of Virginia Biography*, November 4, 2014, https://tinyurl.com/y7oqht6b. The inscription in Davies's Bible is described by Thomas Talbot Ellis in "Samuel Davies: Apostle of Virginia," *Banner of Truth Magazine*, no. 235 (April 1983): 21–27.

86 John Caldwell, *An Impartial Trial of the Spirit Operating in This Part of the World; By Comparing the Nature, Effects, and Evidences* [. . .] (Williamsburg, VA: William Parks, 1747). Quotation is from the sermon as printed in Boston in 1742: John Caldwell, *An Impartial Trial of the Spirit Operating in This Part of the World; By*

Comparing the Nature, Effects and Evidences [. . .] (Glasgow: Boston printed, Glasgow reprinted, and sold by Robert Foulis and by the booksellers in Edinburgh, London, Dublin, and Belfast, 1742), 7, 11, https://digital.nls.uk/119115620.

87 Samuel Davies, *The Impartial Trial, Impartially Tried, and Convicted of Partiality: In Remarks on Mr. Caldwell's, Alias Thornton's Sermon* [. . .] (Williamsburg, VA: William Parks, 1748), cover page.

88 Albert J. Raboteau, *Slave Religion: The "Invisible Institution" in the Antebellum South* (New York: Oxford University Press, 1978), 130.

89 As John Marrant—who would go on to become one of the first Black itinerant preachers in North America—remembered his response to hearing George Whitefield's call to conversion, "The Lord accompanied the word with such power, that I was struck to the ground, and lay both speechless and senseless for near half an hour." Mark A. Noll, *In the Beginning Was the Word: The Bible in American Public Life, 1492–1783* (Oxford: Oxford University Press, 2016), 223. In her 1987 *The World They Made Together*, Mechal Sobel chronicled "a long period of intensive racial interaction" in colonial Virginia, during which "blacks and whites lived together in great intimacy, affecting each other in both small and large ways." Perhaps generalizing a bit too much, Sobel observed that "whites and blacks witnessed together, shouted together, and shared ecstatic experiences at 'dry' and wet christenings, meetings, and burials. . . . They had an experience with the spirit, often marked by tears, moans and fainting." Sobel's lament about the portrayal of Africans and African Americans in earlier scholarship—"blacks are not generally treated as actors nor is their 'divergent culture' seen as having a wide-ranging effect on whites," she wrote—was ahead of the curve, foreshadowing today's scholarly consensus that the environment of the early modern Atlantic was characterized thoroughgoingly by multiracial and cross-cultural encounter. Over time, Sobel argues, English-speaking Virginians came to embrace a more optimistic vision of the afterlife characteristic of African traditions, blending it with more traditional English conceptions of a heavenly realm populated with angelic beings. Mechal Sobel, *The World They Made Together: Black and White Values in Eighteenth-Century Virginia* (Princeton, NJ: Princeton University Press, 1987), 2–3, 174, 180, 183.

90 As Douglas Egerton has described, "West African societies encouraged young men to act out a haughty disdain for physical pain or death. Learning to endure ritual scarification without crying out was an important step in puberty rites meant to direct boy's social integration." Little wonder, Egerton observes, that frequently in colonial Virginia, "the mere hanging of black 'martyrs' not only failed to deter further resistance to enslavement, such displays actually emboldened some witnesses." Douglas R. Egerton, "A Peculiar Mark of Infamy: Dismemberment, Burial and Rebelliousness in Slave Societies," in *Mortal Remains: Death in Early America*, ed. Nancy Isenberg and Andrew Burstein (Philadelphia: University of Pennsylvania Press, 2002), loc. 2956 of 5609, Kindle. See also Douglas R. Egerton, *Death or Liberty: African Americans and Revolutionary America* (Oxford: Oxford University Press, 2009).

91 Raboteau, *Slave Religion*, 130.

92 Samuel Davies, *The Duty of Christians to Propagate Their Religion among Heathens: Earnestly Recommended to the Masters of Negroe Slaves in Virginia* [. . .] (London: printed by John Oliver in Bartholomew Close, 1758), 9.

93 Davies, 8.

94 Davies, 25.

95 On New Year's Day 1761, Davies preached yet another sermon on this theme, this one based on words spoken by the prophet Hananiah in the biblical book of Jeremiah: "Therefore thus saith the Lord; Behold, I will cast thee from off the face of the earth: this year thou shalt die, because thou hast taught rebellion against the Lord" (Jer 28:16). Davies used the verse as a springboard to a litany of admonition:

> *This year you may die, for your*
>   *life is the greatest uncertainty*
>   *in the world.* . . .
> *This year you may die, for thousands*
>   *of others will die.* . . .
> *This year you may die, though you are*
>   *now in health and vigour.* . . .

*This year you may die, though
you are full of business. . . .
This year you may die, though you have
not yet finished your education. . . .
This year you may die, though you
are not prepared for it. . . .
This year you may die, though
you deliberately delay
your preparation. . . .
This year you may die, though
you are unwilling to admit
the thought of it. . . .
This year you may die, though you may
strongly hope the contrary. . . .
Therefore let each of us (for we know
not on whom the lot may fall)
realize this possibility, this alarming
probability, "This year I may die."*

Davies professed that "it would be easy to enumerate several happy consequences of death with regard to those who have spent their life in preparation for it; and the nearness of death, instead of striking them with terror, may heighten the transport of expectation." Instead, though, he determined to address principally those "who are as near to hell as they are to death, and consequently stand in need of the most powerful and immediate applications, lest they be undone for ever beyond recovery." After "alarming" these listeners with detailed descriptions of what awaits them should they die in their current spiritual condition, Davies counseled them to "now begin to think seriously upon your condition, to break off from your sins, and attend in good earnest upon the means appointed for your salvation." Samuel Davies, trained in the school of life to expect death at any turn, was very clear as to what conclusion any serious consideration ought to bring serious men: "Therefore conclude, everyone for himself, 'It is of little importance to me whether I die this year, or not. But the only important point is, that I make a good use of my future time, whether it be longer or shorter.' This, my brethren, is the only way to secure a happy new year—a year of time, that will lead the way to a holy and happy eternity!" Samuel Davies, "Sermon XXIV. A Sermon on the New Year," in *Sermons on the Most Useful and Important Subjects, Adapted to the Family and Closet* (London: Buckland and Payne, 1764), 379–401.

Chapter 3

1   Bernard Bailyn, *The Ideological Origins of the American Revolution* (Cambridge, MA: Harvard University Press, 1967), v–x, 54.

2   Sarah Knott, *Sensibility and the American Revolution* (Chapel Hill: University of North Carolina Press, 2009); Nicole Eustace, *Passion Is the Gale: Emotion, Power, and the Coming of the American Revolution* (Chapel Hill: University of North Carolina Press, 2008); Catherine L. Albanese, *A Republic of Mind and Spirit* (New Haven, CT: Yale University Press, 2007).

3   As chronicled by Parkinson, the phrase *common cause* had deep roots, stretching back generations, as "a vague call to Protestants to join forces against their religious foes, whether Catholic or Muslims" and would become "hegemonic" in the period of the American Revolution. Robert G. Parkinson, *The Common Cause: Creating Race and Nation in the American Revolution* (Chapel Hill: University of North Carolina Press, 2016), loc. 345 of 17188, Kindle.

4   Thanks to Peter Mancall for helping me understand the extent of this. Peter Mancall, History 566, University of Southern California, fall 2014. As the historian John Shy has chronicled, this experience of war and violence shaped the very character of life in the British colonies at its most elemental level by the simple fact that "almost all white men had guns." By the middle decades of the eighteenth century, the English in North America had become, in Shy's encapsulation, "a people numerous and armed." Shy, *People Numerous and Armed*, 123. See also Sarah J. Purcell, *Sealed with Blood: War, Sacrifice, and Memory in Revolutionary America* (Philadelphia: University of Pennsylvania Press, 2002); and James Byrd, *Sacred Scripture, Sacred War* (Oxford: Oxford University Press, 2013).

5   David Copeland in Carol Sue Humphrey, *The American Revolution and the Press: The Promise of Independence* (Evanston, IL: Medill

School of Journalism / Northwestern University Press, 2013), xi.

6 As Carol Sue Humphrey has documented, the typical printer's capacity more than tripled between the 1730s and the mid-1760s—from fewer than 500 to more than 1,500 pages per week—and by the end of this period, "there was at least one printing establishment in each of the thirteen mainland colonies and the number of newspapers had grown from eleven in 1736 to twenty-three." Humphrey, *American Revolution*, 33.

7 Benjamin Franklin was instrumental in this expansion. As James N. Green has chronicled, Franklin provided the press and type to new colonial printers across several colonies and assumed "a share of the expenses and risks in return for one-third share of the income." In this manner, according to Green, Franklin "transformed a brood of potential rivals into a sophisticated intercolonial communications network, with himself at the center." Green, "English Books and Printing," 270–71.

8 Robert Parkinson has carefully chronicled how the printers of colonial newspapers came to collaborate in ways "akin to modern newswires": "through the common practice of 'exchanges'—the clipping of pieces from other papers to insert into your own." In this way, "colonists across colony and region learned much of the same information and read many of the same stories." Parkinson, *Common Cause*, loc. 490 of 17188.

9 See Humphrey, *American Revolution*, 35. For examples from which these quotations were taken, see "Virginia Centinel, No. 1," *Boston Evening-Post*, June 28, 1756; "From the Virginia Gazette, August 20. The Virginia Centinel, No. IX," *Pennsylvania Gazette*, September 16, 1756; and "The Virginia-Centinel, No. X," *New-York Mercury*, October 25, 1756.

10 In 1943 Sidney Kobre famously described this new identity as "a consciousness of kind, an emotional, intellectual and economic sympathy for distant colonies." Sidney Kobre, "The Revolutionary Colonial Press—a Social Interpretation," *Journalism Quarterly* 20 (September 1943): 193–204, cited in Wroth, *Colonial Printer*, 20. A quarter century later, Bernard Bailyn's monumental study *Ideological Origins* showed how the production and distribution of pamphlets in the pre-Revolutionary period produced "a peculiar configuration of ideas" akin to "an intellectual switchboard wired so that certain combinations of events would activate a distinct set of signals." Bailyn, *Ideological Origins*, 22.

11 "From the Virginia Gazette," 1.

12 Robert Eastburn, *A Faithful Narrative, of the Many Dangers and Sufferings, as Well as Wonderful and Surprizing Deliverances of Robert Eastburn* [. . .] (Philadelphia: printed by William Dunlap, 1758; Boston: repr. and sold by Green & Russell, opposite the probate office in Queen Street, 1758), 10. See also William and Elizabeth Fleming's *Narrative of the Sufferings and Surprising Deliverances of William and Elizabeth Fleming*; Thomas Brown's *A Plain Narrative of the Uncommon Sufferings, and Remarkable Deliverance of Thomas Brown*; and Isaac Hollister's *A Brief Narration of the Captivity of Isaac Hollister*.

13 Smith, *Account of the Remarkable*, 285.

14 From my phone conversation with Colin Calloway, May 2017. For more, see Colin G. Calloway, *One Vast Winter Count* (Lincoln: University of Nebraska Press, 2003).

15 The description of the torture is as follows:

> They first broiled his Feet between two red-hot Stones, then they put his Fingers into red hot Pipes, and tho' he had his Arms at Liberty, he would not pull his Fingers out; They cut his Joints, and taking hold of the Sinews, twisted them round small Bars of iron. All this while he kept singing and recounting his own brave Actions against the French. At last they flead his Scalp from his Scull, and poured scalding hot Sand upon it; at which Time the Intendant's Lady obtained Leave to have the *Coup de Grace* given, which put an End to the unspeakable Miseries of the heroic Sufferer, and to the farther cruelties of his inhuman Tormentors.

"From the Gentlemen's Magazine for May, 1756," *Pennsylvania Gazette*, August 19, 1756, 1.

16 Samuel Finley, *The Power of Gospel Ministers, and the Efficacy of Their Ministrations, Represented in a Sermon, Preached at New-Ark* [. . .] (New York: Hugh Gaine, 1755), 4.

17 Jonathan Ellis, *The Justice of the Present War against the French in America, and the Principles That Should Influence Us in This Undertaking, Asserted* [. . .] (Newport, RI: James Franklin, 1755); John Lowell, *The Advantages of God's Presence with His People in an Expedition against Their Enemies. A Sermon Preached at Newbury, May 22. 1755* [. . .] (Boston: John Draper, 1755); Isaac Morrill, *The Soldier Exhorted to Courage in the Service of His King and Country, from a Sense of God and Religion: In a Sermon Preach'd at Wilmington* [. . .] (Boston: John Draper, 1755); Isaac Stiles, *The Character and Duty of Soldiers Illustrated, in a Sermon Preached May 25. 1755, in the Rev. Mr. Noyes's Meeting-House in New-Haven* [. . .] (New Haven, CT: James Parker, 1755); Philip Reading, *The Protestant's Danger, and the Protestant's Duty. A Sermon on Occasion of the Present Encroachments of the French. Preached at Christ-Church* [. . .] (Philadelphia: Benjamin Franklin and David Hall, 1755); Theodorus Frelinghuysen, *Wars and Rumors of Wars, Heaven's Decree over the World. A Sermon, Preached in the Camp of the New-England Forces* [. . .] (New York: Hugh Gaine, 1755).

18 Patricia Bonomi's characterization is apt, if not precise: "Presbyterianism did not secure a firm base in Virginia until the outbreak of the French and Indian War, when the interests of Presbyterians—settled in greatest numbers in the exposed western section—and those of the royal government converged." Patricia U. Bonomi, *Under the Cope of Heaven: Religion, Society, and Politics in Colonial America*, updated ed. (New York: Oxford University Press, 2003), 183.

19 McKenna, *Puritan Origins*, 68.

20 Samuel Davies, *Religion and Patriotism the Constituents of a Good Soldier. A Sermon Preached to Captain Overton's Independent Company of Volunteers* [. . .] (Philadelphia: printed by James Chattin, 1755), 3.

21 Davies, 4.

22 Davies, 5.

23 Samuel Davies, *The Curse of Cowardice. A Sermon Preached to the Militia of Hanover County, in Virginia, at a General Muster, May 8, 1758* [. . .] (London, 1758; Boston: repr. and sold by Zechariah Fowle and Samuel Draper, opposite the Lion & Bell, in Marlborough Street, 1759), 3, 4, 16–17, 26–27.

24 Davies; Samuel Davies, *Curse of Cowardice* [. . .] (London, 1758; Woodbridge, NJ: repr. and sold by James Parker in Woodbridge, 1759; New York: repr. and sold by Samuel Parker at the New-Printing Office in Beaver Street, 1759).

25 George Whitefield, *A Short Address to Persons of All Denominations, Occasioned by the Alarm of an Intended Invasion. By George Whitefield* [. . .] (London: 1756; New York: repr. and sold by Hugh Gaine at the Bible & Crown in Queen Street, 1756, 2nd ed.; Philadelphia: repr. and sold by Benjamin Franklin and David Hall at the new-printing office in Market Street, 1756, 3rd ed.; Boston: repr. and sold by Green & Russell at their printing office near the Custom House and next to the Writing School in Queen Street, 1756, 4th ed.; Boston: repr. and sold by Edes and Gill, next to the prison in Queen Street, 1756, 5th ed.; Boston: repr. and sold by Daniel Fowle in Ann Street and Zechariah Fowle in Middle Street, 1756, 6th ed.).

26 James Byrd has characterized these sermons as demonstrating a "developing alignment between Protestantism and republicanism" and describes these preachers as having increasingly "envisioned the Protestant struggle against Catholicism as parallel to Britain's struggle for freedom against French tyranny." The notion that republican ideology was the best protector of human liberties was indeed ascendant, but this should not be construed as a novel mixing of "religion" and "politics." Civil and religious liberties had never been unlinked in the English imagination to this point, and the Protestant battle against the tyrannies of French Catholicism stretched back generations. Byrd, *Sacred Scripture*, 22. George McKenna has more neatly described this potent admixture as composed of centuries-old "anti-Catholicism," pan-Protestant celebrations of religious "liberty," and new conceptions of "republican freedom." This admixture lit a fire in the period of the French and Indian War that in the war's aftermath, McKenna observes, would fuel "an apocalyptic rage against British policies." McKenna, *Puritan Origins*, 69.

27 That pan-Protestant ties were instrumental to English colonists in their eighteenth-century wars with the French and the

Indians is well established, and so too that Protestant preachers like Samuel Davies and George Whitefield proved indispensable in their forging. Building on the earlier work of Alan Heimert and others, George McKenna has aptly summarized that the French and Indian War combined with these preachers' practices of itineracy and revivalism to accelerate the further "breakdown of local, particular allegiances and social structures, a turning away from inherited hierarchies, classes, and patterns of deference,"

and the emergence of a new "emphasis on the spiritual brotherhood of all Americans." McKenna, *Puritan Origins*, 51. As Mark Noll has put it, the "public biblical religion in the Revolutionary era descended directly from public religion during the French and Indian War." Noll, *In the Beginning*, 292.

28 Richard Saunders [Benjamin Franklin], *Poor Richard Improved: Being an Almanack* [. . .] *for the Year of Our Lord 1764* (Philadelphia: Benjamin Franklin and David Hall, 1764).

Chapter 4

1 For a good summary, see Woody Holton, *Forced Founders* (Chapel Hill: University of North Carolina Press, 1999), 7–8. Holton has summarized how leaders of both the English Crown and Parliament came to think of the colonists in North America in the aftermath of the war: "Here were two million British subjects that—at a time when English, Welsh, and Scottish taxpayers reeled under a load of taxes and often resisted them—did not pay a penny in direct taxes." Holton, 52.

2 As Henry Mayer, the biographer of Patrick Henry the younger, tells the story, there were "immediate domestic consequences" to Sarah Henry's personal awakening—she "withdrew much of her participation in genteel social life [and] set herself against the drinking, gambling, and dancing that comprised her husband's chief diversions and the stuff of gentry political life." Mayer, *Son of Thunder*, 139.

3 Mayer, 139.

4 William Wirt, *Sketches of the Life and Character of Patrick Henry* (Philadelphia: James Webster, 1817), 13. Davies, in a 1750 letter to the bishop of London, explained, "The extremes of my congregation lie eighty or ninety miles apart, and the dissenters under my care are scattered through six or seven different counties." Bonomi, *Under the Cope*, 182.

5 Like other Anglican clergy, Maury had been paid his 1759 salary in notes for tobacco, a long-standing practice in Virginia, where the warehouse notes for standardized bales of tobacco were routinely substituted for currency. In response to a poor harvest in

1758, however, free market tobacco prices had inflated dramatically to almost sixpence per pound, several times what most Virginians were accustomed to thinking of as the going rate. In response, Virginia's colonial assembly had endorsed a "Two Penny Act," fixing the value of the tobacco notes for 1759 at the prior year's price of "twopence per pound." As a result, the 1759 salaries of Anglican clerics like Maury were reduced to approximately one-third their projected value. As far as Virginia's clergy were concerned, the action of the assembly was manifestly unfair. The payment of clergy salaries in tobacco had been an established custom for generations, and everyone knew how the system worked—as Henry's biographer Moses Coit Tyler summarized, "When the price of tobacco was down, the parson was expected to suffer the loss; when the price of tobacco was up, he was allowed to enjoy the gain." Banding together, the clergy appealed to the bishop of London, their ecclesiastical superior, who requested that King George repeal the Two Penny Act. Desiring to support the bishop and reinforce the standing of the Anglican clergy in the colonies, the king did exactly that, setting the stage for each Virginia priest to sue for back pay. The suits were to be heard in Virginia's county courts. The first two cases ended with ambiguous outcomes: in one, the jury had awarded damages, but the court's justices had refused to order the damages paid; in another, the justices had given the whole matter to the jury, who simply threw out the case. Moses Coit Tyler, *Patrick Henry* (Ithaca, NY: Cornell University Press, 1887), 34–40.

6 According to Mayer, Lyons calculated aloud the difference between what the reverend had been paid under the Two Penny Act and what he could have rightly recouped from the sale of his tobacco notes at the prevailing market rates of 1759. He asked the jury to award Rev. Maury the amount of this difference in back pay and promptly took his seat. Mayer, *Son of Thunder*, 65–67.

7 The quotations from Maury's letter are found in Tyler, *Patrick Henry*, 47–48.

8 Patrick Henry, "Virginia Resolves on the Stamp Act (1765)," Encyclopedia Virginia, December 7, 2020, https://tinyurl.com/24kx4cd4.

9 Edmund S. Morgan and Helen Morgan, *The Stamp Act Crisis*, 2nd ed. (Chapel Hill: University of North Carolina Press, 1962), 88–91. As Edmund Morgan and Helen Morgan summarized, "What Henry said and what the Burgesses did are clear in legend but cloudy in history. The first newspaper to report what happened was some five hundred miles away. The first attempt to reconstruct the event was twenty-five years and a revolution later, and the second attempt was forty to fifty years later and only succeeded in giving form to a legend. . . . Thirty-nine Burgesses were present in the Chamber, and several spectators were watching in the lobby, but so far as we know today only one, a visiting stranger, wrote down any part of what he heard and saw." According to Morgan and Morgan, a Frenchman's account (the only contemporaneous account) suggests that when Henry was accused of having spoken treason, he asked pardon for his comments and professed himself ready to "shew his loyalty to his majesty King G. the third, at the Expence of the last Drop of his blood, but what he has said must be attributed to the Interest of his Country's Dying liberty which he had at heart, and the heat of passion might have lead him to have said something more than he intended, but, again, if he said anything wrong, he begged the speaker and houses pardon. Some other members stood up and backed him, on which that afaire was dropped."

10 Benson Bobrick, *Angel in the Whirlwind: The Triumph of the American Revolution* (New York: Simon & Schuster, 1997), 73.

11 Humphrey, *American Revolution*, 43.

12 Wirt, *Patrick Henry*, 24–25. Emphasizing Henry's predilection for the backcountry and his lack of the William and Mary education afforded to so many of Virginia's elite, Wirt embraced the English poet Lord Henry's description of Henry as "a forest-born Demosthenes." "He was styled 'the orator of nature,'" Wirt wrote, "and was, on that account, much more revered by the people than if he had been formed by the severest discipline of the schools; for they considered him as bringing his credentials directly from heaven, and owning no part of his greatness to human institutions." Wirt, 28.

13 Taves, *Fits, Trances, and Visions*, 72–75.

14 Typical is the conclusion of Eva C. Hartless, who, in her 1977 biography of Patrick Henry's mother, Sarah, wrote, "From Davies, young Patrick grasped the force and devastating effect of well-directed forensics. The skills of speaking—measured enunciation, carefully structured thinking, the harmony of words, the rhythm of language, the subtle persuasion of spontaneous gesticulation—all were evidenced in Davies's sermons. Patrick looked upon him as the greatest orator he ever heard." Eva C. Hartless, *Sarah Winston Syme Henry, Mother of Patrick Henry* (Boston: Branden Press, 1977), 10.

15 Robert Douthat Meade, *Patrick Henry: Practical Revolutionary* (Philadelphia: Lippincott, 1969), 6.

16 Statistics and quotes from J. L. Bell, "From Saucy Boys to Sons of Liberty: Politicizing Youth in Pre-Revolutionary Boston," in *Children and Youth in America: Children in Colonial America*, ed. James Marten (New York: NYU Press, 2006), 204.

17 Russell Bourne, *Cradle of Violence: How Boston's Waterfront Mobs Ignited the American Revolution* (Hoboken, NJ: Wiley & Sons, 2006), 46.

18 Eric Hinderaker, *Boston's Massacre* (Cambridge, MA: Harvard University Press, 2017), 47, 61.

19 According to Samuel Adams's biographer John C. Miller, Deacon Adams was "among the first of Boston's 'martyrs' to be deprived of office by the royal governor." John C. Miller, *John Adams: Pioneer in Propaganda* (Boston: Little, Brown, 1936), 11.

20 Mark Puls, *Samuel Adams: Father of the Revolution* (New York: St. Martin's, 2006), 32.

21 As Bernard Bailyn summarized in his landmark 1968 *Ideological Origins*, "In pamphlet after pamphlet, the Americans cited Locke on natural rights and on the social and governmental contract . . . [often] in the most offhand way." Bailyn, *Ideological Origins*, 27–28.

22 Miller, *John Adams*, 16.

23 Miller concludes, "The *Independent Advertiser* contains the germ of the ideas for which Adams was to fight for the greater part of his life, ideas which were later to form the political testament of the Whig Party in the American Revolution." Miller, *John Adams*, 17.

24 Quotations are from John Locke, *Two Treatises of Government*, in *The Works of John Locke. A New Edition, Corrected. In Ten Volumes* (London: printed for Thomas Tegg, W. Sharpe and Son, G. Offor, G. and J. Robinson, and J. Evans; Glasgow: R. Griffin; and Dublin: J. Gumming, 1823), 5:107, 163, 159, 193.

25 Samuel Adams, "Instructions of the Town of Boston to Its Representatives in the General Court, May 1764," in *The Writings of Samuel Adams*, ed. Harry Alonzo Cushing, vol. 1, *1764–1769* (New York: G. P. Putnam's Sons, 1904), 5.

26 Samuel Adams, John Ruddock, and John Hancock, "To the Inhabitants of the Town of Plymouth, March 24, 1766," in *Writings of Samuel Adams*, 72.

27 "Article Submitted to Edes & Gill, Editors, Boston Gazette, October 17, 1768," in *Writings of Samuel Adams*, 251.

28 "Article Signed Vindex to Boston Gazette, December 5, 1768," in *Writings of Samuel Adams*, 258.

29 McKenna, *Puritan Origins*, 70.

30 David Copeland in Humphrey, *American Revolution*, xii.

31 "Article Signed Alfred to Boston Gazette, October 2, 1769," in *Writings of Samuel Adams*, 362–63.

32 Jane E. Calvert, *Quaker Constitutionalism and the Political Thought of John Dickinson* (Cambridge: Cambridge University Press, 2009), 38.

33 Calvert, 67.

34 John Dickinson, *Letters from a Farmer in Pennsylvania* (Philadelphia: Hall and Sellers, 1768).

35 Humphrey, *American Revolution*, 53–55.

36 "Liberty Song," *Connecticut Journal* and *New-Haven Post-Boy*, August 12, 1768, 2; "Liberty Song," *Virginia Gazette*, December 8, 1768, 1. For an example of the broadside advertised, see "Advertisement," *Boston Chronicle*, December 12–19, 1768.

37 John Dickinson, *A New Song: To the Tune of Hearts of Oak* (Philadelphia: printed by David Hall and William Sellers, 1768).

38 For an early and brief mention of the importance of Revolutionary song, see Arthur M. Schlesinger, "A Note on Songs as Patriot Propaganda 1765–1776," *William and Mary Quarterly* 11, no. 1 (1954): 78–88. Schlesinger's brief note is not informed by recent developments in musicological scholarship.

39 Carolyn Rabson and Nancy V. A. Hansen, *Songbook of the American Revolution* (Peaks Island, ME: NEO, 1974), 1.

40 As John Knapp has summarized, "The genre in this period was never confined to churches and meeting houses, to uniform tetrameter stanzas, to biblical paraphrases or scripture-anchored meditation, or to the eyes and voices of worshiping British Christians. Quite to the contrary, it was a dynamic, shape-shifting, aspirant genre, often prized for its novelty, that could be found as well in streets, studies, and coffeehouses." Knapp, "Isaac Watts's Unfixed," 465.

41 Rabson and Hansen, *Songbook*, 9.

42 "The Parody Paradized," *Boston Evening-Post*, October 3, 1768, 3.

43 Historians of the Revolutionary period have long understood—and continue to expand their understanding of—both the diverse sources of American discontent and the ways in which these sources galvanized around common themes. Among these themes was the ancient Protestant suspicion, as Mark Noll has articulated, that the concentrations of authority, whether civil or ecclesial, were invitations to the abuse of power and inherent threats to "the potential for virtue in a society." Mark Noll, "Episode 073 Mark Noll, the Bible in Early America," interview by Liz Covart, *Ben Franklin's World*, March 15, 2016, https://tinyurl.com/y9fx43cd.

44 Samuel Johnson, *Taxation No Tyranny*, in *The Works of Samuel Johnson* (Troy, NY: Pafraets, 1903), 14:93–144, https://www.samueljohnson.com/tnt.html.

45 Watts, *Horae Lyricae. Poems Chiefly*, 79–80.

Chapter 5

1 *Boston-Gazette, and Country Journal*, February 26, 1770.

2 *Boston-Gazette, and Country Journal*, March 5, 1770.

3 *Boston-Gazette, and Country Journal*, February 26, March 5, March 12, and March 19, 1770.

4 Hinderaker's recent and excellent analysis of the Boston Massacre, for instance, considers the "story as a series of narratives that unfolded in real time rather than as a disconnected body of individual recollections." Chronicling how Bostonians "shaped the narrative of events to bolster long-standing complaints" about English colonial policy, especially about the quartering of British troops in the city, Hinderaker argues, "Its malleability is its most striking feature." Hinderaker, *Boston's Massacre*, 9, 159.

5 "Boston Massacre Engraving by Paul Revere," Paul Revere Heritage Project, accessed March 1, 2019, https://tinyurl.com/y8epo5hr. The inspiration of Pelham's title cannot be known for certain, but a likely candidate would be a 1763 sermon by the Reverend Thomas Barnard delivered to the members of the Massachusetts Bay Colony Council in 1763 and then printed by Richard Draper: "The Tyrant's Nod, the Caprice of his Minions and Parasites, have disposed of Liberty, Property, Life, in spite of the most venerable Rights, descended from distant Ages; the Voice of Reason; the Maxims of Equity and Claims of Conscience. . . . O that for the human Species, the horrible Fruits of arbitrary Power were Matter of Theory only, or the painting of a lively Imagination." Thomas Barnard, *A Sermon Preached before His Excellency Francis Bernard, Esq; Governor and Commander in Chief, the Honourable His Majesty's Council* [. . .] (Boston: Richard Draper, 1763).

6 Hinderaker, *Boston's Massacre*, 228. Pelham had placed beneath his original image his own rendering of lines from the ninety-fourth Psalm: "How long shall they utter and speak hard things and all the workers of iniquity boast themselves. They break in pieces thy people, O Lord and afflict thine heritage. They slay the widow and the stranger, and murder the fatherless. Yet they say the Lord shall not see, neither shall the God of Jacob regard it.—Ps. XCIV." Hinderaker, 228. But perhaps Revere consulted the entirety of Psalm 94 as he copied Pelham's image. While it opens in tones of lament, the psalm concludes with the same sentiment Revere struck in his composition:

> *Shall the throne of iniquity have*
> *fellowship with thee, which*
> *frameth mischief by a law?*
> *They gather themselves together*
> *against the soul of the righteous,*
> *and condemn the innocent blood.*
> *But the Lord is my defence; and my*
> *God is the rock of my refuge.*
> *And he shall bring upon them their*
> *own iniquity, and shall cut them*
> *off in their own wickedness;*
> *yea, the Lord our God shall*
> *cut them off. (Psalm 94)*

7 According to the Paul Revere Heritage Project, "Pelham publicly accused P. R. in Boston Gazette of copying his drawing without permission. In Revere's defence we could note that copying somebody's work at that time was not considered a crime and the feud was probably more about the silversmith not sharing the proceeds from selling the print with Pelham." "Boston Massacre Engraving."

8 For a biography of Pelham, see John William Wilkes, *A Whig in Power: The Political Career of Henry Pelham* (Evanston, IL: Northwestern University Press, 1964).

9 For a recent biography of Revere, from which some details in this opening vignette are drawn, see Joel J. Miller, *The Revolutionary Paul Revere* (Nashville: Thomas Nelson, 2010). For a concise summary of the Revere/Pelham controversy, see "The Bloody Massacre," Boston Athenæum, accessed March 1, 2019, https://tinyurl.com/oto7dlr. For more on Revere's engraving, see "Boston Massacre Engraving."

10 Isaiah Thomas, *A Monumental Inscription on the Fifth of March. Together with a Few Lines on the Enlargement of Ebenezer Richardson, Convicted of Murder* (Boston: printed by Isaiah Thomas, 1772), https://tinyurl.com/sz82nhtm.

11 Thomas.

12 See, for instance, *The New-England Primer Enlarged* (Boston: Samuel Kneeland, 1727).

13 See, for instance, *The New-England Primer Enlarged* (Boston: printed and sold by Samuel Kneeland and Timothy Green, 1752).

14 The quotations are from *The New-England Primre [sic] Improved. For the More Easy Attaining the True Reading of English. To Which Is Added, the Assembly of Divines Catechism* (Boston: Samuel Kneeland, 1727).

15 Wright, *Revolutionary Generation*, 14–18.

16 As Gordon Wood has summarized, referencing the work of Josiah Quincy II, a graduate of Harvard in the class of 1763, the "mandates of covenantal theology" were seen not as contradictory but rather as complementary to "knowledge about society reached through the use of history and reason. It seemed indeed to be a peculiar moment in history when all knowledge coincided, when classical antiquity, Christian theology, English empiricism, and European rationalism could all be linked. Thus Quincy, like other Americans, could without any sense of incongruity cite Rousseau, Plutarch, Blackstone, and a seventeenth-century Puritan all on the same page." Gordon Wood, *The Creation of the American Republic* (Chapel Hill: University of North Carolina Press, 1969), 7.

17 James Lovell, *An Oration Delivered April 2nd, 1771. At the Request of the Inhabitants of the Town of Boston; To Commemorate the Bloody Tragedy* [. . .] (Boston: Edes and Gill, 1771), 7–9; Joseph Warren, *An Oration Delivered March 5th, 1772. At the Request of the Inhabitants of the Town of Boston; To Commemorate the Bloody Tragedy* [. . .] (Boston: Edes and Gill, 1772), 12; Benjamin Church, *An Oration, Delivered March Fifth, 1773. At the Request of the Inhabitants of the Town of Boston; To Commemorate the Bloody Tragedy* [. . .] (Boston: printed and sold at the New Printing-Office, 1773), 29.

18 See note 10 on page 215.

19 Church, *Oration, Delivered March Fifth*, 29.

20 Hancock, *An Oration Delivered March 5, 1774, at the Request of the Inhabitants of the Town of Boston; To Commemorate the Bloody Tragedy* [. . .] (Boston: printed by Edes and Gill in Queen Street, 1774; Newport, RI: repr. and sold by S. Southwick in Queen Street, 1774; New Haven, CT: repr. by Thomas and Samuel Green, 1774; Philadelphia: printed by J. Douglass .M'Dougall in Chestnut Street, 1775).

21 Hancock, 6–7, 9–12, 19–20.

22 Hancock, 20.

23 Joseph Warren, *An Oration Delivered March the 6th, 1775. At the Request of the Inhabitants of the Town of Boston; To Commemorate the Bloody Tragedy* [. . .] (New York: printed by John Anderson at Beekman's Slip, 1775), 3.

24 Warren, 12–13.

25 Warren, 15–16.

26 Ethan S. Rafuse, "Warren, Joseph (1741–1775), Physician and Patriot Leader," *American National Biography*, February 2000, https://tinyurl.com/yarukg6b.

27 As the historian A. J. Bell has observed, these youth were not motivated by abstract questions of rights, nor even did they need to feel the sting of taxation that fell disproportionately on property-holding Bostonians. "Their most basic motivation seems to have been simple affiliation: being on the right side. . . . [They] didn't need to understand tax policy and parliamentary factions; they simply showed the flag." Bell, "Saucy Boys to Sons," 209.

28 Over time, as Eric Hinderaker has ably documented, the place of highest privilege in the memory of the massacre was transferred to one of the five victims: Crispus Attucks, a young man of African and Wampanoag descent. In the aftermath of the Civil War, Attucks came to be celebrated as "the first martyr" of the American Revolution, as he was in the handbill printed by C. C. Mead in 1863 advertising the ninety-third anniversary commemoration of the historic event. Hinderaker, *Boston's Massacre*.

Chapter 6

1   "John Adams to Abigail Adams, 14 September 1774," Founders Online, National Archives, accessed January 18, 2019, https://tinyurl.com/y7vletvj (original source: Butterfield, *Adams Papers*, 1:155).

2   "John Adams to Abigail Adams, 16 September 1774," Founders Online, National Archives, accessed February 20, 2021, https://tinyurl.com/4msdmc59.

3   "John Adams to Abigail Adams, 16 September 1774."

4   For a detailed accounting of this, see Spencer W. McBride, *Pulpit and Nation: Clergymen and the Politics of Revolutionary America* (Charlottesville: University of Virginia Press, 2016), 54–57.

5   In the historian Spencer McBride's assessment, these chaplains encouraged soldiers to conceive of themselves "as Christian soldiers, part of a carefully constructed modern Army of Israel dispatched to protect America's providential destiny." McBride, *Pulpit and Nation*, 12, 35, 41.

6   Byrd, *Sacred Scripture*, 12.

7   As the historian James Byrd has summarized, "Congregationalist ministers alone preached over 2000 sermons each week" through the period of the revolution, reaching an audience of listeners and readers far larger than that reached by the pamphlets that have traditionally garnered most attention from historians. Byrd elaborates, "Sermons were published at four times the rate of political pamphlets and were more influential as well. Whereas pamphlets were aimed at an elite readership, sermons began as oral communication for everyone and, as such, proved even more persuasive in printed form. The sermon buttressed the Revolution in ways that the pamphlet could not." These preachers simply took for granted that "great preachers would be great patriots," Byrd concludes, routinely drawing connections "between their zeal for the gospel and their zeal for the American cause." Byrd, *Sacred Scripture*, 16–17.

8   Willison, *Henry and His World*, 264.

9   Tyler, *Patrick Henry*, 143. For recent biographies—from which the details of this opening vignette were drawn—see Mayer, *Son of Thunder*; Unger, *Lion of Liberty*; and Thomas S. Kidd, *Patrick Henry: First among Patriots* (New York: Basic Books, 2011).

10 Wirt, *Patrick Henry*, xii. Some historians have embraced Wirt's as a reliable account of well-transmitted oral tradition, while others have dismissed it as largely "apocryphal." Kidd is the most recent among Henry's many biographers who take Wirt's rendering of the oral tradition as largely reliable. Others see the attribution of the slogan to Henry as part of a romantic tradition that, across the course of the nineteenth century, embellished this and other episodes from the American Revolution with an abundance of dramatic detail. According to Morgan, "The first newspaper to report what happened was some five hundred miles away. The first attempt to reconstruct the event was twenty-five years and a revolution later, and the second attempt was forty to fifty years later and only succeeded in giving form to a legend." Morgan and Morgan, *Stamp Act Crisis*, 88–91. In one rendering of this tradition, Henry is portrayed as having grasped a letter opener to simulate a dagger and thrusting it toward his breast when he reached his final declaration. In yet another, the other delegates are portrayed as having sat in stunned silence until a young man, Edward Carrington, who had been listening to the speech from outside the church through an open window, was moved to exclaim, "Let me be buried on this spot!" While there is no way of ascertaining the accuracy of this legend, when he died thirty-five years later in 1810, Carrington was indeed buried in a grave outside the window of the Williamsburg church. For one rendering of this story, see Mrs. Mecomber, "The Story of Edward Carrington and Patrick Henry's Speech," New York Traveler, July 12, 2011, https://tinyurl.com/6jul4k5.

11 Daniel Boorstin notes that "of the more than a hundred members of the Virginia constitutional convention of 1776, only three were not vestrymen." The membership of this body was virtually identical to that of the preceding year's convention, at which Henry gave his famous speech. Daniel J. Boorstin, *The Americans: The Colonial Experience* (New York: Random House, 1958), 131.

12 Of the biblical allusions in Henry's speech, Thomas Kidd, who leans toward crediting the received version of the speech, writes, "They are easily missed now, but they would have been familiar to the audience at the Virginia Convention. . . . Several phrases came directly from the prophet Jeremiah. For example, Henry warned that British assurances of benevolent intentions would 'prove a snare to your feet' (Jeremiah 18:22). He worried that Virginians would become like those 'who having eyes, see not, and having ears, hear not (Jeremiah 5:21). And he warned that 'gentlemen may cry peace, peace—but there is no peace' (Jeremiah 6:14)." Kidd, *Patrick Henry*, 98.

13 See Wirt, *Patrick Henry*, xii. For a discussion of the connection to Addison's *Cato*, see Julie Ellison, *Cato's Tears and the Making of Anglo-American Emotion* (Chicago: University of Chicago Press, 1999), 68. For examples of the slogan in colonial newspapers, see *Massachusetts Spy*, May 10, 1775; and *Pennsylvania Gazette*, September 20, 1775.

14 "To John Adams from Jonathan Williams Austin, 7 July 1775," Founders Online, National Archives, accessed September 29, 2019, https://tinyurl.com/ybsz937c (original source: Robert J. Taylor, ed., *The Adams Papers*, Papers of John Adams, vol. 3, *May 1775–January 1776* [Cambridge, MA: Harvard University Press, 1979], 66–68).

15 Daniel George, *George's Cambridge Almanack or, the Essex Calendar, for the Year of Our Redemption, 1776* (Boston: E. Russell, 1775).

16 Continental Congress, *A Declaration by the Representatives of the United Colonies of North-America, Now Met in General Congress at Philadelphia* [. . .] (New York: printed by John Holt in Water Street, 1775), 3.

17 See *Journals of the Continental Congress*, July 1, 1775: "That in case any Agent of the ministry, shall induce the Indian tribes, or any of them to commit actual hostilities against these colonies, or to enter into an offensive Alliance with the British troops, thereupon the colonies ought to avail themselves of an Alliance with such Indian Nations as will enter into the same to oppose such British troops and their Indian allies." "Journals of the Continental Congress, 1774–1789: Saturday, July 1, 1775," American Memory: Remaining Collections,

Library of Congress, accessed February 17, 2021, https://tinyurl.com/y8sdpsa8.

18 Pauline Maier, *American Scripture: Making the Declaration of Independence*, 1st ed. (New York: Knopf, 1997), 7.

19 *Dunlap's Pennsylvania Packet and General Advertiser*, Monday, August 7, 1775, 5.

20 See, for instance, *New-York Journal*, August 24, 1775, 4; and *New-Hampshire Gazette and Historical Chronicle*, September 12, 1775, 2.

21 Purcell, *Sealed with Blood*, 28–32.

22 William Smith, *An Oration in Memory of General Montgomery and of the Officers and Soldiers, Who Fell with Him, December 31, 1775, before Quebec* [. . .] (Philadelphia, 1776), https://tinyurl.com/yd5qbm29.

23 Samuel Ward to Henry Ward, December 27, 1775, Ward Collection, box 1, folder 11, cited in J. F. Guy, *The Public Life of a Private Man: Samuel Ward, 1725–1776* (PhD diss., Kent State University, Kent, Ohio, 2003), 217, ProQuest (Dissertations & Theses Global 305318302).

24 Samuel Stillman, *Two Sermons Occasioned by the Condemnation and Execution of Levi Ames* (Boston: John Kneeland, 1773), front cover. Many studies of New England funeral practices emphasize the eighteenth century as a time of transition away from the more austere imagery exemplified by the "death's-head," or skull and crossbones—see, for instance, Stannard, *Puritan Way of Death*. While indeed the transition was underway, these images remained powerfully present in Boston's public life, as suggested by the fact that Kneeland chose this format for Stillman's execution sermons in the year 1773. The popularity of his published sermons about Levi Ames is probably what earned Stillman an invitation to preach before the Continental Congress as a memorial to his fellow Baptist, Ward.

25 Samuel Stillman, *Death, the Last Enemy, Destroyed by Christ* (Philadelphia: Joseph Crukshank, 1776), 14.

26 Stillman, 14–15.

27 Stillman, iv.

28 Thomas Paine, *Common Sense; Addressed to the Inhabitants of America on the following Interesting Subjects*, 3rd ed. (Philadelphia: Robert Bell, 1776), 7. In Paine's reading of the Hebrew scriptures, "Government by

kings was first introduced into the world by the Heathens, from whom the children of Israel copied the custom. It was the most prosperous invention the Devil ever set on foot for the promotion of idolatry." Citing "portions of scripture" that he described as "direct and positive" and "admit[ing] of no equivocal construction," Paine declared that "the Almighty hath here entered his protest against monarchical government. . . . For monarchy in every instance is the Popery of government." Paine, 13–14.

29 Paine, 30.

30 Paine, front cover.

31 *The Poetical Works of James Thomson, James Beattie, Gilbert West and John Bampfylde* (Edinburgh: William P. Nimmo, 1864), 338.

32 See Thomas Paine, *The Writings of Thomas Paine*, vol. 1, prod. Norman M. Wolcott and David Widger, available at Project Gutenberg (2010), https://tinyurl.com/yahwjcr3.

33 Thomas Paine, *The Writings of Thomas Paine* (New York: G. P. Putnam's Sons, 1906), https://www.bartleby.com/184/118.html #txt1.

34 Paine.

35 Jay Fliegelman, *Declaring Independence: Jefferson, Natural Language, and the Culture of Performance* (Palo Alto, CA: Stanford University Press, 1993), 99.

36 Marveling at Jefferson's spirit in the face of this unrelenting loss, the biographer Andrew Burstein has drawn a compelling portrait of Jefferson as "a grieving optimist." Jefferson, Burstein writes, while "outwardly so durable . . . , was assaulted from within by an unstoical weakness he could not deny in attempting to face the losses of those he loved." Still, in the face of it all, he continued to navigate life "with Hope in the head, leaving Fear astern." Andrew Burstein, *The Inner Jefferson: Portrait of a Grieving Optimist* (Charlottesville: University Press of Virginia, 1995), 261.

37 For a good timeline of these events, see "Declaring Independence: Drafting the Documents," Library of Congress, accessed February 17, 2021, https://tinyurl.com/4wf8ycv2.

38 Darren Staloff, *Hamilton, Adams, Jefferson: The Politics of Enlightenment and the American Founding* (New York: Hill & Wang, 2005), 132.

39 Jefferson's most immediate source of inspiration was clearly the Virginia Declaration of Rights, a document by which Jefferson's colleagues in Virginia had recently announced their colony's independence. Drafted by George Mason, and adopted by Virginia's constitutional convention on June 12, 1776, the declaration named as its first right "that all men are by nature equally free and independent and have certain inherent rights, of which, when they enter into a state of society, they cannot, by any compact, deprive or divest their posterity; namely, the enjoyment of life and liberty, with the means of acquiring and possessing property, and pursuing and obtaining happiness and safety." "The Virginia Declaration of Rights," National Archives, accessed February 20, 2021, https://tinyurl .com/vc4u4mde. As to the deeper root of this way of framing things, John Locke's influence is easiest to see. In his *Two Treatises of Government*, Locke had asserted that good government should be founded on the "natural law" of reason. This law, he declared, "teaches all Mankind, who would but consult it, that being all equal and independent, no one ought to harm another in his Life, Health, Liberty, or Possessions." John Locke, *Two Treatises of Government*, ed. Thomas Hollis (London, 1764; Online Library of Liberty, n.d.), chap. 2, sec. 6, https://tinyurl.com/wux8rna8. Elsewhere Locke reduced his listing of essential rights to three: "life, liberty and property," and he also used the phrase "the pursuit of happiness" in his widely read *Essays Concerning Human Understanding*, published in 1690. See, for instance, John Locke, "An Essay concerning Human Understanding," in *The Works of John Locke in Nine Volumes*, 12th ed. (London: Rivington, 1824), 1: chap. 19, sec. 43, https://tinyurl.com/ye6pfcbn. For these reasons, most historians are content to cast Mason's articulation of essential human rights, and Jefferson's elegant encapsulation of them, quite simply, as a recasting of "Lockean" themes. In his splendid commentary on Jefferson's correspondence, *Letters from the Head and Heart*, however, Andrew Burstein has noted that the phrase "the pursuit of happiness" was also a favorite of the Anglican clergyman Laurence Sterne, whose writings were enormously popular among the landed gentry of colonial Virginia. In a 1787 letter to his nephew Peter

Carr, Jefferson recommended Sterne's sermons with an extraordinary endorsement: "The writings of Sterne particularly form the best course of morality that ever was written." Jefferson's felicitous phrase "the pursuit of happiness" and indeed the whole of his philosophy, Burstein concludes, was "both Lockean and Sternean." Andrew Burstein, *Letters from the Head and Heart* (Chapel Hill: University of North Carolina Press, 2002), 18–19.

40 Thomas Jefferson, *A Summary View of the Rights of British America* (Williamsburg, VA: Clemantina Rind, 1774), 9, 12, 15, http://hdl.loc.gov/loc.rbc/jeff.16823.

41 Maier, *American Scripture*, 37. Jefferson's draft included this additional statement: "Future ages will scarce believe that the hardiness of one man adventured within the short compass of twelve years only, to build a foundation, so broad and undisguised for tyranny over a people fostered & fixed in principles of freedom." Maier, 37.

42 Maier, 22.

43 Daniel Dreisbach has summarized this discourse: "To resist a prince lawfully it must first be established that the monarch is a tyrant . . . a prince who willfully disregards or violates the compacts with God and the people." Dreisbach traces this discourse, appropriately, to "the resistance theology that emerged in European Protestant communities in the wake of the Reformation and the wars of religion that followed" and cites as foundational the *Vindiciae contra tyrannos*: "The political theory advanced in the Vindiciae can be summarized briefly: legitimate political order in all civil states is based on two contracts (or national covenants). . . . The first contract is between God, on the one side, and the prince and the people jointly, on the other. . . . The second contract is between the prince and the people. . . . If the prince fails to fulfill his commitment to this joint agreement, the contract is abrogated and the people may resist or depose the 'tyrannical' prince for the sake of the people's promise to God." Daniel L. Dreisbach, *Reading the Bible with the Founding Fathers* (New York: Oxford University Press, 2017), 120–21. See also Dustin Gish and Daniel Klinghard, eds., *Resistance to Tyrants, Obedience to God: Reason, Religion, and Republicanism at the American Founding* (Lanham, MD: Lexington Books, 2013).

44 See "Benjamin Franklin's Great Seal Design," greatseal.com, accessed February 27, 2021, https://tinyurl.com/qfqorde.

45 "From Thomas Jefferson to William Stephens Smith, 13 November 1787," Founders Online, National Archives, last modified June 29, 2017, https://tinyurl.com/ycxy8q72 (original source: Julian P. Boyd, ed., *The Papers of Thomas Jefferson*, vol. 12, *7 August 1787–31 March 1788* [Princeton, NJ: Princeton University Press, 1955], 355–57).

46 See "English Bill of Rights 1689: An Act Declaring the Rights and Liberties of the Subject and Settling the Succession of the Crown," Lillian Goldman Law Library, accessed February 17, 2021, https://tinyurl.com/agm47h.

47 As Pauline Maier has concluded, "To attack the King was, in short, a constitutional form. It was the way Englishmen announced revolution." Maier, *American Scripture*, 38.

48 See "English Bill of Rights 1689."

49 For accounts of this extensive practice, see Fliegelman, *Declaring Independence*, 4–15; Maier, *American Scripture*, 69–75; and Humphrey, *American Revolution*, 123–26.

50 "Declaration of Independence: A Transcription," National Archives, accessed February 19, 2021, https://tinyurl.com/4dnmfm7z. By this time, many Americans were accustomed to pledging their lives to the Revolutionary cause in ways that were more than merely symbolic. In 1766, the New York Sons of Liberty approved resolutions formalizing their organization, including the resolution to go to the "last Extremity, and venture our lives and fortunes, effectually to prevent the Stamp-Act from ever taking place in this city and Province." Les Standiford, *Desperate Sons: Samuel Adams, Patrick Henry, John Hancock, and the Secret Bands of Radicals Who Led the Colonies to War* (New York: HarperCollins, 2012), 91. In 1775, the Massachusetts assembly had asked inhabitants of each town if "honorable Continental Congress" were to decide that separation from Britain was required, if "they the said Inhabitants [would] . . . solemnly engage with their Lives and Fortunes to Support the Congress in the Measure." Maier, *American Scripture*, 59. These are just two of countless examples.

51 In Maier's summation, this closing to the Declaration of Independence was "a public confession of treason. And conviction for treason meant death and confiscation of estate." Maier, 156.

52 As Thomas Kidd has summarized, in the buildup to revolution, colonists from across the theological spectrum became more and more convinced that "God was raising up America for some special purpose" and that Britain "had abandoned its providential role, descending into corruption and evil." Thomas S. Kidd, *God of Liberty: A Religious History of the American Revolution* (New York: Basic Books, 2010), 9. McBride calls this "American providentialism," arguing that the colonists sometimes "used [it] as an ideology or worldview, while at other times they used it as a sociopolitical rhetoric to assign divine approbation to an event, cause or idea." McBride, *Pulpit and Nation*, 13.

53 For an excellent historiographic treatment of this concept, see Purcell, *Sealed with Blood*, 6–10. Purcell sums up, "Revolutionary bloodshed legitimized the American nation by providing a specific focus for American self-fashioning." Purcell, 7. McBride conjures this same historiography in his 2016 *Pulpit and Nation*, arguing that clergy played a critical role in "forging a national polity and national identity because they helped Americans from Massachusetts to Georgia to view themselves as part of a larger imagined community." McBride, *Pulpit and Nation*, 35.

Chapter 7

1 Phelps, *Nathan Hale*, 11. Unless otherwise noted, I have drawn biographical facts about Hale's life from Phelps, Hale's most fastidious biographer, whose portrait is imaginatively presented but built on a solid foundation of documentary evidence extracted from the dozens of hagiographic Hale biographies published in the nineteenth and early twentieth centuries. For a genealogy of Nathan Hale, see Holloway, *Nathan Hale*, 237–62.

2 See "Hale Genealogy" in Holloway, 179.

3 Phelps, *Nathan Hale*, 13.

4 No surviving records detail the precise sequence of these events, but each would have been a necessary precursor to admission to Yale College. Gerald F. Moran and Maris A. Vinovskis, "The Great Care of Godly Parents: Early Childhood in Puritan New England," *Monographs of the Society for Research in Child Development* 50, no. 4/5 (1985): 24–37.

5 The quote is from the minutes of a 1753 meeting of President Thomas Clap and the fellows of Yale College. Ebenezer Baldwin, *Annals of Yale College, from Its Foundation, to the Year 1831*, 2nd ed. (New Haven, CT: William Noyes, 1838), 68.

6 Joseph Huntington, *College Almanack, 1761. An Astronomical Diary; Or an Almanack for the Year of Our Lord Christ, 1761* (New Haven, CT: Parker, 1761), 2.

7 Huntington, *College Almanack, 1761*, 16.

8 Joseph Huntington, *College Almanack, 1762. An Astronomical Diary; Or an Almanack for the Year of Our Lord Christ, 1762* (New Haven, CT: Parker, 1762).

9 According to Christopher Grasso, "Yale into the 1740s and 1750s reflected an eclectic mixture of old and new learning in place of what had once been thought of as a coherent body of knowledge. . . . As New England opened to the new ideas animating the larger European world, . . . genteel, cosmopolitan attitudes toward cultural life and a liberal acceptance of the new learning merged to produce the Anglicization of the colonial American gentry in the eighteenth century." Christopher Grasso, *A Speaking Aristocracy: Transforming Public Discourse in Eighteenth-Century Connecticut* (Chapel Hill: University of North Carolina Press, 1999), 187.

10 Cornelius Tacitus and Centre Traditio Litterarum Occidentalum, *Historiae* (Turnhout, Belgium: Brepols, 2010), iv, 5.

11 Moss, *Ancient Christian Martyrdom*, 29. Moss says that in this period, "dying nobly became the prime location for the display of virtus and thus, of masculinity" and, citing the work of Catharine Edwards, concludes, "An opportunity to demonstrate self-restraint, courage, and clear-headedness, the noble death came to supplant military victory as the finest articulation of virtue."

See also Castelli, *Martyrdom and Memory*, 62–65.

12 Joseph Huntington, *A Discourse, at the Ordination of the Reverend Mr. Enoch Hale* (Hartford, CT: Hudson and Goodwin, 1780), 19, 21.

13 Holloway, *Nathan Hale*, 266.

14 Holloway, 286.

15 Samuel Bird, *The Importance of the Divine Presence with Our Host* (New Haven, CT: James Parker, 1759), 3, 13, 5, 16.

16 Bird, 17, 22–23.

17 "I shoud th(ink) my time more agreable spent believe me, in playing a part in Cato with the Company you mention," Washington wrote to Sarah Cary Fairfax on September 25, 1758. "From George Washington to Sarah Cary Fairfax, 25 September 1758," National Archives, accessed February 20, 2021, https://tinyurl.com/yxj7bwuy.

18 Jason Shaffer, "Mourning, and Patriotism in the Propaganda Plays of the American Revolution," *Early American Literature* 41, no. 1 (2006): 1–27.

19 Joseph Addison, *Cato: A Tragedy and Selected Essays*, ed. by Christine Dunn Henderson and Mark E. Yellin, with a foreword by Forrest McDonald (Indianapolis: Liberty Fund, 2004), 84, https://tinyurl.com/vta998wb, accessed February 19, 2021.

20 Addison.

21 Maier, *American Scripture*, 156.

22 "Declaration of Independence: A Transcription."

23 "Thomas Jefferson to William Stephens Smith."

24 See note 24 in chapter 3.

25 Eastburn, *Faithful Narrative.*

26 Hancock, *Oration Delivered March 5.*

27 The letter first appeared in the *New-York Journal* (June 22, 1775) and then in the *Connecticut Journal* and the *New-Haven Post-Boy* (June 28, 1775), the *Providence Gazette* and *Country Journal* (July 1, 1775), the *Essex Journal* (July 7, 1775), and the *New-England Chronicle* (November 9–16, 1775).

28 The *New-England Chronicle* and the *Essex Gazette*, November 9–16, 1775. Within weeks, the same letter appeared in the *Pennsylvania Gazette* (November 29, 1775), the *Maryland Journal* (December 6, 1775), Dunlap's *Maryland Gazette* (December 12, 1775), the *Virginia Gazette* (December 20, 1775).

29 Abiel Leonard, *A Prayer, Composed for the Benefit of the Soldiery, in the American Army, to Assist Them in Their Private Devotions* [. . .] (Cambridge, MA: printed and sold by S. and E. Hall, 1775), 5.

30 Ebenezer Watson, *Watson's Register, and Connecticut Almanack, for the Year of Our Lord, 1776. Calculated for the Meridian of Hartford, Lat. 41 Deg. 56 Min. North* [. . .] (Hartford, CT: Ebenezer Watson, 1775), 8, 24.

31 The phrase appears at least 150 times between the years 1776 and 1836 in a simple word search of the Early American Imprints database: "Early American Imprints, Series I Evans, 1639–1800," Readex, accessed February 17, 2021, https://tinyurl.com/2y2reer4.

Conclusion

1 Hugh M. Brackenridge, *An Eulogium of the Brave Men Who Have Fallen in the Contest with Great-Britain: Delivered on Monday, July 5. 1779* [. . .] (Philadelphia: printed by Francis Bailey in Market Street, 1779).

2 Israel Evans, *A Discourse Delivered near York in Virginia, on the Memorable Occasion of the Surrender of the British Army to the Allied Forces of America and France* (Philadelphia: Francis Bailey, 1782), 24, cited in Byrd, *Sacred Scripture*, 12.

3 See the afterword for an extended historiographic comment.

4 For an exposition of how the ideals of martyrdom served as a spur to pacifism in the German Moravian tradition, for instance, see Patrick M. Erben, *A Harmony of the Spirits: Translation and the Language of Community in Early Pennsylvania* (Chapel Hill: University of North Carolina Press, 2012).

5 As Carla Gardina Pestana has summarized, "The American Revolution reprised the very issues that had been at stake a century before. . . . As colonies moved fitfully toward separation and the creation of the United States, disloyal individuals, many

of them religious dissenters, failed to respect their duty to God and King, and instead participated in revolt." Pestana, *Protestant Empire*, 220.

Afterword

1 John Demos's early demographic study of the English colony of Plymouth, Massachusetts, was extraordinarily influential in establishing this narrative of increased longevity in the eighteenth century, but even he projected "a maximum of 25 percent mortality for the entire age span between birth and maturity (age 21)" while acknowledging that "this is a difficult matter to study systematically because some deaths among the very young were not recorded in the usual fashion." John Demos, *A Little Commonwealth: Family Life in Plymouth Colony*, 2nd ed., 30th anniversary ed. (New York: Oxford University Press, 2000), 66. It is important to note that neither rapid overall population growth nor increases in average longevity can be presumed to translate directly into a diminished awareness of death. Both measures obscure how deaths can appear randomly, on the one hand, and cluster in specific times and places, on the other, both dynamics with far-reaching implications for how people perceive the threat of mortality. Rates of infant and maternal mortality remained shockingly high and were subject to occasional unpredictable spikes. Communicable disease ran rampant, and its method of spread defied not just popular but also "expert" comprehension. Epidemics—from smallpox to yellow fever—continued to terrorize populations in growing urban settlements and along the busy shorefronts of colonial harbor towns. The English enterprise in North America continued to be characterized by the kinds of violence that were inherent in slavery and that were born from encounters infused with racism and cross-cultural misunderstanding. Many English colonists, especially those living at the ever-expanding circumferences of territory claimed by the English, were engaged in near-perpetual war with their Indian neighbors and with their colonial competitors, the hated Catholic French. For all these reasons and more, death remained a central preoccupation of English speakers living in eighteenth-century British North America.

2 Seeman, *Pious Persuasions*, 53.
3 Bernard Bailyn's 1967 *Ideological Origins* remains among the most important and lasting contributions to this ongoing conversation. In this landmark work, Bailyn characterized the American Revolution as "above all else an ideological, constitutional, political struggle" and described the Americans' distinctive conception of liberty as resulting from a "surprising mix" of Enlightenment philosophy and what he described as a "peculiar strain of antiauthoritarianism" rooted in centuries of English civil strife. Writing against what was then the scholarly consensus that the Revolution could be understood as "primarily a controversy between social groups," Bailyn argued that this "peculiar configuration of ideas constituted in effect an intellectual switchboard" that connected people across America's Revolutionary generation. While agreeing that the revolutionaries were producers and consumers of a novel set of ideas, more recent generations of historians have chafed at the notion that the Revolution can be accounted for, principally, in ideological terms, preferring instead to excavate the many layers of culture that underlay the formal articulations of Revolutionary ideology. Nonetheless, a full half century after its publication, Bailyn's masterwork remains widely heralded for having transformed our understanding of the revolutionaries' unique use of terms like *slavery* and *corruption* and *conspiracy*, demonstrating that terms like these were not mere rhetorical devices but were infused with "real fears, real anxieties, a sense of real danger." Bailyn, *Ideological Origins*, v–x, 22–23, 29. Just as Bailyn surfaced distinctly American appropriations of an ancient English oppositional vernacular, cultural historians have sought to describe the inner lives of Americans in the Revolutionary and early Republican eras using an entirely distinct set of actor's categories like "sensibility" and "passion" and "spirit." Knott, *Sensibility*; Eustace, *Passion Is the Gale*; Albanese, *Mind and Spirit*.

4 By focusing on circumstances of extremis in which perceptions of death and practices of dying are brought to the fore—war, slavery, travel, captivity, plague—a traditional historiography of religion in eighteenth-century British North America is thrust into dialogue with other bodies of scholarship touching on diverse themes: the decimation of Native peoples, the catastrophic experience of African slaves and their descendants, the pervasiveness of ethnic (or tribal) conflict and the varied practices of warfare, and the conveyance of perceptions of death and practices of dying beyond those parts of North America settled by English colonists. With this litany, I am conjuring works like these: Calloway, *Vast Winter Count*; Brown, *The Reaper's Garden: Death and Power in the World of Atlantic Slavery* (Cambridge: Harvard University Press, 2008); Martina Will de Chaparro and Miruna Achim, *Death and Dying in Colonial Spanish America* (Tucson: University of Arizona Press, 2011); Martina Will de Chaparro, *Death and Dying in New Mexico* (Albuquerque: University of New Mexico Press, 2007); Gish and Klinghard, *Resistance to Tyrants*; and Mary Terrall and Helen Deutsch, *Vital Matters: Eighteenth-Century Views of Conception, Life, and Death* (Toronto: University of Toronto Press, 2012). Erik Seeman's 2010 *Death in the New World* represents perhaps the most comprehensive attempt to analyze the central role played by death and dying in the cross-cultural encounters foundational to the creation of European colonies in the Eastern Seaboard of North America and the Caribbean. Erik Seeman, *Death in the New World: Cross-Cultural Encounters, 1492–1800* (Philadelphia: University of Pennsylvania Press, 2010). There remains, however, room for more scholarship about death and dying as experienced by those who lived between the early generations of English colonists in North America (in the seventeenth century) and the catastrophic experience of mortality resulting from the US Civil War (in the nineteenth century). If not on the same scale as they experienced in the Civil War, Americans of diverse racial, ethnic, and religious backgrounds knew well the realm of suffering long before white Northerners and Southerners turned their sights on each other.

5 Thanks to the work of David Hall and others. Scholars who began as "historians of the book" have turned more and more to consider the myriad ways that people in early modern England engaged with printed texts. In his groundbreaking 1989 *Worlds of Wonder, Days of Judgment*, Hall searched "beyond the text" to examine not just the beliefs, as these could be found articulate in printed works, but also the experiences and practices of early New Englanders. In doing so, he found evidence of a world in which people were indeed influenced by questions of doctrine and the transatlantic book trade but also by folk wisdom and the occult, by preoccupation with the proper observance of the Christian sacraments, and by the rhythms of life rooted in rituals like fast days, confessions, and executions. David D. Hall, *Worlds of Wonder, Days of Judgment: Popular Religious Belief in Early New England* (New York: Knopf, 1989). Hall's history of publication tracks this evolution, from *Worlds of Wonder* to two edited volumes—the 1996 *Cultures of Print* and the 1997 *Lived Religion in America: Toward a History of Practice*—to his own 2010 *Lived Religion*. Hall, *Cultures of Print*; David D. Hall, *Lived Religion in America: Toward a History of Practice* (Princeton, NJ: Princeton University Press, 1997); David Hall, *Lived Religion: Toward a History of Practice* (Princeton, NJ: Princeton University Press, 2010). What Hall and many scholars call "lived religion," still others call "popular religion," expressions of which Peter Williams has characterized as "usually 1) found outside formal church structures, 2) transmitted outside the established channels of religious instruction and communication employed by these structures, and 3) preoccupied with concrete manifestations of the supernatural in the midst of the secular world." Commenting on Hall's "close analysis of 'meaning' and . . . attention to ambivalence and contradiction," Stephen Marini elaborates, "In such quotidian contexts religious practice becomes less systematized and more eclectic, attaining coherence defined by the practitioners themselves, rather than by ecclesiastical authority." Peter Williams, *Popular Religion in America*, cited in Stephen Marini, "Hymnody as History: Early Evangelical Hymns and the Recovery of

American Popular Religion," *Church History* 71, no. 2 (2002): 302.

6   See the extended commentary in note 19 below.

7   Weimer, *Martyrs' Mirror*, 218. Weimer chose as the title for her book the title of the first book printed in German in North America, a landmark Anabaptist martyrology containing, according to its subtitle, "the story of seventeen centuries of Christian martyrdom from the time of Christ to A.D. 1660." The book had first been published in Dutch in 1660 and was foundational to the identity of Amish, Hutterite, and Mennonite communities on both sides of the Atlantic. Beginning in 1745, the Mennonite preacher Jacob Gottschalk, one of thousands of Germans who immigrated to Pennsylvania in the middle decades of the eighteenth century, oversaw its translation into German and published a complete edition in 1749 in Ephrata, Pennsylvania. Over time it became most widely known in North America as the "Ephrata Book of Martyrs." For an online version, see: https://www.homecomers.org/mirror/contents.htm.

8   Sarah J. Purcell, *Sealed with Blood*, 6–7, 19. Consistent with scholarly investigation of the ancient tradition of martyrdom, Purcell concluded that the martyrs and heroes of the American Revolution "were not created by death itself, but rather by the search for meaning among the community of the living." In many varied acts of commemoration, leading Americans in the early national period "transformed the heroic martyrs of the Revolutionary War into symbols of a new kind of national political commitment that their very deaths made possible." Purcell, 19, 21. But this process of commemoration was just part of a much longer process. The legend that grew up around Nathan Hale in the decades following his death, for instance, cannot be separated from the lived experience of the young man who died on September 22, 1776. To do so fails to take him seriously as an individual, as a historical agent in his own right, shaped as he was by a lengthy process of cultural and spiritual formation. The legend of Nathan Hale was birthed decades after his death because he was identified as someone who exemplified how countless young men were remembered as having faced their deaths in the Revolutionary War. But Nathan Hale also exemplified how countless young revolutionaries were raised to confront their own mortality and how they were rallied to the patriot cause. The legend of Nathan Hale was not merely manufactured commemoration—it was also the fruit of a tradition that unfolded across a much longer arc of time, the tradition of English Protestant martyrdom appropriated and adapted to the unique circumstances of Revolutionary America. The same is true of other legendary sayings from the Revolution that resonate with this same sentiment, like "Give me liberty or give me death!" and "Live free or die!"

9   Byrd, *Sacred Scripture*, 2. As was true in earlier wars, appeals to martyrdom were "everywhere" in the American Revolution, Byrd observes, as Protestant clergy issued calls for enlistment, muster sermons, and battlefield rallying cries.

10   McBride, *Pulpit and Nation*, 1–2. McBride describes this role as "intermediary," such that both the Revolution and the project of nation building "became popular movements and not just undertakings confined to society's elite."

11   Quotations are from Susan Juster's helpful response to my dissertation proposal as shared with participants in a seminar hosted by the USC-Huntington Early Modern Studies Institute in March 2015. The Reformation, Juster commented, "redefined martyrdom as a more capacious category of suffering," a "corollary to the Reformation's redefinition of a saint as an ordinary Christian rather than a spiritual intercessory." For Quakers, for instance, "martyrdom came perilously close to meaning persecution of any kind, no matter how mild or unspectacular." To make her point, Juster went so far as to claim that in eighteenth-century British North America, "martyrdom was increasingly a rhetorical exercise in special pleading" such that "there was only room for martyr tales, not martyrs."

12   Fanestil, "Print Practice."

13   Thomas Laqueur, *The Work of the Dead: A Cultural History of Mortal Remains* (Princeton, NJ: Princeton University Press, 2016), 10, 113.

14   Philippe Ariès, "The Reversal of Death: Changes in Attitudes toward Death in Western Societies," *American Quarterly* 26,

no. 5 (December 1974): 536–60, 546. In this period, Ariès claimed, "the desire to assert one's identity and to come to terms with the pleasures of life gave a new and formidable importance to the hour of death." In his landmark 1977 *L'homme devant le mort*—which four years later was translated into English as *The Hour of Our Death*—Ariès broke the millennium into five stages. While acknowledging that remnant attitudes and practices continued to exist in successive stages, he nonetheless presented these stages as essentially chronological, hanging a provocatively crafted banner over each: "The Tamed Death," "The Death of the Self," "Remote and Imminent Death," "The Death of the Other," and "The Invisible Death." A companion volume published in 1985 shortly after Ariès's death, *Images of Man and Death*, employed these same categories to present visual representations of Ariès's extraordinary archival haul. Ariès earned near-universal acclaim for the expansive research that he invested in *The Hour of Our Death*, but his commitment to the grand intellectual gesture provoked sharp criticism of several kinds. Most widespread were charges of presumptuousness (with reference to the chronological scope of his interest) and of elitism (with regard to his selection of data). Philippe Ariès, *The Hour of Our Death* (New York: Knopf, 1981); Philippe Ariès, *Images of Man and Death* (Cambridge, MA: Harvard University Press, 1985).

15 "Family members needed to witness a death in order to assess the state of the dying person's soul," Faust summarized, "for these critical moments of life would epitomize his or her spiritual condition." According to Faust, this proper consolation of loved ones (denied to those who lost their next of kin on the battlefield) required that the "hour of death . . . be witnessed, scrutinized, interpreted, narrated—not to mention carefully prepared for by any sinner who sought to be worthy of salvation." Drew Gilpin Faust, *This Republic of Suffering: Death and the American Civil War*, 1st ed. (New York: Alfred A. Knopf, 2008), 9–10. With its unwavering focus on both the "incidence and experience" of death, Faust's *This Republic of Suffering* is rightly recognized as having made a lasting contribution

to the historiography of the US Civil War. Faust marshals a tremendous array of evidence—battlefield reminiscences and photographs, personal correspondence, popular literature and poetry, sermons and hymnody, cemetery records, and more—to demonstrate that the Civil War not just affected the millions of families who lost loved ones but transformed American customs of burying the dead and accounting for death and in fact caused Americans to question fundamental beliefs about death and the afterlife. Its method alone—which takes seriously that people occupying different social positions, including the dying themselves, play an important role in "the work of death"—makes *This Republic of Suffering* an important and inspiring contribution. The book's overall excellence makes all the more surprising the relative shallowness with which Faust treats the point of departure for her narrative: her analysis of those American attitudes toward death and practices of dying that prevailed before the Civil War. In her opening chapter, entitled simply "Death," she hangs a single banner over these antecedents, writing, "The Good Death proved to be a concern shared by almost all Americans of every religious background." And in attempting to give it brief definition, Faust grounds her understanding of the Good Death in just a few landmark resources—the Catholic tradition of *Ars Moriendi* and the Anglican Jeremy Taylor's *Rule and Exercises for Holy Dying*. Faust, *This Republic of Suffering*, 7–10. But the tradition of the *Ars Moriendi* dates to the fifteenth century, and Taylor's work was first published in 1651. While both had lasting influence, they were by no means the only traditions to shape the cultural landscape of North American in the intervening centuries. Making only glancing reference even to extraordinarily well-documented Puritan attitudes toward death and dying (citing a few dated resources in footnotes [Faust, *This Republic of Suffering*, 276–77]), Faust fails to address with any depth the experience of death in colonial North America and in the antebellum United States. In doing so, she leaves her readers, if only by omission, to suspect that the practices and perspectives inspired by these few landmark resources remained largely static across many generations. Faust, 276–77. These familiar "Old World" cultural resources were themselves appropriated and transformed in the environment of the North American "New World," profoundly shaped as this environment was in the seventeenth and eighteenth centuries by the widespread and traumatic experiences of war, disease, conquest, and slavery.

16 See my own *Mrs. Hunter's Happy Death*. Or consider the climactic chapters of Harriet Beecher Stowe, *Uncle Tom's Cabin* (Boston: John P. Jewett, 1852), which tell of Tom's "martyrdom."

17 Edwards, *Faithful Narrative*; Edwards, *Sinners in the Hands*.

18 Butler, *Awash in a Sea*, 164–65.

19 Through copious narrating of accounts in his 1966 *Religion and the American Mind*, Alan Heimert, a contemporary of Bernard Bailyn, made a strong case that mid-eighteenth-century religious revivals, commonly referred to as a first "Great Awakening," had helped lay a cultural foundation for the American Revolution. Alan Heimert, *Religion and the American Mind* (Cambridge, MA: Harvard University Press, 1966), 668. Heimert's student William McLoughlin later brought brevity and clarity to this thesis. William McLoughlin, *Revivals, Awakenings, and Reform: An Essay on Religion and Social Change in America, 1607–1977* (Chicago: University of Chicago Press, 1978). In a landmark *Journal of American History* article in 1982, Jon Butler declared the whole notion of Great Awakenings an "interpretive fiction," arguing that generations of scholars had taken the theological and ecclesial disputations of localized religious revivals in New England and generalized them onto the whole of the American colonial experience. Butler did not deny the reality of eighteenth- and nineteenth-century revivals but called on his colleagues to consider them in proper perspective—in his view, for instance, the so-called First Great Awakening was more accurately characterized as "a short-lived Calvinist revival in New England during the early 1740s." Jon Butler, "Enthusiasm Described and Decried: The Great Awakening as Interpretative Fiction," *Journal of American History* 69, no. 2 (September 1982): 309. The impact of Butler's essay was far-reaching—"Rarely in the space of one essay has so much damage been done to so many historical reputations," wrote Allen C. Guelzo in 1997—and a spirited response to it effectively polarized the field. Allen C. Guelzo, "God's Designs: The Literature of the Colonial Revivals of Religion, 1735–1760," in *New Directions in American Religious History*, ed. D. G. Hart and Harry S. Stout (New York: Oxford University Press, 1997), 146. McLoughlin responded, enumerating some of the benefits afforded by the traditional framework, "The construct [of 'revivalism'] has helped us to understand the shifts from a Calvinistic to an evangelical world view in the eighteenth century; it has helped us to understand the new sense of American identity which emerged after 1735; it has thrown new light on the basic question of separation of church and state, on the shift from a corporate ideal of the state to an individualistic ideal, and from a top-down, deferential theory of politics toward a bottom-up, government-by-consent theory of politics and from admiration of England to anxiety over its corruption." William G. McLoughlin, "Timepieces and Butterflies: A Note on the Great-Awakening-Construct and Its Critics," *Sociological Analysis* 44, no. 2 (1983): 103.

In his 1989 *The Democratization of American Christianity*, Nathan Hatch effectively rehabilitated Heimert's thesis, linking religious fervor and republican politics but in a way that suggested correspondence more than causation: "America's non-restrictive environment," he wrote, "permitted an unexpected and often explosive conjunction of evangelical fervor and popular sovereignty." While chronicling the explosion of Methodist, Baptist, and other movements between the American Revolution and 1845, this rise of a "democratic religious culture" was deeply rooted in earlier generations of religious expression often dismissed by historians of colonial America as mere "enthusiasm." Seeking to identify "common developments rather than those characteristic of a given region . . . or of a local town or county," Hatch said this democratic impulse—both ecclesial and political—distinguished the American experience from that of the

European nations to which most Americans traced their ancestry. Nathan O. Hatch, *The Democratization of American Christianity* (New Haven, CT: Yale University Press, 1989), 312. More recently, Thomas Kidd has embraced the frame of linking "Great Awakenings" and "democratization" in a series of books, adding new dimension to traditional characterizations of the revivalists and those who embraced the fervor they promoted while identifying them correctly as the forerunners of an authentically American movement, "Evangelicalism," that is active today in every corner of the globe. Thomas S. Kidd, *The Great Awakening: The Roots of Evangelical Christianity in Colonial America* (New Haven, CT: Yale University Press, 2007), 392; Kidd, *God of Liberty*, 298; Kidd, *Patrick Henry*, 306; Thomas S. Kidd, *George Whitefield: America's Spiritual Founding Father* (New Haven, CT: Yale University Press, 2014). Kidd's argument in sum is this: "The Great Awakening of the 1730s and 1740s was the most profound social upheaval in the history of colonial America" and "the first widespread popular uprising against established authority in the history of British colonial America." Noting that "it heavily influenced many of those who would fill the rank and file of the Patriot movement in the American Revolution," Kidd says "this first American revolution would herald the political revolution of 1776. . . . A new era of spiritual democracy had begun." Kidd, *God of Liberty*, 21.

In the end, this attempt to characterize early American religious experience by a single pattern of "democratization" suffers the same fundamental limitation as traditional scholarship on revivalism. For a helpful counterpoint to Hatch's thesis of democratization, for instance, see Christine Heyrman's portrayal of ascendant paternalism and authoritarianism in the early nineteenth-century American south: Christine Heyrman, *Southern Cross: The Beginnings of the Bible Belt* (Chapel Hill: University of North Carolina Press, 1997), 336, cited in Richard Wightman Fox, *Jesus in America: Personal Savior, Cultural Hero, National Obsession*, 1st ed. (San Francisco: HarperSanFrancisco, 2004), 488. And for an excellent critical review of Kidd's attempt to rehabilitate the framework of

"Great Awakening," albeit based only on his earlier work, see Christopher Grasso, "A 'Great Awakening'?," *Reviews in American History* 37, no. 1 (2009): 13–21.

Moving into the space cleared by Butler and Hatch, many talented historians have embraced interpretive frameworks other than revivalism in telling a religiously inflected story of life in early America. In *Fits, Trances, and Visions*, Ann Taves charted the evolution of religious experience in America across a wider span of time ("from Wesley to James") than is customary for studies of early American religion, characterizing the essential religious tension in Revolutionary and republican America as one between "formalism" and "enthusiasm." Taves, *Fits, Trances, and Visions*, 449. Susan Juster has highlighted prophetic streams of thought and practice that cut across regional and denominational lines in America's Revolutionary and republican generations. Susan Juster, *Doomsayers: Anglo-American Prophecy in the Age of Revolution* (Philadelphia: University of Pennsylvania Press, 2003). Carla Gardina Pestana and Katherine Carté Engel have emphasized the pervasively transatlantic and frequently transdenominational nature of religious movements in eighteenth- and nineteenth-century America, while they and countless others have also focused on the inner complexities of specific populations and particular religious traditions. Pestana, *Protestant Empire*, 302; Katherine Carté Engel, *Religion and Profit: Moravians in Early America* (Philadelphia: University of Pennsylvania Press, 2009), 313; Dee Andrews, *The Methodists and Revolutionary America, 1760–1800: The Shaping of an Evangelical Culture* (Princeton, NJ: Princeton University Press, 2000), 367.

Today, few scholars would contest at least a minimalist version of Butler's essential claim as he presented it in expanded (and less rhetorically charged) form in his 1990 book *Awash in a Sea*: "Since its first elucidation in Joseph Tracy's *The Great Awakening*, which was published in 1841 to provide historical support for America's nineteenth-century revivals, its interpretive significance has multiplied a thousandfold. . . . [And yet] an obsessive concern with it distorts important historical subtleties and obscures other crucial realities." Butler, *Awash in a Sea*, 360. Put simply, the enormous regional, cultural, and ethnic diversity of religious expression in early America cannot be made to conform to any unilinear process of historical change such as "democratization." The same criticism could be leveled at any of a number of alternate descriptions of the period as characterized by "secularization" or "individualism" or "enthusiasm" or "Evangelicalism" or "Romanticism." Given this enormous variety of early American religious life, the scholarly concern that the lens of "awakenings" obscures more than it illumines still warrants great respect.

20 Christopher Grasso, for instance, has rightly observed that the famous revivals spearheaded by Edwards, George Whitefield, and others in the 1740s "were dominated by a single question: 'What must I do to be saved?'" Grasso, *Speaking Aristocracy*, 96. More precisely, though, they were dominated by the question, "What must I do to be saved from the powers of sin, and from the wages of sin, which is death?" This is the classical formulation of the ancient Christian question, which found its way in various forms into every English Protestant catechism for several centuries. See, for among countless examples, the catechism of John Cotton, Cotton Mather's namesake grandfather: John Cotton, *Spiritual Milk for Babes, Drawn Out of the Breasts of Both Testaments, for Their Souls Nourishment: But May Be of like Use for Any Children* (London: printed for Peter Parker near Cree Church, 1688), 6. Grasso observes that "the Awakening ended as factions formed that proclaimed different answers." Grasso, *Speaking Aristocracy*, 96. Note, however, that the end of revivals did not put an end to the question, nor the struggle to find the best answer to it.

21 I disagree, for instance, with McBride's conclusion that "religious expression was common in the political culture of the Revolutionary era, yet it was as much the calculated design of ambitious men seeking power as it was the natural outgrowth of a devoutly religious people." McBride, *Pulpit and Nation*, 174. Kidd's assessment is more subtle: "During the Revolution, a new blend of Christian and republican ideology led religious traditionalists to embrace wholesale the concept of republican virtue. Conservative Protestants had traditionally been uneasy with the ideal of republican virtue, because its defenders often held a high view of human potential for goodness independent of the practice of Christianity. But by the 1770s, even Calvinists and other conservative believers agreed with Samuel Adams when he declared that if they remained virtuous, Americans could create a 'Christian Sparta,' a unique amalgamation of the Christian and classical republican traditions." But in my view, Kidd goes too far when he argues, "The Great Awakening and the Seven Years' War forged a visceral bond among Protestantism, anti-Catholicism and liberty." This bond required no special forging—it had remained solid across centuries, and in my view the Americans were simply improvising off well-established themes. Kidd, *God of Liberty*, 4, 8, 16. In this, I come much closer to McKenna's assessment: "What makes this dichotomy between the 'religious world' of seventeenth-century America and the 'political world' of eighteenth-century America so unconvincing is the fact that in *both* centuries politics and theology were so thoroughly intertwined that it was often impossible to say where one left off and the other began." McKenna, *Puritan Origins*, 48.

22 Robert Middlekauff, *The Glorious Cause: The American Revolution, 1763–1789* (Oxford: Oxford University Press, 2005), 52. See also Gordon Wood's description of Josiah Quincy II's worldview: chap. 5, n. 16.

23 Noll, *In the Beginning*, 16, 17, 327. Noll argues that this process of "disengaging church and society" was working its way toward completion by the end of the eighteenth century, but George McKenna is right to observe, "The idea of separation of church and state was really quite suspect in the eighteenth century (as it was in previous centuries). . . . Not until the 1840s and 1850s did separation of church and state become a rallying cry in America, and then its intent was not to exclude religion in general from the public arena, but only Roman Catholicism." McKenna, *Puritan Origins*, 47.

Index

265